COGNITIVE ENTERPRISE

ARCHITECTING BUSINESS TRANSFORMATION WITH ARTIFICIAL INTELLIGENCE.

AF679754

SHEKHAR KULKARNI

Copyright © 2025
Shekhar Kulkarni

eBook ISBN: 979-8-89795-271-7
Paperback ISBN: 979-8-89795-329-5
Hardcover ISBN: 979-8-89795-330-1

All © Reserved. Any unauthorized reprint or use of this material is strictly prohibited. No part of this book may be reproduced or transmitted in any form or by any means, electronic or mechanical, including photocopying, recording, or by any information storage and retrieval system without express written permission from the author.

All reasonable attempts have been made to verify the accuracy of the information provided in this publication. Nevertheless, the author assumes no responsibility for any errors and/or omissions.

Contents

Foreword

In early 2023, Generative AI stepped into the spotlight as ChatGPT captured global attention. For years, organizations had quietly used machine learning and traditional AI—largely predictive models—to enhance specific processes in isolated, siloed ways. But with the explosion of interest in Generative AI, often driven from the C-suite down, it became clear that AI would reshape much of how we operate in business. It was only a matter of time before we'd need to explore how AI could be meaningfully integrated to enable progress and transformation in **Enterprise Architecture**.

This book is a timely and important step forward. It offers a clear path to understanding how AI can be infused across all aspects of an organization—not just as a tool but as a catalyst for turning a static business structure into a dynamic, adaptive, and intelligent **"Cognitive Enterprise."**

In today's fast-moving world, organizations must evolve to stay relevant. The scale and urgency of that change depend on many factors: competition, emerging technologies, rising costs, shifting customer demands, new products, market volatility, and, most critically, organizational culture. Poorly executed change can be disastrous. This is where the **Enterprise Architect** plays a vital role—someone with a deep understanding of business strategy, systems, data, and operations who can lead transformation with clarity and purpose.

Building a Cognitive Enterprise is not merely a technical upgrade—it's a **business change journey**. Yes, there will be technical shifts, but the most valuable outcome will be organizational alignment and shared responsibility for change. The **Cognitive Enterprise Architecture Framework (CeAF)** presented in this book offers a comprehensive, logical, and practical approach to embedding AI within the architecture of a business. It outlines how to create operational processes that can learn, adapt, and continuously optimize performance.

The book opens by addressing common challenges facing modern organizations, using relatable examples to bring these concepts to life. It then introduces the CeAF model and shows readers how to apply it within their own context—step by step. From tackling legacy systems and fragmented data to addressing talent shortages, governance misalignment, cultural barriers, and unnecessary complexity, the book equips readers with a roadmap to transformation.

By the end, this isn't just a guide to rethinking enterprise architecture—it's a journey toward building a smarter, more agile, and forward-thinking organization with intelligence embedded into its core.

W. George Glass
Chief Technology Officer, TM Forum

Preface

As I pen these words, we stand at a pivotal moment in the evolution of enterprise technology. The rapid ascent of Artificial Intelligence, particularly Generative AI, represents not merely another technological shift but a fundamental reimagining of how enterprises operate, compete, and create value. This book emerges from my journey through successive waves of technological transformation-from the rise of the internet and distributed computing to cloud computing, service-oriented architecture, big data, digital transformation and now the cognitive revolution powered by AI.

Throughout my career architecting technology solutions for global enterprises, I have observed a consistent pattern: organisations that thrive during technological transitions are those that approach transformation holistically, with clear architectural vision and pragmatic implementation paths. Each wave brings both tremendous opportunity and significant challenges, especially for established enterprises with substantial legacy investments. The cognitive revolution amplifies this dynamic exponentially-offering unprecedented possibilities for innovation while demanding a fundamental rethinking of how we architect systems, manage data and enable human-technology collaboration.

The genesis of this book lies in a realisation that struck me while working with large enterprises struggling to move beyond initial AI implementations. While chatbots and simple automation offer visible quick wins, they barely scratch the surface of AI's transformative potential. The true opportunity lies in reimagining every business process with embedded intelligence, transforming application landscapes into intelligent services, implementing federated data architectures for real-time analytics, and orchestrating AI agents that can make informed decisions by accessing enterprise capabilities and data.

This deeper transformation introduces complex challenges: managing AI models and their lifecycle, considering infrastructure requirements for hosting and deployment, implementing runtime governance to enforce ethical boundaries, evaluating agent performance, and ensuring human centricity throughout. Organisations need a comprehensive architectural approach that addresses these interrelated challenges while providing a practical path forward.

The Cognitive Enterprise Architecture Framework (CeAF) introduced in this book represents my response to this need a structured blueprint that brings together business processes, capabilities, and technology in a holistic framework. It builds upon proven architectural principles while introducing new patterns and approaches uniquely enabled by AI. The framework is designed to help organisations navigate the complexity of cognitive transformation with confidence.

My journey in developing this framework has been one of both learning and unlearning. While core architectural principles remain foundational, AI-powered systems introduce dynamics that challenge conventional approaches to design, governance, and human-system interaction. The process of architecting AI agents revealed the need for new patterns, considerations and implementation strategies that this book aims to share.

As I was writing this book, new developments were already emerging- for example, Anthropic's Model Context Protocol and Google's A2A (Agent-to-Agent) protocol were launched, both of which significantly impact how tools integrate with agents. I expect this evolution in technology, practices and approaches to continue accelerating. To reflect this rapid pace of change, I have created a companion website (https://cognitive.enterprises), where I will update the framework, principles, and patterns as technology advances.

This work would not have been possible without the collaboration and insights gained from working with forward-thinking organisations and exceptional teams. I am particularly grateful to Deutsche Telekom's Product Innovation and Experience (PIX) team, led by Jonathan Abrahamson, Chief Product & Digital Officer, whose vision and conviction regarding AI's transformative potential have been inspiring. The practical experience gained working alongside the talented software engineers at Deutsche Telekom Digital Labs (DTDL), led by Kanwardeep Singh Ahluwalia (K.D.), Managing Director at DTDL and

CIO, Digital, has been invaluable in refining the framework and testing its principles in real-world implementations.

On a personal note, I am deeply indebted to my father, a talented fiction author who filled my childhood with stories and books that sparked my love for writing. His work has always been a source of fascination and motivation for me. My mother, on the other hand, instilled in me a deep passion for learning that continues to fuel me every single day. I am especially thankful to my wife, Neelima, who has supported me tremendously during this entire journey. Her patience, understanding, and encouragement during the long hours of research, writing, and revision made this book possible. I am also deeply grateful to my daughters and son, whose boundless enthusiasm, understanding, and constant encouragement provided me with both motivation and perspective throughout this writing process. I would like to extend my sincere gratitude to Penguin Publishers, whose editorial expertise, unwavering support, and thoughtful guidance through multiple revisions have been instrumental in shaping this book into its final form.

Throughout this book, we will explore the CeAF through two contrasting case studies-ComPlus, a large telecommunications provider, and LegalDeal, a specialised legal practice. These composite examples, drawn from real transformation journeys, illustrate how the framework adapts to different organisational contexts while maintaining consistent principles. From modernising legacy applications to implementing multi-agent orchestration, from building cognitive data platforms to ensuring ethical AI governance, we will examine practical approaches for each component of the cognitive enterprise.

My hope is that this book provides both inspiration and practical guidance for your organisation's cognitive transformation journey. Whether you are a business leader setting strategic direction, an architect designing future systems, or a technologist implementing AI capabilities, the frameworks, principles, and examples shared here offer a structured path towards becoming a truly cognitive enterprise-one that harnesses AI not just as a technology but as a transformative force that amplifies human potential, creates new value and builds lasting competitive advantage.

The road to cognitive transformation is not simple, but with clear architecture and systematic implementation, it is a journey every enterprise can undertake successfully. Let us begin.

Chapter 1: Setting the Stage

The Cognitive Enterprise Revolution

In a world where digital innovation sets the pace, businesses are scrambling to adapt, evolve, and stay relevant. It's no longer just about using data and AI; it's about integrating them so deeply into the DNA of an organisation that they drive every decision and action. From retail giants crafting shopping experiences that feel almost psychic to healthcare providers predicting patient needs before they arise, this is the age of the cognitive enterprise. It's not about chasing shiny new tools; it's about building smart systems into the heart of your business so you can innovate, adapt, and stay ahead in an unforgiving, competitive world.

The transformation toward cognitive capabilities reflects a fundamental shift in how businesses operate. Traditional enterprises typically process information in linear ways—collecting data, analysing it through predefined methods, and making decisions through hierarchical structures. This approach worked in stable markets but falters in today's volatile business environment, where conditions change rapidly, and new competitors emerge from unexpected quarters. Organisations find themselves hampered by legacy thinking as much as by legacy technology.

AI, in general, and Generative AI, in particular, are rewriting the rules of how businesses work, shaking up industries, and pushing organisations to rethink everything. For clarity, Generative AI refers to artificial intelligence systems capable of creating new content, insights, and solutions rather than simply analysing existing information. These technologies represent a paradigm shift from AI that merely assists human decision-making to AI that actively generates novel options and approaches.

Cognitive enterprises are leading this charge, ditching outdated systems and static processes for ones that are flexible, fast, and powered by real-time data. But it's not just about shiny tech. It's about creating a partnership between humans and AI, where machines amplify what people do best instead of trying to replace them. It's about building businesses that don't just react to change but drive it, setting new standards for innovation, agility, and success.

The Challenge of Transformation

Despite recognising the need for change, many organisations find themselves stuck in transformation limbo. Sarah Chen, CIO of a mid-sized insurance company, describes this common predicament: "*We know where we need to go, but the path is blocked by decades of technical debt, siloed departments that resist collaboration and uncertainty about which AI capabilities will deliver real value rather than just impressive demos.*"

This sentiment captures the reality faced by countless business leaders. The journey toward becoming a cognitive enterprise is far from straightforward. Despite the promise of advanced AI systems, many organisations remain trapped in a web of legacy applications, siloed data platforms, and outdated processes that hinder their ability to adapt and compete. The challenges are numerous, and the stakes are high: organisations that fail to evolve risk being left behind in a world that demands real-time insights, seamless collaboration, and continuous innovation.

These obstacles aren't merely technical—they're organisational, cultural, and strategic. When systems can't talk to each other, when data is locked in departmental silos, and when business processes are designed for stability rather than adaptability, even the most sophisticated AI tools will fail to deliver transformative value. This fundamental mismatch between traditional enterprise structures and cognitive capabilities creates the central tension that organisations must resolve to move forward.

Introducing the Cognitive Enterprise Architecture Framework

This book, Cognitive Enterprise Architecture: Transforming Business with AI, explores these challenges and offers a structured, actionable roadmap to overcoming them. It introduces the Cognitive Enterprise Architecture Framework (CeAF), a modular and scalable blueprint designed to help organisations navigate the complexities of cognitive transformation.

The CeAF isn't just another technical framework—it's a comprehensive approach that addresses technology, processes, organisational structures, and human factors in an integrated way. It provides organisations with a systematic method for assessing their current state, envisioning their cognitive future, and plotting a realistic path between these two points.

Before diving into the specifics of CeAF, it is important to understand the forces driving this revolution, the obstacles organisations face and the profound opportunities that await those who successfully embrace this transformation. Throughout this book, we'll explore not just what cognitive enterprises are but how your organisation can become one through practical, proven strategies that balance ambition with pragmatism.

Who This Book Is For

Transforming into a cognitive enterprise is not the responsibility of a single department or a select group of professionals. It is a holistic endeavor that requires alignment across the organisation. This book is intentionally structured to support a wide range of readers, each with unique perspectives and needs but united by a common goal: leveraging AI and data to create organisations that are smarter, more adaptable, and more human-centric.

Key Audiences and What They Will Gain

- Business Leaders and Executives
  For CEOs, CIOs, CTOs, COOs, and other decision-makers, this book translates the promise of cognitive transformation into tangible business outcomes. It offers clear strategies for aligning business goals with technology initiatives, managing risks, and fostering a culture of innovation and trust.

- Enterprise and Technology Architects & Engineers
  Enterprise, solution, and data architects will find a comprehensive framework for integrating AI, breaking down data silos, and modernizing legacy systems. The book provides practical patterns and real-world examples to bridge business vision with technical reality, ensuring scalable and adaptive architectures.
- Data Scientists, AI Engineers and Technologists
  For those building and deploying AI systems, the book offers practical guidance on integrating models into workflows, ensuring data quality, and deploying ethical, human-centric AI. The focus is on operationalizing AI for business value rather than on deep technical theory, making the content approachable yet actionable.
- Anyone Interested in the Future of Enterprises
  Whether you are a student, academic, entrepreneur, or policymaker, this book provides a comprehensive understanding of how organisations can harness AI and data to thrive in a complex world. The cognitive revolution is relevant to startups, governments, non-profits, and established corporations alike.

Making Technical Content Accessible: Guidance for All Readers

Beginning with Chapter 10, the book explores the technical foundations of the Cognitive Enterprise Architecture Framework (CeAF), including intelligent networks, integration platforms, and advanced AI orchestration. To ensure these chapters remain accessible:

- Clear Explanations and Context
  Each technical concept is introduced with plain-language explanations and real-world analogies before delving into detailed architectures or algorithms. For example, before presenting the Multiagent Orchestrator Platform (MOP), the book explains its role in everyday business scenarios, such as resolving a broadband customer's issue through a blend of AI and human support.

- Case Studies and User Stories
  Fictional yet relatable case studies such as ComPlus (a telecommunications provider) and LegalDeal (a legal services firm)-illustrate how technical solutions translate into business value and improved user experiences. These narratives ground abstract concepts in practical, human-centric outcomes.
- Visual Aids and Summaries
  Diagrams, tables, and end-of-chapter summaries highlight key takeaways, making it easy for non-technical readers to grasp the essentials and for technical readers to dive deeper as needed.

Structure and Flow: Layered Learning for All Levels

The book is structured to first build foundational understanding before introducing technical depth:

- Early Chapters:
  Focus on the business case for cognitive transformation, the challenges organisations face, and the principles of human-centric AI. These chapters are accessible to all readers, regardless of technical background.
- Middle Chapters:
  Introduce the Cognitive Enterprise Architecture Framework (CeAF) and its components, using case studies and practical examples to bridge theory and practice.
- Later Chapters (10 onwards):
  Provide technical deep-dives for those interested in implementation details while maintaining clear signposting and summaries for readers who wish to focus on outcomes rather than technical mechanics. Each technical section is prefaced with a non-technical overview and concludes with a recap of business implications.

By adopting this layered, reader-centric approach, the book ensures that every stakeholder from the boardroom to the data center engages with cognitive enterprise transformation. Whether you are seeking strategic insights, architectural guidance, or practical implementation tips, you will find content tailored to your needs, all within a unified, accessible framework.

A Shared Journey

While the specific goals and challenges of these audiences may differ, they are united by a shared objective: to navigate the complexities of cognitive transformation and unlock the full potential of AI, data, and innovation. This book is designed to provide actionable insights and practical tools for every stakeholder in this journey, ensuring that the transformation is not only successful but also sustainable, ethical, and aligned with the organisation's long-term vision.

The cognitive transformation journey often evokes both excitement and apprehension. Leaders may worry about making the right investments, technologists may feel pressure to deliver immediate results, and employees may fear changes to their roles and responsibilities. This book acknowledges these human concerns alongside technical considerations, recognising that successful transformation addresses both rational and emotional aspects of change.

No matter your role, this book will equip you with the knowledge and inspiration to drive meaningful change in your organisation. The Cognitive Enterprise Architecture Framework (CeAF) is your weapon in this transformation journey, enabling you to:

Integrate AI seamlessly into business processes rather than treating it as a separate technology layer. You'll learn how to embed intelligence into workflows in ways that feel natural to users while delivering unprecedented capabilities.

Exploit your data's full potential through architectures that unlock insights across organisational boundaries. You'll discover approaches for creating a unified data fabric that fuels innovation while maintaining appropriate governance and security.

Build an organisation that's intelligent, adaptable, and human. Beyond technology, you'll learn how to foster a culture where human creativity and AI capabilities complement each other, creating an enterprise that's greater than the sum of its parts.

As we begin this exploration of cognitive enterprise architecture, remember that transformation is not a destination but a continuous evolution. The organisations that thrive will be those that build not just intelligent systems but learning organisations capable of constant renewal and adaptation in an ever-changing world.

Chapter 2: The Cognitive Revolution: A Human-Centric Approach

Tina Davis, the Chief Strategy Officer at Global Shipping Enterprises, stared at the dashboard on her tablet. Just six months ago, she would have been surrounded by printouts, Excel sheets, and a team of analysts scrambling to make sense of a supply chain disruption like the one they were facing today. Instead, she watched as the company's cognitive system analysed the hurricane's projected path, evaluated the impact on nineteen shipping routes, identified vulnerable inventory across three continents, and recommended alternative logistics strategies—all within minutes. More impressively, the system didn't just present cold data; it outlined how each potential decision would affect customer commitments, provided confidence scores for each recommendation, and highlighted where human judgment would be most valuable.

"This is what transformation looks like," Tina thought, not because technology had replaced her team but because it had elevated them. The analysts who once spent days compiling reports were now focusing on strategic decisions that only humans could make, combining their industry expertise with AI-powered insights to navigate complexity with unprecedented agility.

Building on Foundations: From Traditional to Cognitive

A cognitive enterprise isn't just a smarter business—it's a living, breathing system of intelligence woven into every part of its operations. Unlike traditional organisations stuck in static workflows, cognitive enterprises thrive on adaptability. With Generative AI, machine learning, and cloud-native technologies, they create processes that evolve in real-time, delivering not just efficiency but groundbreaking innovation and deeply personalised customer experiences.

Traditional enterprises function like complex but ultimately static machines, with predetermined processes designed for consistency and control. Cognitive enterprises function more like biological systems—

adaptive, self-healing, and capable of evolution without disruption. This biological metaphor is apt: just as natural systems sense environmental changes and adapt accordingly, cognitive enterprises continuously sense market shifts, customer needs, and operational conditions, adjusting in real-time to maintain optimal performance.

The Human-Centric AI Vision

At the core of this revolution is Human-Centric AI—a radical shift that puts humans back in control. This isn't about AI taking over; it's about AI amplifying human intelligence and empowering better decisions. It's designed with a purpose: to uphold ethical principles, prioritize user needs, and remain transparent and accountable at every turn.

For years, the narrative around AI has centred on what the technology could do rather than whom it was serving. Human-centric AI flips that narrative entirely, starting with human needs, values, and potential and then designing AI systems that enhance rather than replace these uniquely human qualities. This approach addresses the widespread anxiety about AI replacing human jobs—a fear that pervades many organisations undertaking digital transformation. By explicitly designing systems that augment human capabilities rather than replacing them, Human-Centric AI creates space for the emotional aspects of transformation, acknowledging that technological change affects not just processes but people's sense of purpose and value.

Human-centric AI makes machines collaborators, not competitors. It doesn't just enhance workflows; it builds trust, drives innovation, and pushes productivity to new heights. This is a technology with a conscience—intelligent, ethical, and unapologetically focused on empowering people to lead the charge.

Key Principles of Human-Centric AI

The Human-Centric AI vision is guided by several core principles that ensure AI serves human needs and values. These principles aren't abstract concepts—they're practical guidelines that shape how cognitive systems are designed, deployed, and governed.

Transparency and Explainability

AI must make sense. If a system makes a decision, users should know why. Transparency isn't optional—it's non-negotiable. Whether it's a loan approval or a medical diagnosis, the reasoning needs to be clear and actionable, building trust and ensuring accountability.

In healthcare, this principle manifests when AI tools empower doctors with insights rather than leaving them guessing with vague results. Diagnostic systems that highlight the patterns they've detected in medical images link to relevant research and explain their confidence levels, giving physicians the information they need to make informed decisions while maintaining their authority and responsibility for patient care.

Loan officers at community banks benefit from transparent AI-powered underwriting systems that show exactly which factors influenced decisions, helping explain outcomes to customers and sometimes identifying situations where the AI might be missing important context. Rather than following a machine's orders, these professionals collaborate with tools that respect their expertise enough to show their work.

Humans in Charge

AI should assist, not replace. Critical decisions need human oversight, especially when lives or livelihoods are on the line. From healthcare to autonomous driving, humans must have the final say. This collaboration ensures AI enhances human judgment rather than overriding it.

Commercial aircraft with AI-assisted navigation systems exemplify this principle in action. Modern planes can identify and suggest responses to thousands of potential issues, from weather patterns to mechanical anomalies. However, these systems are designed to recognize the boundaries of their expertise, presenting options rather than taking control and acknowledging that human experience and judgment remain irreplaceable, especially in novel or complex situations.

This principle extends beyond high-risk contexts to everyday business decisions. When an AI suggests a particular marketing strategy or inventory allocation, humans retain the authority to accept, modify, or reject these recommendations based on factors the AI might not fully comprehend, such as emerging market trends or competitive intelligence that hasn't yet appeared in the data.

Fairness and Equity

AI can't be trusted without ethical safeguards. Companies must address issues like bias, fairness, and data privacy head-on. Systems should be designed to promote accountability, whether it's mitigating biases in hiring algorithms or ensuring compliance with regulations. Ethical AI isn't a buzzword—it's the foundation of trust.

Leading recruitment firms implement this principle by subjecting every algorithm to rigorous testing for bias across dozens of demographic factors. This monitoring continues after deployment, with AI recommendations regularly compared against diverse panels of human recruiters. Organisations increasingly recognize that ethical considerations aren't merely technical problems to solve but ongoing commitments that require constant vigilance, especially as AI systems learn and evolve in production environments.

Empowerment, Not Replacement

AI is here to support people, not make them obsolete. It should handle the repetitive, time-consuming stuff, leaving humans free to focus on creativity, strategy, and empathy. Think chatbots managing routine questions while customer service reps handle complex, nuanced conversations. The goal? Amplify human potential, not sideline it.

In the telecommunications industry, the introduction of AI-powered chatbots has transformed customer service roles. Instead of eliminating jobs, AI has taken over password resets and basic troubleshooting—the monotonous tasks that drain energy. Service representatives now focus exclusively on complex problems where they can apply creativity and empathy, resulting in increased job satisfaction and higher customer satisfaction scores.

This principle rejects the false binary between human and machine intelligence, recognising that the most powerful results come from combining the complementary strengths of each. AI excels at processing vast amounts of data and identifying patterns, while humans bring creativity, ethical judgment, and emotional intelligence that remains beyond the reach of even the most sophisticated algorithms.

Inclusive by Design

AI must work for everyone, not just a select few. Systems should be built with accessibility and inclusivity in mind—voice commands for those with disabilities and multilingual interfaces for global users. If AI doesn't serve diverse needs, it's failing its purpose.

Educational technology companies incorporate this principle by testing learning algorithms with students from different cultural backgrounds, socioeconomic levels, and abilities. When systems assume certain cultural references that confuse international students, designers completely redesign the content generation system. Inclusivity isn't just a moral imperative—it makes products better for everyone.

This principle acknowledges that AI systems can perpetuate or even amplify existing social inequalities if not deliberately designed for inclusion. By considering diverse needs and perspectives from the outset, Human-Centric AI ensures technology serves as a force for equity rather than exclusion.

Continuous Learning and Adaptation

AI should adapt, not stagnate. Continuous learning ensures systems stay relevant, responsive, and effective. Whether it's tailoring educational tools to individual learning styles or evolving based on user feedback, AI must keep growing alongside the people it serves.

In personalised medicine, diagnostic systems don't just apply fixed algorithms to patient data. They continuously learn from outcomes, integrating new research findings automatically and adapting to population-specific patterns. When these systems encounter cases that don't fit existing patterns, they flag them for human review, creating a virtuous cycle where human expertise guides machine learning and machine insights extend human capabilities.

This principle recognizes that static AI systems quickly become outdated in rapidly changing environments. By designing for continuous learning and adaptation, cognitive enterprises ensure their systems remain valuable even as conditions evolve.

Visible and Accountable

AI can't operate in the shadows. Users need to see how decisions are made, how data is used, and who's responsible when things go wrong. Audit trails and accountability measures are essential, especially in high-stakes fields like finance or healthcare. Transparency builds trust; accountability keeps it.

Community development financial institutions exemplify this principle through loan approval systems that show both applicants and loan officers exactly which factors influenced decisions. When loans are denied, these systems provide specific reasons and suggest steps applicants might take to improve their chances in the future. Every decision is logged with a clear attribution of responsibility between AI recommendations and human judgments. This transparency reduces complaints about loan decisions while improving regulatory compliance.

This principle ensures that AI systems remain answerable to human oversight, creating the conditions for trust even in sensitive domains where decisions have significant consequences for individuals and communities.

Safe and Reliable

AI must be dependable, even under pressure. Systems need rigorous testing and safeguards to prevent errors or failures. Whether it's emergency protocols in industrial automation or fail-safes in self-driving cars, safety isn't a feature—it's a mandate.

Industrial automation companies design with the assumption that things will go wrong. Their systems undergo thousands of simulated failure scenarios, and engineers build redundant safety mechanisms that can operate even if primary AI systems fail. They also ensure humans can always take control in emergencies. This approach might slow development somewhat, but it's non-negotiable when safety is at stake.

This principle acknowledges that while AI systems can achieve impressive performance in controlled environments, they must be designed with robust safeguards to handle the complexity and unpredictability of real-world deployment, especially in critical applications.

Key Drivers of the Cognitive Revolution

The cognitive revolution is being powered by several key trends that are redefining how organisations operate and compete. These drivers aren't merely technological innovations—they represent fundamental shifts in how businesses create value, make decisions, and engage with customers and employees.

Adaptive, Dynamic Processes Enabled by AI

Traditional business processes are like trains on fixed tracks—efficient but inflexible. Cognitive processes are more like autonomous vehicles, constantly sensing their environment and adapting their route to changing conditions. This shift from static to dynamic processes represents one of the most profound changes in how organisations operate.

Cognitive enterprises move away from rigid, pre-defined workflows to embrace adaptive, dynamic processes that can adjust in real time based on evolving business contexts. These processes are powered by AI models that are capable of understanding and responding to complex scenarios.

When the pandemic hit, traditional, static supply chain models completely failed many global food distributors. Companies simply couldn't adapt fast enough to the daily changes in demand, supply, and logistics capacity. After implementing adaptive supply chain platforms, the difference was immediate. These systems continuously recalibrate based on real-time conditions—identifying alternate suppliers, adjusting delivery routes, and even recommending temporary changes to product formulations when ingredients are scarce. What used to take weeks of emergency meetings now happens automatically, with humans focusing on strategic decisions rather than reactive firefighting.

This adaptability extends across industries and functions:

Retail: AI-driven inventory systems dynamically adjust stock levels based on real-time demand, supply chain disruptions, or even external factors like weather patterns. Consider how a clothing retailer's system might automatically increase umbrella inventory at specific stores when rain is forecast or shift summer merchandise allocations based on unexpected temperature trends—all without human intervention.

Healthcare: AI systems continuously analyse patient data to recommend personalised treatment plans that evolve with the patient's condition. Rather than following standardised protocols, these systems consider the unique characteristics of each patient, learning from outcomes and adjusting recommendations as new information becomes available.

Manufacturing: Predictive maintenance solutions powered by reasoning models monitor equipment usage and performance, dynamically scheduling repairs to minimize downtime. Unlike traditional maintenance schedules based on average failure rates, these systems learn the specific patterns and anomalies of individual machines, allowing for precisely timed interventions that optimize both equipment lifespan and operational efficiency.

These adaptive processes enable organisations to move beyond reactive operations and embrace proactive, data-driven decision-making. By doing so, they not only improve efficiency but also create value at every step of the workflow. The shift is comparable to the difference between a traditional map and a GPS navigation system—both can guide you to a destination, but only one adapts in real-time to changing conditions, offering alternative routes when obstacles arise.

Productivity Improvements Through AI-Driven Automation

AI is forcing a reality check on how work gets done. The repetitive, mindless tasks? Gone. AI is taking those off the table, and if you're still clinging to them, you're wasting time. This isn't about fear; it's about freedom—freedom to focus on what actually matters: ideas, strategy, and impact. The industries that get it are already pulling ahead, turning AI into their unfair advantage.

Legal professionals are experiencing this transformation first-hand. Paralegals who once spent about 70% of their time on document review—scanning through thousands of pages to find relevant information for cases—now have that ratio completely flipped. AI-powered legal research platforms handle the initial document filtering and classification, allowing legal staff to focus on analysing the findings, identifying case strategy implications, and collaborating more closely with attorneys. They're doing more valuable work and firms can handle more cases without increasing headcount.

This productivity revolution extends across sectors:

Marketing: Generative AI can produce personalised campaigns, product descriptions, and even social media posts, allowing marketing teams to focus on strategy and creative innovation. A small marketing team can now produce content at the scale previously requiring dozens of copywriters while maintaining brand consistency and tailoring messages to specific audience segments.

Legal Operations: AI-powered tools analyse contracts, identify risks, and recommend changes, reducing the time required for manual reviews. Legal professionals can focus on negotiation strategy and relationship management rather than combing through dense legal language for potential issues.

Customer Service: AI chatbots handle routine inquiries, freeing human agents to address more nuanced and emotionally complex customer needs. When a customer contacts their bank's customer service about a missing payment, the AI system handles the authentication process, locates the payment details, and resolves the simple tracking issue—all in minutes. For more complex situations involving financial hardship or a dispute, the system seamlessly transfers customers to human agents, providing those agents with full context so customers don't need to repeat information.

These productivity improvements not only drive cost savings but also enhance employee satisfaction by eliminating mundane tasks and enabling them to contribute more meaningfully to the organisation's goals. The result is a workforce that's more engaged, more strategic, and more aligned with activities that create genuine value for customers and the business.

Generative AI: Unlocking Creativity and Innovation

Generative AI models, such as large language models and generative design tools, enable enterprises to innovate at an unprecedented scale. These models can generate creative outputs tailored to specific contexts, from product designs to personalised marketing, fundamentally changing how organisations approach innovation and creative work.

Product designers at consumer electronics companies have witnessed this transformation first-hand. Before generative AI, teams might explore 5-10 design concepts for a new product based on initial ideas. Now, they can generate hundreds of design variations based on specific parameters, discover unexpected approaches never previously considered, and focus human creativity on refining and enhancing the most promising concepts. Technology hasn't replaced creative roles—it's expanded creative capacity exponentially.

The impact of generative AI spans multiple domains:

Product Development: AI can generate prototypes, optimize designs, and simulate performance, reducing time-to-market for new products. An automotive manufacturer using generative design might input requirements for a new bracket—specifying materials, load requirements, and manufacturing constraints—and receive dozens of optimized designs that might never occur to human engineers, some using 30% less material while improving performance.

Content Creation: Marketing teams can use AI to generate unique, engaging content customized for individual customer segments. Rather than creating a single product description, marketers can generate variations tailored to different customer personas, each emphasizing features most relevant to that audience, written in the appropriate tone, and optimized for specific platforms or contexts.

Software Development: AI tools assist developers by generating boilerplate code, identifying bugs, and suggesting improvements. A programmer can describe a desired function in natural language, and AI can generate the corresponding code, complete with error handling and optimisation, allowing developers to focus on more complex architectural decisions rather than routine implementation details.

Generative AI enables organisations to experiment more freely, reduce costs associated with innovation, and generate solutions faster than ever before. This isn't about replacing human creativity but amplifying it—allowing people to explore more possibilities, iterate more quickly, and focus their unique human insights on evaluation and refinement rather than routine production.

Productivity and Customer-Centricity as Core Outcomes

The goal of the cognitive revolution is to create organisations that are not only efficient but also customer-centric. By embedding intelligence into every layer of their operations, cognitive enterprises can anticipate customer needs, deliver personalised experiences and build lasting relationships.

Five years ago, telecommunications companies operated with fundamentally reactive customer interactions—waiting for customers to contact them with problems and then scrambling to solve them. Today, cognitive systems analyse usage patterns, network performance, and even social media sentiment to identify potential issues before customers are affected. When a network anomaly suggests certain customers might experience degraded service, the system proactively notifies them, offers temporary alternatives and keeps them updated on resolution progress. The shift from apologizing for problems to preventing them has completely transformed customer relationships.

This customer-centric approach takes numerous forms across industries:

Retailers can use AI to analyse customer preferences and generate tailored recommendations, creating shopping experiences that feel intuitive and engaging. When customers visit their favourite online clothing stores, the sites don't just show similar items to past purchases—they understand style preferences, consider seasonal trends, recognise browsing patterns across devices, and present personalised collections that feel like they were curated specifically for each individual. The experience feels less like transactional shopping and more like working with a personal stylist who understands unique tastes.

Financial institutions can leverage reasoning models to provide personalised investment advice, helping customers achieve their financial goals with confidence. Instead of generic asset allocation models based solely on age and risk tolerance, these systems consider a customer's complete financial picture—income patterns, spending habits, life goals, and even region-specific economic factors—to create truly personalised recommendations that adapt as circumstances change.

Hospitality companies can use AI-powered chatbots and dynamic pricing models to deliver seamless, customized booking experiences. When planning a family vacation, travellers might interact with a hotel's AI system that remembers previous stays, recognizes the presence of children, and automatically highlights family-friendly amenities and room configurations. The system might also offer personalised pricing based on length of stay, season, and room availability, creating a win-win scenario where guests get value, and hotels optimize occupancy.

These innovations drive customer loyalty while enabling enterprises to operate more efficiently, creating a virtuous cycle of competitiveness and growth. By deeply understanding customer needs and preferences, cognitive enterprises can deliver experiences that feel personal and attentive at scale without the prohibitive costs associated with traditional high-touch service models.

Challenges on the Road to Becoming a Cognitive Enterprise

While the promise of cognitive transformation is compelling, the journey is rarely straightforward. Organisations face numerous obstacles that can slow or derail their efforts if not addressed strategically. Understanding these challenges is the first step toward overcoming them.

Many organisations begin their cognitive transformation journey with naive optimism. They have the vision, executive support, and access to cutting-edge AI technologies. What they often underestimate is how deeply legacy systems, siloed data, and traditional operating models constrain their ability to implement that vision. After years of investment and effort, organisations must frequently rethink their approach—focusing much more on architectural foundations and organisational alignment before racing to implement AI use cases.

This reality reflects what many organisations face as they pursue cognitive transformation—enthusiasm meets entrenched obstacles that require thoughtful, systematic solutions.

Legacy Systems Holding You Back

Legacy systems are the chains that keep businesses stuck in the past. These outdated platforms weren't built for the demands of modern AI or dynamic, data-driven workflows. They're expensive, rigid, and drag agility to a crawl. And it's not just the tech—outdated processes add layers of inefficiency, making change feel impossible.

Core systems built decades ago present particular challenges. Consider insurance claims processing systems from the 1980s. They're stable but designed for a different era—batch processing, limited data capacity, and no API capabilities. When companies try to implement modern claims analytics platforms, they discover that simply extracting the necessary data is nearly impossible without risking the stability of the entire system. They're effectively trying to build smart homes on top of foundations designed for completely different structures.

Legacy challenges manifest in several dimensions:

Technical Debt: Over decades, enterprises have accumulated layers of outdated technology and ad hoc fixes. This "technical debt" slows down innovation and increases the cost of adopting innovative solutions. Each new system added without retiring old ones creates a more tangled web of dependencies and integration challenges.

Inflexibility: Legacy systems are often rigid, with architectures that cannot easily integrate with modern AI, cloud-based platforms, or real-time data pipelines. They were designed for stability and predictability in a world that now demands adaptability and responsiveness.

Maintenance Costs: A disproportionate share of IT budgets is spent maintaining outdated systems, leaving little room for investment in innovation. Many organisations find themselves allocating 70-80% of their technology resources to "keeping the lights on" rather than driving transformation.

Security Risks: Older systems are more vulnerable to cyber threats, creating risks for data breaches and compliance violations. As vendors end support for legacy platforms, security patches become unavailable, creating growing vulnerability over time.

The impact of these challenges can be severe. Consider a financial services firm with legacy mainframe systems managing its core banking operations. These systems are incapable of integrating with modern AI-powered customer service tools or real-time fraud detection systems. This limitation not only prevents the firm from delivering seamless, AI-driven customer experiences but also hampers its ability to respond to market changes dynamically. The result is a growing competitive disadvantage as more agile, digitally-native competitors capture market share.

Data Locked in Silos

Siloed data isn't just an inconvenience; it's a roadblock to innovation. When information is scattered across departments and systems, organisations can't see the full picture. The result? Missed insights, fractured workflows, and an inability to unleash AI's true potential.

Data is the foundation of everything organisations do with AI. But when many healthcare networks started their journey, they discovered data locked in dozens of different systems that didn't communicate with each other. Patient information is in the electronic health record, billing data is in the financial system, scheduling is in another platform, and imaging is in yet another repository. Building a comprehensive view of a patient journey was nearly impossible, let alone training AI models to identify patterns across that journey.

This fragmentation creates numerous obstacles:

Fragmentation: Customer data, operational metrics, financial records, and other critical information are often stored in isolated systems that do not communicate with one another. Each department may have its own version of the truth, leading to inconsistent decision-making and customer experiences.

Inconsistent Data Quality: Without centralized governance, data from diverse sources often lacks standardisation, resulting in inaccuracies and duplication. Field definitions, formats, and quality standards vary across systems, making integration extremely challenging.

Missed Opportunities: Siloed data prevents organisations from gaining a unified view of their operations, customers, or markets, limiting their ability to make informed decisions. Patterns and correlations that exist across data domains remain invisible when those domains cannot be analysed together.

The impact of data silos is perhaps most vividly illustrated through failed AI initiatives. Imagine a global retailer betting big on an AI-powered recommendation engine to revolutionize customer experience. Sounds bold, right? But here's the problem: purchase history is locked in one system, inventory data buried in another, and browsing patterns scattered everywhere else. The AI can't work with scraps, and instead of delivering killer recommendations, it churns out useless noise. Data silos are innovation killers. Without smashing these barriers, that dream of transformation is dead in the water.

Not Ready for AI

AI might be the future, but many organisations are stuck at the starting line. Lacking the infrastructure, expertise, or clear alignment with business goals, AI initiatives often stall in pilot phases. The potential is there, but the readiness is not.

Many organisations have executives demanding AI solutions after reading about them in business magazines, but they lack the fundamental capabilities to deploy these solutions successfully. Their data isn't prepared, their infrastructure can't support the computational requirements, and their teams don't have the skills to develop or maintain AI models. They waste months on pilots that can never scale because they haven't addressed these foundational issues first.

This lack of readiness manifests in several areas:

Infrastructure Gaps: AI systems require robust computing power, scalable data platforms, and real-time integration capabilities, which many organisations lack. Traditional IT infrastructure designed for transaction processing and reporting is inadequate for the demands of modern AI workloads.

Talent Shortages: The rapid pace of AI development has created a significant talent gap, with organisations struggling to hire or upskill professionals in data science, machine learning, and AI governance. Competition for this talent is fierce, putting smaller organisations at a particular disadvantage.

Isolated AI Initiatives: Many enterprises launch disconnected AI projects without a clear strategy for scaling or aligning them with broader business goals. These isolated efforts rarely deliver sustained value and often fail to progress beyond the proof-of-concept stages.

The consequences of these gaps are reflected in the high failure rate of AI initiatives. For example, a healthcare provider may deploy an AI model to predict patient readmissions but fail to integrate it with its electronic health record (EHR) system. Without operational integration, the AI model remains an isolated tool, unable to influence day-to-day decision-making or improve patient outcomes. Clinicians continue their work unaware of the insights the model could provide, and the initiative fails to deliver meaningful value despite technical success in a controlled environment.

Governance is a Minefield

AI adoption comes with its own set of challenges—navigating regulatory frameworks, addressing bias, and ensuring ethical accountability. From GDPR compliance to tackling data privacy concerns, organisations face a maze of governance complexities that demand constant attention.

Every AI model deployed introduces new governance considerations. Is the model fair and unbiased? Are we using customer data appropriately? Can we explain how decisions are made? Are we in compliance with evolving regulations across different jurisdictions? The governance workload has grown exponentially alongside AI capabilities, and failure in any of these areas could have serious consequences for both customers and businesses.

These governance challenges take multiple forms:

Data Privacy and Security: Regulations such as GDPR and the EU AI Act impose strict requirements for how data is collected, stored, and used. Organisations must implement robust processes for consent management, data minimization, and security protocols, especially when sensitive information is involved.

Bias and Fairness: AI systems are prone to biases that can lead to unethical or discriminatory outcomes, potentially damaging an organisation's reputation and eroding trust. Identifying and mitigating these biases requires ongoing vigilance and specialised expertise, which many organisations lack.

Transparency: Stakeholders increasingly demand explainable AI systems that provide clear, interpretable insights into how decisions are made. This transparency is particularly important in regulated industries and in high-stakes decisions that affect individuals.

The impact of governance failures can be severe. Consider an insurance company deploying an AI model to calculate premiums. If the model inadvertently discriminates against certain demographics due to biased training data, the company could face regulatory penalties, reputational damage, and customer backlash. Robust governance frameworks are essential to mitigating such risks and ensuring responsible AI use.

Cultural Resistance to Change

Technology can evolve quickly; mindsets, not so much. Resistance to change, silos between IT and business teams, and leadership without a clear vision all slow the transformation process. Becoming a cognitive enterprise isn't just about upgrading tools; it's about shifting how an organisation thinks and works.

The biggest challenges in digital transformation are often human, not technical. Organisations frequently encounter managers who feel threatened by AI, teams protective of their domains and data, and employees worried about job security. The technology implementation is straightforward compared to navigating these cultural and emotional responses. Transformation success depends 20% on technology and 80% on people and culture.

This cultural resistance manifests in several ways:

Fear of Change: Employees may resist modern technologies due to concerns about job displacement or a lack of familiarity with AI systems. Without clear communication about how AI will augment rather than replace human roles, this fear can derail even well-designed initiatives.

Siloed Teams: A lack of collaboration between IT, business, and operations teams often leads to misaligned priorities and conflicting goals. When technical teams develop solutions without deep business context or when business teams demand capabilities without understanding technical constraints, the result is often failed initiatives and mutual frustration.

Leadership Gaps: Without a clear vision and commitment from leadership, transformation efforts often lose momentum. When executives treat cognitive transformation as a technology project rather than a business imperative, they fail to create the conditions necessary for success.

These cultural challenges can have profound effects on transformation efforts. For example, a manufacturing company implementing AI-powered predictive maintenance may face pushback from technicians who distrust the system's accuracy or fear that it will make their roles obsolete. If this resistance isn't addressed through training, involvement in the implementation process, and clear communication about how the technology will enhance rather than replace their expertise, the initiative is likely to fail despite its technical merit. Overcoming such resistance requires strong leadership, clear communication, and a focus on change management.

The Talent Crunch

AI is advancing faster than the workforce can keep up. The talent gap in AI, data science, and enterprise architecture is widening, leaving businesses scrambling for skilled professionals. Upskilling teams and fostering collaboration are non-negotiable, but they're far from easy.

Every organisation is struggling to find and retain AI talent. The demand for data scientists, machine learning engineers, and AI architects far exceeds supply, and traditional educational pipelines aren't producing graduates fast enough. Organisations are competing for a limited pool of experts while also trying to upskill their existing workforce—a dual challenge that requires creative approaches and significant investment.

This talent gap creates several specific challenges:

Shortage of Expertise: There is a global shortage of professionals with expertise in AI, data engineering, and cognitive system design. This scarcity drives up costs and creates delays in critical projects as organisations compete for limited talent.

Need for Cross-Disciplinary Skills: Cognitive transformation requires collaboration across technical, business, and operational domains, which can be difficult to achieve with siloed skill sets. The most valuable professionals are those who can bridge these domains, combining technical depth with business acumen and communication skills.

Upskilling Requirements: Organisations must invest in upskilling their existing workforce to ensure employees can effectively leverage new tools and technologies. This represents a significant investment of time and resources, particularly for larger enterprises with diverse workforces.

The impact of these talent challenges can significantly impede transformation efforts. For instance, a logistics company implementing an AI-driven route optimisation system may struggle to find data engineers capable of integrating the system with existing platforms, delaying deployment and reducing ROI. Even after successful implementation, the organisation may face ongoing challenges in maintaining and enhancing the system if it lacks the necessary in-house expertise.

The Interconnected Nature of Challenges

These challenges—legacy complexity, siloed data, lack of AI readiness, governance pressures, cultural resistance, and skills gaps—are not isolated. They are deeply interconnected, creating a cycle of inefficiency and resistance that hinders progress.

When working with clients, experienced consultants often show how these challenges form a self-reinforcing cycle. Legacy systems make it difficult to break down data silos, which in turn, limits an organisation's ability to deploy AI solutions effectively. The technical limitations reinforce cultural resistance as teams become frustrated with failed initiatives and grow more sceptical of transformation efforts. This scepticism makes it harder to attract top talent, further widening the skills gap. Breaking this cycle requires a holistic approach that addresses these challenges simultaneously.

The interconnections are numerous:

Legacy systems make it difficult to break down data silos, which in turn, limits an organisation's ability to deploy AI solutions effectively.

Cultural resistance exacerbates governance challenges, as employees may be reluctant to adopt transparent, ethical practices without strong leadership support.

Talent shortages make it harder to modernise legacy systems, creating a vicious cycle of technical debt and continuing dependence on outdated platforms.

Understanding these interconnections is crucial for developing effective transformation strategies. Organisations that attempt to address individual challenges in isolation often find their efforts stalled by the pull of related issues. Breaking this cycle requires a holistic approach that addresses these challenges simultaneously. This is precisely where the Cognitive Enterprise Architecture Framework (CeAF) comes into play.

Making AI Work for Your Organisation: The Cognitive Enterprise Architecture Framework

This book introduces a powerful solution to today's complex AI implementation challenges: the Cognitive Enterprise Architecture Framework (CeAF). This framework serves as your organisation's roadmap for successful AI integration and digital transformation.

What is the Cognitive Enterprise Architecture Framework?

The Cognitive Enterprise Architecture Framework (CeAF) is a structured blueprint designed to help organisations systematically implement and scale AI technologies. Unlike piecemeal approaches that create disconnected AI systems, CeAF provides a cohesive architecture that aligns technology with business goals.

Rather than presenting abstract theories, CeAF offers practical guidance through:

- A well-defined architecture framework that provides a clear set of architecture principles and patterns to transform application, data, and integration architecture by using AI.
- A modular design that allows organisations to implement components based on their specific needs and readiness
- Clear integration pathways that connect AI capabilities with existing enterprise systems and data resources

By applying this structured approach, organisations can transform theoretical AI potential into practical business advantages while navigating the complexities of cognitive transformation with confidence.

What sets CeAF apart is how it addresses the full spectrum of technical transformation challenges—not just isolated technical implementations but processes, governance, and systemic integration. It provides organisations with a structured method for aligning technical capabilities with operational workflows while maintaining compliance across complex enterprise ecosystems. It gives organisations a structured way to assess their current state, define their target architecture, and create a realistic roadmap that acknowledges constraints while still driving meaningful progress. Most importantly, it helps communicate complex transformation in ways that resonate with different stakeholders, from executive leadership to technical teams.

In the following chapters, we will explore the CeAF in detail, examining its components, principles, and practical applications across diverse industries and organisational contexts. We'll provide concrete guidance on how to apply this framework to your specific challenges, whether you're just beginning your cognitive journey or looking to accelerate existing initiatives.

Conclusion

The cognitive revolution represents a fundamental shift in how organisations operate, compete, and create value. By embracing Human-Centric AI, adaptive processes, and generative capabilities, enterprises can achieve unprecedented levels of productivity, innovation, and customer-centricity. However, this transformation journey is fraught with challenges—from legacy systems and data silos to cultural resistance and talent shortages.

Success requires more than just implementing new technologies; it demands a holistic approach that addresses these interconnected challenges systematically. The Cognitive Enterprise Architecture Framework (CeAF) provides this comprehensive approach, offering a structured path forward that balances ambition with pragmatism.

As we move into the subsequent chapters, we'll dive deeper into the specifics of CeAF, exploring its components, methodologies, and real-world applications. You'll learn how to assess your organisation's current state, design your cognitive future, and navigate the journey between these points with confidence and clarity. The roadmap to becoming a cognitive enterprise may be complex, but with the right framework and approach, it's a journey that any organisation can undertake successfully.

Chapter 3: Key Components of the Cognitive Enterprise Architecture Framework (CeAF)

Bridging Vision and Reality: The CeAF Approach

In Chapter 2, we explored the profound challenges organisations face on their journey to becoming cognitive enterprises—legacy systems, data silos, governance complexities, cultural resistance, and talent gaps. The Cognitive Enterprise Architecture Framework (CeAF) is specifically designed to address these interconnected challenges through a holistic, adaptable architecture that balances technical innovation with human needs.

CeAF represents a fundamental shift from traditional enterprise architecture approaches. Rather than treating AI as a separate technology layer bolted onto existing systems, it weaves intelligence, adaptability, and human-centricity into every aspect of the organisation. This integrated approach ensures that cognitive capabilities serve business outcomes while embodying the Human-centric AI principles we explored in Chapter 2.

Before diving into the individual components, it's important to understand how they work together as an integrated system. Imagine an orchestra where each section contributes distinct elements to create a harmonious whole. Similarly, CeAF's components operate both independently and in concert, creating a framework that is greater than the sum of its parts. From user interactions to data management, from application modernisation to governance, each layer addresses specific challenges while supporting the overall cognitive transformation journey.

Human-centric AI: The Philosophical Foundation

At the core of CeAF lies a fundamental commitment to human-centric AI (HCAI), which ensures that technology serves human needs and values rather than the reverse. This isn't merely a philosophical statement but a practical design principle that shapes how each component functions and interacts. Rather than treating HCAI as a separate layer, it serves as the connective tissue that binds the framework together with a consistent purpose: to amplify human capabilities, ensure ethical operations, and build systems worthy of trust.

The principles of HCAI introduced in Chapter 2—clarity over confusion, humans in charge, ethics at the core, empowerment, not replacement, inclusive by design, always learning, visible and accountable, and safe and reliable—influence how each component is designed and implemented. This human-centred foundation is particularly evident in components that directly interface with users, orchestrate intelligent workflows, and govern AI operations.

By embedding these principles throughout the framework, CeAF ensures that even the most technically sophisticated systems remain aligned with human priorities. As we examine each component, we'll highlight where HCAI principles have the most significant influence while recognising that this human-centred philosophy permeates the entire architecture.

The CeAF Components: An Integrated System

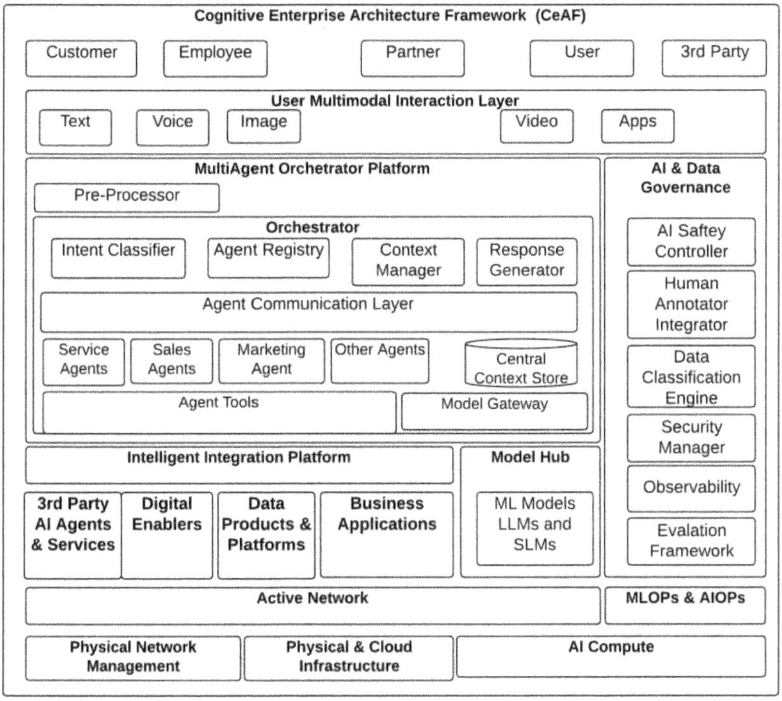

The CeAF consists of ten interconnected layers, each addressing specific challenges while contributing to a unified cognitive architecture:

1. **User Multimodal Interaction Layer** serves as the interface between people and systems, creating intuitive, adaptive experiences across channels and modalities.
2. **Multi-Agent Orchestrator Platform (MOP)** coordinates the actions of various AI agents and business workflows. It interprets user intent, manages context, and intelligently routes tasks to the right agents or systems. This orchestration ensures that responses are not only fast but also context-aware and relevant, enabling the enterprise to deliver intelligent, end-to-end solutions.
3. **Business Application Layer** modernises traditional, often rigid, business applications by transforming legacy systems into

modular, AI-enhanced services; it allows organisations to adapt quickly to changing needs, embeds intelligence into everyday processes, and supports innovation without the constraints of outdated technology.

4. **Data Products and Platform** unify fragmented enterprise data into a single, accessible foundation that enables the delivery of high-value data products. These data products, enrich AI agents with curated, contextualised information-fueling more intelligent, context-aware decisions.
5. **Digital Enabler Layer** bridges traditional systems with modern engagement tools, enabling personalised experiences.
6. **Intelligent Integration Platform** acts as the connective tissue of the cognitive enterprise, providing seamless, secure access to a wide variety of enterprise resources, including data, applications, and services for both human users and AI agents.
7. **Model Hub** manages the lifecycle of AI and machine learning models from development and validation to deployment and monitoring. It ensures that the right models are available, governed, and continuously improved, supporting a wide range of business and technical use cases.
8. **AI Compute Layer** provides the computational power required to train, fine-tune, and deploy AI models at scale. It supports flexible deployment options-on-premises, in the cloud, or hybrid, ensuring organisations can match their infrastructure to their unique needs and workloads.
9. **Active and Intelligent Network Systems** create self-healing, adaptive networks that optimize performance automatically.
10. **AI & Data Governance Layer** embeds governance controls across all AI and data activities, ensuring responsible use of technology. It monitors for bias, enforces regulatory compliance, and provides human oversight where necessary, building confidence among users, customers, and regulators alike.

Now, let's explore each component in depth, understanding not just its technical function but how it addresses specific challenges and transforms business operations in tangible ways.

1. User Multimodal Interaction Layer: Creating Intuitive Human Experiences

The User Multimodal Interaction Layer sits at the forefront of CeAF and redefines how people and systems engage with enterprise systems. It creates seamless, personalised interactions across multiple channels and modalities, ensuring that every touchpoint—whether through text, voice, video, or other formats—feels intuitive and human-centred.

In retail banking, this transformation is particularly evident. Customers who once navigated a frustrating maze of disconnected systems—starting in a mobile app, then calling a service centre only to repeat information, and finally visiting a branch to complete transactions—now experience something entirely different. Today, a customer can begin applying for a mortgage on their phone while commuting, continue the conversation with a virtual assistant at home via their smart speaker, and seamlessly transition to a video call with a mortgage specialist when they have complex questions—all while the system maintains the context of their journey.

How It Works

The User Multimodal Interaction Layer serves as an intelligent interface that understands and responds to various forms of communication. It incorporates:

Multimodal Support that enables natural interactions through text, voice, video, and images across platforms like chatbots, voice assistants, websites, and mobile apps. This versatility allows users to engage with systems in ways that feel most natural to them.

Omnichannel Experiences that maintain context and continuity across different touchpoints, from social media and mobile apps to physical locations and customer service calls. When a customer begins a transaction on their phone and later continues on a computer, the system remembers where they left off, eliminating frustrating repetition.

Emotion-Aware Interactions that use sentiment analysis to recognize emotional cues and adapt responses accordingly. The system can detect frustration, confusion, or satisfaction in a user's communication and adjust its tone and approach to provide more empathetic support.

AI-Powered Assistants that deliver intuitive, real-time support across multiple contexts. These digital assistants understand natural language, remember past interactions, and continuously learn from user behaviour to provide increasingly personalised experiences.

Addressing Key Challenges

This layer directly addresses several challenges identified in Chapter 2:

Data Silos: By creating a unified interaction layer, it bridges previously disconnected customer touchpoints, overcoming the fragmentation that frustrates users and limits organisational effectiveness.

Legacy Systems: It provides a modern, consistent interface that can sit on top of older systems, delivering improved user experiences even before the complete modernisation of backend infrastructure.

Cultural Resistance: By demonstrating immediate value through improved user experiences helps build organisational support for broader cognitive transformation.

Value Across Industries

The impact of this layer extends across diverse sectors:

In healthcare, patients can describe symptoms through natural conversation, upload photos of physical conditions, and receive guidance through multiple channels—all while the system maintains a coherent understanding of their health journey.

In financial services, advisors can review investment options with clients using interactive visualisations during video calls, with the system capturing decisions and automatically initiating appropriate transactions.

In retail, customers can snap a photo of a product they like, ask questions about it via voice, and complete purchases through their preferred channel, with the system providing consistent, personalised recommendations throughout.

By transforming how users interact with enterprise systems, this layer creates experiences that feel human-centred rather than technology-driven—a crucial step toward becoming a truly cognitive enterprise.

2. Multi-Agent Orchestrator Platform (MOP): The Cognitive Nervous System

The Multi-Agent Orchestrator Platform (MOP) functions as the "central nervous system" of the cognitive enterprise. Like the human nervous system coordinates signals between different parts of the body, MOP orchestrates intelligent workflows across various AI agents and enterprise systems, ensuring cohesive operation and optimal performance.

This orchestration capability transforms operations across industries. In global logistics, for example, companies have evolved from having disconnected AI tools that each performed one function well—route optimisation, inventory prediction, weather impact analysis—but didn't work together. Previously, when a customer asked about a delayed shipment, support teams had to check multiple systems and piece together answers manually. Today, when that same question comes in, systems automatically coordinate between different AI agents—one checks shipment status, another analyses weather patterns affecting the route, and a third examines inventory at nearby facilities. All this happens in seconds, giving teams a complete picture without any manual coordination.

How It Works

The Multi-Agent Orchestrator Platform is a sophisticated coordination system consisting of several key components:

Pre-Processor that converts diverse inputs—text, audio, images, structured data—into formats that downstream systems can process effectively. This translation layer enables the seamless handling of information regardless of its original form.

Orchestrator that serves as the central intelligence mapping user requests to appropriate actions and coordinating workflows across multiple agents. It includes:

- An Intent Classifier that interprets what users are trying to accomplish
- A Context Manager that maintains the thread of interactions over time
- Task Planners that break complex requests into manageable steps

Specialised Agents that execute specific tasks autonomously or collaboratively. These might include:

- Knowledge agents that retrieve and synthesise information
- Reasoning agents that analyse complex scenarios
- Action agents that execute transactions or updates in enterprise systems

Model Gateway provides access to appropriate AI models for different situations, ensuring optimal performance, accuracy, and efficiency. This component selects the right model for each task while managing computational resources effectively.

Agent Communication Layer enables seamless, real-time interaction and data exchange between autonomous agents. It ensures agents can collaborate effectively, share intermediate results, synchronize tasks, and resolve conflicts, even in complex, multi-step workflows.

Agent Tools is designed to empower agents with the operational capabilities required to perform tasks effectively. Agent Tools focuses on the execution layer-bridging the gap between agents and external systems by enabling actions such as integrating with third-party APIs, fetching and processing data, managing files and facilitating secure communication with users and systems. These tools ensure that agents can interact seamlessly with the broader enterprise environment, execute complex workflows, and deliver reliable, context-aware outcomes across diverse business scenarios.

Addressing Key Challenges

The MOP directly addresses several key challenges:

Siloed Data and Systems: enables seamless information flow through its Pre-Processor, which standardises diverse inputs (text, audio, images, structured data) into actionable formats. This ensures that downstream systems and agents can operate cohesively, regardless of the original data source or format, creating a unified operational experience.

Lack of AI Readiness: provides a structured way to integrate AI capabilities into existing workflows, allowing organisations to implement cognitive functions incrementally rather than requiring wholesale transformation.

Inter-Agent Collaboration: ensures seamless, real-time interaction among internal and external agents, enabling effective collaboration, data exchange, and task synchronisation.

Value Across Industries

In customer service, inquiries are automatically routed to appropriate agents based on content, with the system gathering relevant information from multiple sources before generating comprehensive responses. A customer asking about retirement planning might trigger coordination between a financial calculator agent, a regulatory compliance agent, and a personalised recommendation agent.

In healthcare, it facilitates coordinated care by connecting diagnostic systems, treatment protocols, and patient history. When new test results arrive, relevant information is automatically extracted, compared with treatment guidelines, and presented to clinicians in context.

By orchestrating previously disconnected AI capabilities into coherent workflows, the MOP transforms siloed technologies into an integrated cognitive system that can address complex, real-world challenges.

3. Data Products and Platform: Transforming Information into Insight

The Data Products and Platform component reshapes how organisations harness their information assets. It transforms scattered, inaccessible data into cohesive, trusted resources that drive intelligence throughout the enterprise.

Financial services firms exemplify the power of this transformation. Where once customer information was spread across different systems, market data lived in another silo, and risk assessments were managed in spreadsheets, today, unified data approaches provide on-demand access to complete, trusted information. Financial advisors can instantly see a holistic client picture, risk teams get real-time exposure updates, and marketing accesses integrated customer journeys. The result is not just faster operations but fundamentally better decisions.

How It Works

The Data Products and Platform layer creates a comprehensive foundation for data-driven operations through several integrated capabilities:

Data Fabric connects disparate data sources across the organisation, creating a unified network of information that transcends traditional silos. This interconnected approach enables data to flow where it's needed without requiring massive centralization efforts.

Metadata Management automatically tracks the origins, transformations, and relationships of data assets, making them discoverable and trustworthy. This "data about data" helps users understand what information exists, where it came from, how it's been processed, and how it can be appropriately used.

Knowledge Graphs that map relationships between data entities, creating a context that enhances understanding. These graphs connect concepts like customers, products, transactions, and locations, revealing patterns and insights that might otherwise remain hidden.

Ontology Management establishes consistent terminology and frameworks across the organisation, ensuring that everyone shares a common language when discussing data. This standardisation is particularly valuable in large enterprises where different departments might use varying terms for the same concepts.

Data Products that package information into reusable, governed resources that can be easily consumed by various applications and users. Like physical products, these data assets are designed with specific use cases in mind, with appropriate controls, documentation, and quality assurance built in.

Addressing Key Challenges

This component directly addresses some of the most persistent challenges in cognitive transformation:

Data Silos: By creating a unified data fabric with standardised access methods, it breaks down the barriers that prevent comprehensive analysis and insight generation.

Inconsistent Data Quality: Through metadata management and standardised data products, it improves data trust and reliability, addressing the quality issues that often undermine AI initiatives.

Governance Complexity: By embedding governance controls into data products themselves, compliance is simplified, and risk across the organisation is reduced.

Value Across Industries

This data transformation creates significant value across sectors:

In healthcare, organisations create unified patient profiles that combine clinical records, imaging studies, genetic information, and social determinants of health. Clinicians access comprehensive views that inform personalised treatment plans, while researchers identify patterns across populations to advance medical knowledge.

In retail, unified customer data products combine transaction history, browsing behaviour, loyalty program information, and support interactions. Marketing teams use these comprehensive profiles to create truly personalised experiences, while operations teams gain insights into inventory optimisation and supply chain management.

By transforming fragmented data into accessible, trusted resources, this component provides the foundational information layer upon which cognitive capabilities depend. Without this unified approach to data, even the most sophisticated AI systems would struggle to deliver meaningful value.

4. Digital Enabler Layer: Bridging Legacy and Innovation

The Digital Enabler Layer bridges the gap between traditional systems of record and modern engagement capabilities. It creates a flexible middle layer that enables personalised experiences while leveraging existing investments in core business systems.

Insurance companies illustrate this transformation effectively. Many have decades of policy data in mainframe systems that couldn't easily connect to modern digital channels, requiring agents to use multiple applications to service a single customer request. With digital enabler layers in place, legacy systems feed into unified digital platforms that power consistent experiences across web, mobile, and call centre channels. When customers start claims online and then call for help, agents see exactly what customers see. The experience is modernised without replacing all core systems at once.

How It Works

The Digital Enabler Layer operates as an intelligent bridge between backend systems and frontend experiences through several integrated capabilities:

Content Management that organises and delivers relevant information—from marketing materials to product details to support documentation—across multiple channels in consistent, personalised ways. This capability ensures that users receive the right information at the right time, regardless of how they interact with the organisation.

Engagement Engines that power personalised interactions based on comprehensive user profiles, historical behaviours, and real-time context. These engines drive recommendations, next-best actions, and tailored content that make each interaction feel individually crafted.

Customer 360 Services aggregate information from multiple systems to create holistic views of customers, enabling dynamic, real-time personalisation. These unified profiles bring together transaction history, preferences, service interactions, and other relevant data to inform more relevant experiences.

Addressing Key Challenges

This layer directly addresses several key transformation barriers:

Legacy Systems: It creates modern digital experiences without requiring immediate replacement of core systems, enabling organisations to evolve incrementally while still delivering improved customer and employee experiences.

Siloed Experiences: By providing unified engagement capabilities across channels, it eliminates the fragmented interactions that frustrate users and reduce operational efficiency.

AI Readiness: It creates a platform for embedding AI-powered personalisation and recommendations into customer journeys, even when underlying systems weren't designed for these capabilities.

Value Across Industries

This bridging capability creates significant value across sectors:

In financial services, banks create unified customer experiences across branches, call centres, mobile apps, and websites. Customers enjoy consistent service regardless of channel, while employees access comprehensive information that enables more informed support.

In hospitality, companies deliver personalised guest experiences from booking through checkout. Digital preferences follow guests throughout their journey, from room temperature settings to restaurant recommendations, creating memorable stays without requiring constant preference sharing.

In telecommunications, providers unify customer service across retail stores, contact centres, and self-service channels. When a customer begins troubleshooting online and then calls for additional help, agents see the complete history and can continue the process without repetition.

By bridging traditional systems with modern capabilities, the Digital Enabler Layer allows organisations to evolve incrementally while delivering significant improvements in customer and employee experiences. This approach balances innovation with practical constraints, making cognitive transformation more achievable for organisations with substantial legacy investments.

5. Busienss Application Layer: Modernising Core Business Systems

The Application Layer transforms rigid legacy systems into flexible, intelligent capabilities that respond dynamically to changing conditions. It focuses on modernising core business applications through cloud-native architecture, embedded AI, and continuous delivery approaches.

Manufacturing companies demonstrate this evolution clearly. Many operate with production planning systems that are decades old—monolithic, inflexible, and expensive to maintain. Making small changes takes months, and when market conditions shift, they can't adapt quickly enough. Transformation to modern application architectures changes these dynamics fundamentally. Systems become composed of modular services that can be updated independently, with AI embedded directly into workflows so planning automatically adjusts to supply chain disruptions or demand shifts. What used to take weeks happens in minutes, with better outcomes.

How It Works

The Application Layer transforms traditional business applications through several integrated approaches:

Cognitive Microservices Architecture that decomposes monolithic systems into modular services with embedded intelligence capabilities. Each microservice contains self-optimizing components that adapt to usage patterns, integrate lightweight machine learning models for context-aware processing, and automatically scale reasoning capacity during peak demands.

Example: Retail inventory modules now predict stockouts 14 days in advance while dynamically adjusting reorder logic based on supplier reliability scores and market trends.

AI-Driven Decision-Making that embeds predictive analytics and reasoning capabilities directly into business workflows. Rather than treating AI as a separate capability, these intelligent features become integral parts of everyday processes.

Legacy Transformation uses AI-powered tools to analyse, refactor and modernise legacy codebases. This approach helps organisations understand complex legacy systems and transition them to modern architectures more efficiently.

API-First Design that creates standardised interfaces for business functions, enabling easier integration and reusability across the enterprise. These well-defined APIs allow capabilities to be composed into new solutions without creating deeper dependencies.

Addressing Key Challenges

This layer addresses several critical barriers to cognitive transformation:

Legacy System Constraints: It provides a structured approach to modernising outdated applications that limit an organisation's agility and innovation potential.

Technical Debt: By incrementally refactoring and modernising code, it helps organisations reduce the accumulated technical debt that consumes resources and limits progress.

Integration Complexity: Through standardised APIs and microservices, it simplifies the connections between different systems, reducing the integration challenges that often derail transformation efforts.

Value Across Industries

This application modernisation creates significant benefits across sectors:

In supply chain operations, companies transform rigid planning systems into adaptive platforms that continuously optimize inventory, production, and logistics based on real-time conditions. When disruptions occur, these systems automatically adjust plans and provide transparent explanations of the changes to human operators.

In financial services, loan processing systems evolve from batch-oriented workflows to real-time, event-driven architectures. Applications analyse incoming data continuously, updating risk assessments and processing status without waiting for nightly batch runs, dramatically improving customer experience and operational efficiency.

In healthcare, patient management systems transform from isolated record-keeping tools to intelligent platforms that proactively identify care opportunities and coordinate services across providers. When test results arrive, the system automatically evaluates them against protocols and patient history, alerting clinicians to significant findings that require attention.

By modernising core business applications, organisations create the flexible, intelligent foundation needed to operate as a cognitive enterprise. This transformation isn't merely technical—it fundamentally changes how businesses operate, enabling greater responsiveness, efficiency, and innovation in core processes.

6. AI Compute Layer: Powering Intelligence at Scale

The AI Compute Layer provides the computational foundation necessary to train, fine-tune, and deploy AI models at scale. It enables organisations to move beyond experimental AI to production-grade capabilities that deliver consistent value.

Media companies illustrate this evolution effectively. Many started with data scientists using laptops to build basic recommendation models. But as ambitions grew—analysing video content, generating personalised highlights, translating in real-time—they hit computational walls. Models took weeks to train and couldn't deploy at scale for global audiences. Building proper AI computing infrastructure changes everything, providing flexible platforms that support everything from massive language models to specialised video analysis algorithms. Teams can experiment rapidly, and when they create valuable capabilities, they can scale to millions of users immediately.

How It Works

The AI Compute Layer provides specialised infrastructure through several integrated capabilities:

Support for Diverse AI Models, including large language models, specialised domain models, and custom-trained solutions. This flexibility allows organisations to select the right approach for each use case rather than forcing all problems into the same solution.

Hybrid Deployment Strategies that enable AI capabilities to run in cloud environments, on-premises data centres, or edge devices based on requirements for latency, data gravity, and cost optimisation. This hybrid approach gives organisations the flexibility to place computation where it makes the most sense.

Specialised Hardware Access that provides efficient computing resources like GPUs (Graphics Processing Units) and TPUs (Tensor Processing Units) optimized for AI workloads. These specialised processors dramatically accelerate training and inference compared to general-purpose computing.

Model Management that handles versioning, deployment, monitoring, and lifecycle management for AI models. This capability ensures that models remain current, accurate, and properly governed throughout their operational life.

Addressing Key Challenges

This layer directly addresses several key transformation barriers:

AI Readiness Gap: It provides the technical foundation needed to move beyond experimental AI to production-scale deployment, addressing a common barrier to cognitive transformation.

Resource Constraints: By optimizing computational resources and enabling flexible deployment options helps organisations balance performance needs with cost considerations.

Scaling Limitations: It creates the infrastructure necessary to deploy AI capabilities at an enterprise scale, overcoming the limitations that often restrict pilot projects from expanding.

Value Across Industries

This computational foundation creates significant value across sectors:

In healthcare, organisations deploy sophisticated medical imaging analysis that helps radiologists identify potential issues more accurately and efficiently. The computing infrastructure handles the intensive processing requirements of analysing high-resolution images while maintaining strict performance standards.

In financial services, fraud detection systems analyse transaction patterns in real-time across millions of accounts, identifying suspicious activities that require investigation. The compute layer enables this continuous monitoring without introducing delays that would impact legitimate transactions.

In retail, recommendation engines process massive amounts of behavioural data to generate personalised product suggestions that improve customer experience and drive sales. The flexible infrastructure scales during peak shopping periods to maintain performance despite dramatic increases in traffic.

By providing the computational foundation for AI capabilities, this layer enables organisations to move beyond limited experiments to enterprise-scale cognitive capabilities. Without this foundation, even the most promising AI innovations would remain theoretical rather than operational.

7. Active and Intelligent Network Systems: Creating Self-Optimizing Infrastructure

Active and Intelligent Network Systems transform traditional network infrastructure into self-healing, adaptive systems. While particularly critical for telecommunications providers, this capability extends to any organisation where network performance impacts business operations.

Network operations teams have historically operated in constant firefighting mode—waiting for customers to report problems, then scrambling to diagnose and fix issues. Major outages meant all-hands emergencies lasting days. The shift to intelligent network systems transforms these operations fundamentally. Networks actively monitor themselves, detecting potential problems before customers notice them. When weather threatens infrastructure, systems automatically reroute traffic. When usage patterns suggest potential bottlenecks, capacity adjusts without human intervention. Teams shift from emergency response to strategic improvement.

How It Works

Active and Intelligent Network Systems create adaptive infrastructure through several integrated capabilities:

AI-Driven Network Management uses machine learning to monitor network conditions, detect anomalies, predict potential issues, and optimize performance continuously. These capabilities enable proactive management rather than reactive troubleshooting.

Dynamic Resource Allocation that automatically adjusts network resources based on changing requirements, traffic patterns, and environmental conditions. This adaptability ensures optimal performance while maximizing resource efficiency.

Self-Healing Networks that detect problems and implement corrective measures automatically, often resolving issues before users notice them. When failures occur, these systems reroute traffic, activate redundant systems, or adjust configurations to maintain service continuity.

Enhanced Operational Support Systems (OSS) that integrate AI into network operations, enabling predictive maintenance, automated fault resolution, and continuous optimisation without constant human intervention.

Addressing Key Challenges

This layer directly addresses several key transformation barriers:

Legacy Infrastructure Limitations: It modernises critical network infrastructure, addressing a fundamental barrier to delivering reliable cognitive capabilities.

Operational Inefficiency: By automating routine network management tasks it frees technical teams to focus on innovation rather than maintenance.

Reliability Concerns: It improves service resilience through predictive maintenance and automated recovery, addressing a critical concern for organisations becoming more dependent on digital capabilities.

Value Across Industries

While especially transformative for telecommunications providers, these capabilities create value across sectors:

In healthcare, intelligent networks ensure reliable connectivity for critical systems like patient monitoring and telemedicine. When potential issues arise, the network automatically prioritizes medical applications and initiates backup systems to prevent disruption to patient care.

In manufacturing, smart factory networks continuously optimize communication between production equipment, inventory systems, and logistics operations. When production plans change, network resources automatically adjust to support different workflows and data requirements.

In financial services, intelligent network systems ensure transaction processing remains secure and reliable even during peak volumes or attempted cyberattacks. Automated security measures identify and isolate potential threats while maintaining essential services.

By creating a self-optimizing network infrastructure, this layer ensures that the technical foundation of the cognitive enterprise remains reliable, efficient, and secure. As organisations become increasingly dependent on digital capabilities, this intelligent infrastructure becomes a critical enabler of overall business performance.

8. AI Governance Layer: Ensuring Trust, Ethics and Compliance

The AI Governance Layer ensures that AI systems operate ethically, transparently, and in compliance with regulations. As AI capabilities become more deeply embedded in core business operations, this governance framework becomes essential for managing risk and building trust.

Insurance companies have learned the importance of this layer through experience. Many moved quickly to deploy AI for claims processing but hadn't fully considered all the implications. Some models showed unexpected biases in certain scenarios and companies struggled to explain decisions to customers who questioned their claims assessments. Regulators started asking questions they weren't prepared to answer. Implementing comprehensive AI governance changed this dynamic fundamentally. Now, ethics and governance are built into development processes from the beginning, with clear standards, regular audits, and transparent documentation. When regulators or customers ask questions, companies can show exactly how systems work and what safeguards are implemented.

How It Works

The **AI Safety and Control Component** monitors workflows for compliance with organisational policies, ethical guidelines, and regulatory requirements. It ensures that automated processes operate within appropriate boundaries. Additionally, it monitors models for bias, drift, and other potential issues, ensuring that systems continue to operate as intended over time. The component incorporates regulatory frameworks to ensure AI systems adhere to relevant laws and standards like the EU AI Act, from data privacy regulations like GDPR to industry-specific requirements. These frameworks help organisations navigate the complex and evolving regulatory landscape surrounding AI.

The **Human Annotator** component facilitates expert input for data labelling, output validation, and continuous model improvement. This human-in-the-loop system enhances model accuracy by incorporating domain expertise and addressing edge cases that automated systems might miss, creating a crucial feedback loop for ongoing AI refinement.

The **Observability Framework** provides comprehensive visibility into AI systems' operations, performance metrics, and potential issues through real-time monitoring and detailed logging. This transparency enables organisations to detect anomalies, understand model behaviour patterns, and ensure systems operate as intended across the enterprise landscape.

The **Evaluation Framework** systematically assesses AI model performance, accuracy, and business impact against predefined metrics and standards tailored to organisational objectives. This structured approach to measurement ensures AI investments deliver tangible value while providing the data needed for continuous improvement and stakeholder reporting.

The **Security Manager** safeguards AI systems through robust access controls, encryption, and comprehensive threat protection while ensuring compliance with data privacy regulations. This component maintains a secure environment for sensitive operations by continuously monitoring for vulnerabilities, preventing unauthorized access, and implementing appropriate data governance throughout the AI lifecycle.

Addressing Key Challenges

This layer directly addresses several key transformation barriers:

Governance Complexity: It provides a structured approach to managing the ethical, legal, and operational risks associated with AI deployment.

Trust Barriers: Ensuring transparency and accountability helps build confidence among users, customers, and regulators, which is essential for AI adoption.

Regulatory Uncertainty: It creates adaptable governance frameworks that can evolve as regulations change, reducing compliance risk in a dynamic environment.

Value Across Industries

This governance capability creates significant value across sectors:

In healthcare, robust governance ensures that AI used in diagnostics or treatment recommendations meets strict standards for accuracy, bias mitigation, and explainability. Clinicians can understand the reasoning behind AI suggestions and maintain appropriate oversight of patient care decisions.

In financial services, governance frameworks ensure that credit scoring and fraud detection models operate fairly across different demographic groups. Regular audits identify and address potential biases before they impact customers, while transparent documentation satisfies regulatory requirements.

In human resources, governance controls ensure that AI-assisted hiring and promotion systems avoid reinforcing historical biases. Regular testing identifies potential issues, and human oversight maintains accountability for employment decisions.

By establishing comprehensive governance for AI systems, this layer ensures that cognitive capabilities enhance rather than undermine trust, ethics, and compliance. As AI becomes more deeply embedded in core business operations, this governance framework becomes not just a risk management tool but a competitive advantage in building stakeholder confidence.

9. Model Hub: Centralizing AI Model Management for Enterprise Intelligence

The Model Hub acts as the central repository for managing, storing, and governing AI models. It enables organisations to harness a diverse array of models-from Large Language Models (LLMs) to specialized task-specific solutions-ensuring that agents have access to the most relevant and optimized tools for intelligent decision-making and task execution.

How It Works

The Model Hub operates as the strategic backbone for AI model lifecycle management within MOP, offering several integrated capabilities:

Model Lifecycle Management: It oversees the entire journey of AI models, from onboarding pre-trained models (e.g., GPT, BERT) to fine-tuning them for enterprise-specific tasks. This includes versioning and updates to ensure agents always use the latest, approved iterations tailored to specific needs.

Centralized Model Repository: Acting as a single source of truth, it stores and categorises models by type and domain relevance, eliminating redundancies and ensuring uniformity across workflows.

Performance Monitoring and Feedback Loops: The Model Hub continuously tracks key performance indicators (KPIs), such as accuracy and latency, using feedback from agents and end-users to iteratively improve models. It also identifies underperforming models for retraining or retirement, ensuring sustained quality over time.

Scalability and Security: Designed to scale with enterprise needs, it supports the integration of new models while enforcing enterprise-grade security through encryption and role-based access controls. This ensures that sensitive data and models remain protected as organisations expand their AI capabilities.

By centralising the management and governance of AI models, the Model Hub empowers organisations to transition from fragmented AI experiments to cohesive, enterprise-wide cognitive capabilities.

10. Intelligent Integration Platform

The Intelligent Integration Platform serves as the vital connective tissue within the Cognitive Enterprise Architecture Framework (CeAF), ensuring seamless data and service flow across disparate systems, applications, and platforms. By acting as a centralised layer for interoperability, it empowers organisations to integrate legacy systems with modern AI-driven workflows, enabling real-time decision-making and operational agility for platforms like the Multi-Agent Orchestrator Platform (MOP). Additionally, it plays a critical role in supporting the implementation of model context protocols, ensuring that AI agents and systems can access and utilise contextual data effectively across enterprise resources.

How It Works

The Intelligent Integration Platform operates as a dynamic hub for connectivity and intelligence, leveraging several integrated capabilities:

Service and API Exposure: It provides a unified interface for accessing a wide variety of enterprise resources and services-including data, applications, and external systems for both human users and AI agents within MOP, regardless of the underlying technology stack. This ensures seamless interaction with critical systems, abstracting the complexity of backend integrations.

Real-Time Data Flow: The platform facilitates continuous data streaming across systems, supporting immediate processing and decision-making.

AI-Powered Automation: Features like automated code and API flow generation, semantic data mapping, and real-time data enrichment enhance integration efficiency. AI models can generate integration logic or map data fields between systems.

Scalability and Flexibility: Designed to adapt to evolving business needs, the platform dynamically incorporates new systems and workflows.

Security and Governance: Robust access controls, traffic monitoring, and compliance enforcement safeguard integrations. The platform ensures that data exchanges adhere to organisational policies and regulations like GDPR.

From Framework to Reality: The Path Forward

The Cognitive Enterprise Architecture Framework provides a comprehensive blueprint for organisations seeking to transform into intelligent, adaptive enterprises. Addressing the interconnected challenges identified in Chapter 2—from legacy systems and data silos to governance complexities and cultural resistance—creates a structured pathway toward becoming a cognitive enterprise.

However, a framework is only valuable when applied to real-world challenges. In the chapters that follow, we'll explore how organisations across different industries have implemented CeAF to drive meaningful transformation. We'll examine specific use cases, implementation approaches, and lessons learned, providing practical guidance for your own cognitive journey.

Whether you're a business leader seeking strategic direction, an architect designing future systems, a technologist implementing AI capabilities, or a consultant guiding transformation efforts, these real-world examples will help you translate the framework into actionable plans for your specific context.

The cognitive revolution represents a fundamental shift in how organisations operate, compete, and create value. With CeAF as your guide, you can navigate this transformation with confidence, building an enterprise that's not just more intelligent but more human, adaptive, and future-ready.

Chapter 4: Introducing Our Case Studies – ComPlus and LegalDeal

At ComPlus, a senior network engineer named Maria Chen remembers the frustration of trying to diagnose service outages before their cognitive transformation began. The company had fifteen different monitoring systems that didn't communicate with each other. When customers reported problems, the team would spend hours just figuring out which system to check first. By the time they identified the root cause, customers were already posting complaints on social media. Today, the systems detect patterns indicating potential issues before they affect service. Engineers start their shifts with prioritized lists of potential concerns, complete with recommended actions and underlying reasoning. They spend more time preventing problems than firefighting them—a difference customers have begun to notice.

Across the continent at LegalDeal, a contract attorney named David Torres has experienced a parallel journey in a completely different context. Before their transformation, he spent 70% of his time on document review—essentially hunting for key provisions in massive contracts. The work was tedious but necessary, and it limited how many clients they could serve. Today, their cognitive system handles the initial document analysis, identifying relevant clauses and potential risks. Attorneys now focus on evaluating findings, applying professional judgment to complex issues, and actually advising clients rather than just processing paperwork. They're delivering better service to more clients while using their legal expertise for work that truly requires it.

The Power of Real-World Application

Throughout the previous chapters, we've explored the conceptual foundations of cognitive enterprises and the comprehensive Cognitive Enterprise Architecture Framework (CeAF) designed to enable this transformation. We've examined the Human-centric AI principles that should guide this journey and the specific technical components that make it possible. However, while they are valuable, principles come to life only when applied to real organisational challenges.

In this chapter, we introduce two fictional organisations—ComPlus and LegalDeal—that will serve as concrete examples throughout the remainder of this book. These case studies represent dramatically different organisations in terms of size, industry, and challenges, yet both are embarking on cognitive transformation journeys guided by the CeAF. By following their contrasting yet complementary paths, we can better understand how the framework adapts to different contexts while remaining true to its core principles.

These organisations aren't simply theoretical constructs; they're composites based on real transformation journeys we've observed across multiple industries. They embody the challenges, opportunities, and human experiences that define cognitive transformation. While fictional, they provide a safe space to explore strategies, anticipate obstacles, and envision possibilities that may closely parallel your own organisation's path.

As you read these case studies, you may recognize elements of your own organisation's challenges and aspirations. This recognition is intentional—the principles of cognitive transformation transcend specific industries and scales, though their application naturally varies with context. Whether you work in a global enterprise or a specialised firm, the journeys of ComPlus and LegalDeal offer valuable insights that can inform your own transformation strategy.

ComPlus: Transforming a Global Telecommunications Leader

ComPlus operates in 25 countries, serving over 100 million customers across consumer, business, and wholesale markets. With 85,000 employees and a 50-year history, the company has built extensive infrastructure spanning fixed-line networks, mobile services, and increasingly, digital offerings. While successful and established, ComPlus faces mounting pressures from multiple directions: rising operational costs, legacy systems limiting innovation, and aggressive competition from digital-native providers.

The Chief Customer Officer at ComPlus often points out that customers no longer compare the company just to other telecommunications providers. Instead, they measure their ComPlus experience against the seamless digital interactions they have with streaming services, e-commerce platforms, and social media. Systems built for a different era create friction that customers immediately notice in every interaction.

The company's vast technical estate includes hundreds of applications built over decades, many running on ageing infrastructure with limited integration. Network operations rely on multiple monitoring systems that don't communicate effectively, while customer data remains fragmented across service lines. Meanwhile, competitors unburdened by this technical debt can quickly launch new services and adapt to market changes.

The CEO has set an ambitious target: transform into a fully cognitive enterprise by 2027. This isn't about incremental improvement but about reimagining what a telecommunications company can be when enhanced by AI across every dimension. The vision involves evolving from a provider of connectivity to an intelligent partner in customers' digital lives.

ComPlus's 2027 Vision: Four Pillars of Transformation

ComPlus Transformation Pillars: Driving Business Growth Through Cognitive Enterprise

📈 Pillar 1: Intelligent Networks and Operations

Objective: Achieve industry-leading reliability while reducing operational costs by 30%

From: Reactive maintenance driving high costs and customer dissatisfaction when outages occur
To: Predictive operations delivering superior service quality at lower cost with minimal downtime

Key Results:

- Reduce network-related customer complaints by 70% through proactive issue resolution
- Cut maintenance costs by €45M annually by replacing routine inspections with AI-driven predictive maintenance
- Decrease mean time to resolution by 85%, minimising revenue impact from service disruptions
- Improve network capacity utilization by 40%, deferring €120M in capital expenditure over 3 years

Business Impact: Transforms network operations from a cost centre to a competitive differentiator, delivering superior customer experience at reduced operational expense.

💰 *Pillar 2: Hyper-Personalised Customer Experiences*

Objective: Increase revenue per customer by 15% while reducing churn by 40%

From: Generic offerings with high acquisition costs and elevated churn rates
To: Tailored experiences that deepen customer relationships, drive cross-selling, and create switching barriers

Key Results:

- Improve Net Promoter Score from +7 to +35 through contextually relevant interactions across all touchpoints
- Increase digital sales conversion by 45% through personalised offerings and streamlined purchasing journeys
- Boost cross-sell and upsell success rates by 60%, driving average revenue per user growth
- Reduce customer acquisition costs by 30% through improved targeting and higher referral rates

Business Impact: Creates sustainable competitive advantage through superior customer engagement, transforming transactional relationships into high-value, loyal partnerships.

🚀 *Pillar 3: Data-Driven Enterprise*

Objective: Accelerate decision velocity by 65% while improving decision quality across all business units

From: Intuition-based decisions limited by data accessibility and analysis capabilities
To: Real-time insights driving superior strategic and operational choices throughout the organisation

Key Results:

- Reduce new product time-to-market by 50% through data-informed development and targeting
- Improve marketing campaign ROI by 85% via granular customer segmentation and preference analysis
- Enhance forecast accuracy by 40%, optimizing inventory management and resource allocation
- Identify €75M in efficiency opportunities through cross-functional data pattern analysis

Business Impact: Establishes information superiority that drives competitive advantage through faster, better-informed decisions across marketing, operations, and strategic planning.

💼 *Pillar 4: Adaptive Business Operations*

Objective: Achieve market-leading agility with 70% faster response to changing business conditions

From: Rigid processes requiring months to adapt to market shifts and regulatory changes
To: Flexible operations that rapidly capitalize on opportunities and navigate disruptions

Key Results:

- Launch new services and offers in days rather than months, capturing a first-mover advantage
- Reduce operational overhead by €65M annually through intelligent automation of routine processes
- Decrease regulatory compliance implementation time by 60%, minimising risk exposure
- Enable business teams to implement 80% of operational changes without IT dependence

Business Impact: Builds organisational resilience and adaptability that turns market disruption into competitive opportunity while significantly reducing operational costs.

"This transformation isn't about technology—it's about building a business that can move at the speed of opportunity, deliver exceptional value to customers, and operate with unprecedented efficiency. The cognitive enterprise isn't our destination; it's the vehicle that will drive our next decade of market leadership." — ComPlus CEO.

Human Impact and Considerations

Beyond these technical transformations, ComPlus recognizes that becoming a cognitive enterprise fundamentally changes the nature of work for its employees. Network engineers like Maria Chen will shift from reactive troubleshooting to proactive optimisation. Customer service representatives will evolve from information processors to relationship managers, supported by AI systems that handle routine inquiries and provide real-time guidance for complex issues.

The company's leadership emphasizes that this transformation isn't about replacing people with technology but about augmenting human capabilities and elevating the work people do. They're investing as much in reskilling and cultural change as in technical systems, recognising that a cognitive enterprise requires both technological and human transformation.

This human-centred approach reflects the principles of Human-centric AI discussed in Chapter 2, ensuring that technology serves and enhances human capabilities rather than diminishing them. By embedding these principles throughout its transformation journey, ComPlus aims to create an organisation that's not only more intelligent but also more fulfilling for the people who make it work.

LegalDeal: Cognitive Transformation in a Specialised Legal Practice

In contrast to ComPlus's global scale, LegalDeal represents a different but equally compelling transformation journey. With 100 lawyers across five European cities, LegalDeal specializes in contract negotiation, compliance audits, and litigation support, primarily for small and medium enterprises. The firm has built a reputation for specialised expertise and client focus, but like many legal practices, it faces pressure to deliver more value with greater efficiency.

Senior partners at the firm acknowledge that legal expertise has always been time-intensive and, therefore, expensive. Their clients are businesses that need sophisticated legal guidance but often struggle with traditional legal costs and timeframes. Clients increasingly ask pointed questions about why contract review takes so long and why the firm can't leverage technology like other industries. These fair questions prompted the firm to explore transformation opportunities.

As a ComPlus client, LegalDeal experienced first-hand how cognitive technologies could transform customer experiences. This sparked their CEO, a former technology lawyer, to envision a similar transformation for her own firm. She views the legal industry as standing at a critical inflection point, with Generative AI and cognitive systems fundamentally changing what's possible in legal practice. The choice is clear: lead this transformation or be diminished by it.

Despite its smaller scale, LegalDeal faces many of the same challenges as larger organisations. Legal knowledge remains siloed within practice areas and individual attorneys. Document creation and analysis consume excessive time. Client interactions lack the digital fluidity that characterizes other professional services. Like many specialised firms, LegalDeal operates with limited technical resources and expertise compared to global enterprises like ComPlus.

Pillar 1: Cognitive Legal Knowledge Management

Objective: Transform attorney productivity by 40% while improving service consistency across all practice areas

From: Legal expertise trapped in attorneys' minds or isolated documents, creating redundant work
To: A living knowledge system that captures insights, learns from every matter, and makes collective expertise universally available

Key Results:

- Reduce research and precedent-finding time by 65% through the implementation of a comprehensive legal knowledge graph
- Increase consistency in legal advice by 85% by automatically surfacing relevant firm experience and precedents
- Cut matter ramp-up time by 70% through intelligent provision of applicable expertise from previous similar matters
- Improve new attorney productivity by 50% by providing AI-assisted access to the firm's collective knowledge

Business Impact: Converts the firm's intangible knowledge assets into a measurable competitive advantage that improves margins while delivering superior client outcomes.

CeAF Alignment: Leverages Data Products and Platform and Multi-Agent Orchestrator Platform components to transform collective expertise from intangible assets into an explicit, accessible resource that continuously improves.

Pillar 2: AI-Enhanced Legal Services

Objective: Increase firm capacity by 60% without proportional headcount growth while improving work quality

From: Attorneys spending valuable time on pattern-based tasks that don't fully utilize their expertise

To: AI handling routine aspects while attorneys focus on complex judgment and client counsel that truly require human intelligence

Key Results:

- Reduce contract review time by 75% through AI that identifies key provisions, risks, and non-standard terms.
- Decrease document drafting time by 60% using systems that create high-quality initial drafts based on transaction requirements.
- Cut legal research hours by 50% with AI-assisted research, finding relevant precedents, regulations, and firm knowledge.
- Increase compliance monitoring coverage by 300% through tools tracking regulatory changes and identifying client impacts.

Business Impact: Dramatically improves the firm's economics by enabling higher-value work at lower cost while creating capacity for growth without proportional expense increases.

CeAF Alignment: Implements the Application Layer component to transform core services from time-intensive manual processes to AI-enhanced workflows, delivering greater value more efficiently.

👥 *Pillar 3: Client-Centred Digital Experience*

Objective: Achieve industry-leading 95% client retention while increasing average revenue per client by 30%

From: Opaque legal services, where clients submit requests and wait for results with limited visibility
To: Transparent, collaborative experiences where clients track progress, access information, and engage through preferred channels

Key Results:

- Improve client satisfaction scores from 7.4 to 9.2 through real-time visibility into matter status, documents, and communications

- Increase client collaboration by 85% through secure digital spaces for joint document work and decision-making
- Reduce routine inquiry response time from hours to minutes using conversational interfaces that answer common questions
- Grow client self-service adoption to 75% through intuitive dashboards that translate complex legal concepts into accessible insights.

Business Impact: Transforms client relationships from transactional interactions to strategic partnerships, driving higher retention, expanded services, and a stronger competitive position.

CeAF Alignment: Implements the User Multimodal Interaction Layer to evolve client relationships from transactional interactions to collaborative partnerships enabled by technology.

📊 *Pillar 4: Adaptive Legal Operations*

Objective: Increase firm profitability by 45% through operational excellence and optimized resource allocation

From: Administrative tasks consuming time without creating client value and inconsistent resource allocation
To: Automated operations with AI-assisted decision tools for optimal resource allocation, pricing, and scheduling

Key Results:

- Reduce administrative overhead by 60% through intelligent workflow management for task routing and workload balancing
- Improve matter profitability by 35% using predictive analytics for accurate scoping, pricing, and resource requirements
- Decrease client onboarding time by 80% with automated conflict checking and client intake processes
- Enhance resource utilization by 50% through AI-assisted staffing that matches attorney expertise to matter requirements

Business Impact: Dramatically improves the firm's financial performance by reducing non-billable time, optimizing resource deployment, and ensuring appropriate pricing for services rendered.

CeAF Alignment: Leverages the Multi-Agent Orchestrator Platform and AI Governance Layer components to transform operations from manual processes to intelligent workflows that optimize resource utilization and improve decision quality.

"*Our vision isn't to replace attorneys with AI—it's to eliminate the work that attorneys never should have been doing in the first place. By building a cognitive law firm, we free our professionals to focus on what truly matters: the complex judgment, strategic advice, and human relationships that create exceptional client value.*"
— LegalDeal Managing Partner

Human Impact and Considerations

Like ComPlus, LegalDeal recognizes that cognitive transformation fundamentally changes how people work. Attorneys like David Torres will shift from document processing to strategic counselling. Paralegals will evolve from research assistants to knowledge curators, managing the firm's growing cognitive capabilities. Support staff will transition from administrative tasks to client experience management.

The firm's leadership emphasizes that the practice of law has always been about human judgment, relationships, and trust. Their cognitive transformation aims to enhance these human elements, not replace them. By automating routine aspects of legal work, they create space for deeper client relationships and more meaningful application of legal expertise.

This human-centred approach aligns with the principles of Human-centric AI discussed in Chapter 2, ensuring that technology amplifies rather than diminishes the human elements that define quality legal services. By embedding these principles throughout its transformation, LegalDeal aims to create a practice that combines technological sophistication with deepened human connection.

Contrasting Journeys, Common Principles

The transformation journeys of ComPlus and LegalDeal illustrate how the Cognitive Enterprise Architecture Framework can be applied across dramatically different organisational contexts. Despite their differences in scale, industry, and specific challenges, several common principles emerge:

Human-Centricity Transcends Scale

Both organisations recognize that successful cognitive transformation must enhance human capabilities rather than simply automate existing processes. Whether managing vast telecommunications networks or providing specialised legal services, the focus remains on elevating human work by addressing routine tasks through technology.

Senior partners at LegalDeal often observe that technology is just a means to an end. The real transformation happens when people work differently because they're supported by cognitive systems that handle routine aspects of their work.

Organisational Context Shapes Implementation

While both organisations apply the same CeAF components, their implementation approaches differ significantly based on their scale, resources, and specific challenges:

ComPlus, with its extensive technical resources, can pursue large-scale development of custom cognitive capabilities across multiple domains simultaneously. Its transformation strategy emphasizes enterprise-wide integration and comprehensive modernisation of its vast technical estate.

LegalDeal, with more limited technical resources, adopts a focused approach that leverages specialised legal AI solutions while building targeted integrations between these tools. Its transformation strategy emphasizes maximum impact in core service areas rather than comprehensive technical modernisation.

These contrasting approaches demonstrate the flexibility of the CeAF—it provides a consistent framework while allowing for implementation approaches tailored to organisational realities.

Data Integration Enables Intelligence

Both organisations identify data integration as a foundational element of their cognitive transformation, though the specific challenges differ:

ComPlus must integrate vast operational data across network systems, customer platforms and business applications to enable coherent, intelligent operations at scale.

LegalDeal must transform unstructured legal knowledge into structured, accessible resources that can fuel AI-powered legal services and insights.

Despite these differences, both organisations recognize that fragmented data prevents cognitive capabilities from delivering their full potential, making data integration an essential first step in their transformation journeys.

Ethical Considerations Apply Universally

Both organisations embed ethical considerations throughout their transformation plans, reflecting the importance of responsible AI practices regardless of organisational scale:

ComPlus emphasizes transparent network management practices, customer data privacy, and ethical use of personalisation capabilities to maintain customer trust.

LegalDeal focuses on maintaining client confidentiality, ensuring that AI recommendations can be explained to clients, and preserving attorney oversight of all legal advice.

These ethical dimensions reflect the principles of Human-centric AI discussed in Chapter 2, demonstrating their relevance across different organisational contexts and industries.

The Path Forward

The journeys of ComPlus and LegalDeal will serve as recurring reference points throughout the remainder of this book, illustrating how the Cognitive Enterprise Architecture Framework can be applied to address specific challenges in different contexts. As we explore implementation strategies, technological enablers, and organisational considerations in subsequent chapters, these case studies will provide concrete examples that bring abstract concepts to life.

Whether your organisation resembles ComPlus in scale and complexity, LegalDeal in specialization and focus, or represents an entirely different context, these contrasting journeys offer valuable insights for your own cognitive transformation. By observing how each organisation applies the CeAF components to their unique challenges, you can better envision how similar approaches might be adapted to your specific circumstances.

In the next chapter, we'll explore the concept of 'Human-Centric AI - a philosophy and practice that places humans at the centre of this transformation.

Chapter 5: Human-Centric AI in Cognitive Enterprises

As we explored in Chapter 4, both ComPlus and LegalDeal are embarking on ambitious transformation journeys to become cognitive enterprises. While their industries, scales, and specific challenges differ significantly, both organisations recognize a fundamental truth: successful cognitive transformation centres not on technology alone but on the human experience it enables. This realization brings us to Human-centric AI—the philosophical and practical foundation that ensures technology serves human needs and values rather than the reverse.

Human-centric AI represents the intersection where technological innovation meets human experience. In cognitive enterprises, it serves as the guiding principle that shapes how AI systems are designed, deployed, and governed. By focusing on human empowerment, ethical considerations, and collaborative workflows, this approach ensures that cognitive transformation enhances rather than diminishes the human element in organisations.

Both ComPlus and LegalDeal have placed Human-centric AI at the core of their transformation strategies, recognising that sustainable success requires technology that amplifies human capabilities respects human values, and builds rather than erodes trust. In this chapter, we explore how these organisations are implementing Human-centric AI principles across their operations, the impacts on their employees and customers, and the governance frameworks they've established to ensure responsible innovation.

Understanding Human-Centric AI in Practice

Human-centric AI refers to the design and implementation of artificial intelligence systems that empower, support, and collaborate with people. Rather than focusing solely on technological capabilities or efficiency metrics, this approach ensures that AI enhances decision-making, improves workflows, and upholds ethical values while complementing rather than replacing human roles.

At its core, Human-centric AI embodies three fundamental characteristics. First, it empowers users by working alongside them to improve decisions and performance, providing insights and recommendations that expand human capabilities rather than constraining them. Second, it operates responsibly by adhering to ethical principles such as fairness, transparency, and accountability, ensuring that automated processes align with human values and societal expectations. Third, it fosters collaboration by integrating seamlessly into human workflows, enhancing productivity and creativity through complementary capabilities rather than competitive displacement.

In business contexts, Human-centric AI bridges technological advancement with human outcomes. It ensures that AI-driven workflows align with goals that matter to people—customer satisfaction, employee fulfilment, ethical practice, and sustainable growth. This alignment creates a virtuous cycle where technology serves human needs, building trust that accelerates adoption and further innovation.

The value of this approach extends to all stakeholders in the cognitive enterprise. For customers, it delivers personalised, empathetic experiences that respect individual preferences and needs. For employees, it enhances skills, eliminates repetitive tasks, and creates space for innovation and creativity while supporting meaningful human roles. For the enterprise as a whole, it promotes trust, encourages technology adoption, and ensures compliance with ethical standards and regulatory requirements.

As ComPlus and LegalDeal implement their transformation strategies, this human-centred approach guides their technology decisions, operational changes, and organisational development. By placing people at the centre of their cognitive architecture, they ensure that transformation creates value not just through efficiency but through enhanced human experiences and capabilities.

Human-Centric AI in Daily Operations: Contrasting Examples

To understand how Human-centric AI manifests in practice, let's examine its impact on daily operations at both ComPlus and LegalDeal through the experiences of two professionals whose roles have been transformed by cognitive capabilities.

A Field Technician's Experience at ComPlus

Sarah Chen works as a field technician at ComPlus, responsible for ensuring seamless connectivity for customers by diagnosing and repairing network faults across a major metropolitan area. Before the implementation of Human-centric AI, her daily routine involved manual diagnostics, reactive problem-solving, and considerable time spent travelling between service locations with limited information about what awaited her.

Today, Sarah's workday looks dramatically different, though her expertise remains essential. Her morning begins with an AI-enhanced planning session where her mobile dashboard displays optimized service routes based on fault priorities, traffic conditions, and her specific skills. The system doesn't simply dictate her schedule; it explains the reasoning behind its recommendations and allows Sarah to adjust the plan based on her knowledge of local conditions or specific customer needs.

When Sarah arrives at her first service location, she opens her mobile application to find a detailed analysis of the network issue. The AI-powered diagnostic system has already monitored the affected equipment, analysed performance patterns, and identified the most likely causes of the problem. Rather than starting from scratch, Sarah begins with informed hypotheses that narrow her troubleshooting scope considerably. "*Before, I might spend the first hour just figuring out what was wrong,*" she explains. "*Now I can focus immediately on confirming the diagnosis and implementing the solution.*"

During complex repairs, Sarah accesses an AI Technical Support Agent through her augmented reality glasses. The system overlays visual guides onto the equipment, highlighting components that need attention and providing step-by-step instructions when needed. When Sarah encounters an unfamiliar issue, the system connects her with a senior engineer who can see exactly what she sees and provide real-time guidance. This collaboration ensures that Sarah's hands-on expertise is augmented rather than replaced by digital capabilities.

Perhaps most importantly, Sarah participates actively in improving the AI systems she uses. After completing repairs, she provides feedback on the AI's diagnostic recommendations, noting where they were helpful and where they missed important factors. This input doesn't disappear into a black box; Sarah can track how her feedback influences system updates over time, creating a sense of partnership rather than subordination to technology.

The impact on Sarah's work satisfaction has been profound. "*I still use all my technical skills,*" she notes, "*but I'm not wasting time on the tedious parts of the job anymore. I can help more customers each day and I'm solving more challenging problems rather than just following the same diagnostic scripts over and over.*"

This transformation embodies several key principles of Human-centric AI. The system provides transparency by explaining its recommendations, maintains human oversight by allowing Sarah to adjust automated plans, and incorporates continuous feedback that improves its performance over time while respecting Sarah's expertise and autonomy.

A Legal Analyst's Experience at LegalDeal

Across the continent at LegalDeal, Miguel Rodriguez experiences a different but equally transformative application of Human-centric AI in his role as a legal analyst specializing in contract review. Before the firm's cognitive transformation began, Miguel spent most of his days methodically reviewing lengthy contracts to identify potential risks, non-standard clauses, and compliance issues—work that was intellectually demanding but often tedious and time-consuming.

Today, Miguel's workflow has evolved significantly. He begins his morning by reviewing an AI-generated summary of new contracts that require analysis. The system has already processed these documents, highlighting unusual clauses, potential risks, and compliance considerations based on jurisdiction-specific regulations and LegalDeal's historical approach to similar contracts.

Rather than reading each contract from start to finish, Miguel focuses his attention on the sections flagged by the AI system, applying his legal expertise to evaluate the significance of identified issues and determine appropriate responses. The system doesn't make final determinations about risk or acceptability; instead, it presents its analysis with confidence scores and explicit reasoning that Miguel can evaluate based on his professional judgment.

When Miguel disagrees with the system's assessment, he doesn't simply override it—he provides specific feedback about why the flagged issue isn't problematic in this context or why an unflagged section actually merits attention. The system learns from these interactions, becoming more aligned with LegalDeal's specific approach to contract analysis over time. "*The AI isn't replacing my legal judgment," Miguel observes. "It's handling the initial review that used to take hours, allowing me to focus on the substantive legal analysis where my expertise adds the most value.*"

Perhaps most significantly, Miguel now spends more time directly interacting with clients. While the AI handles initial document processing, Miguel conducts consultations where he explains the identified risks, explores business implications, and develops strategic recommendations. "*Before, I might spend 90% of my time on document review and 10% advising clients," he notes. "Now that ratio has flipped—I'm doing the work I went to law school for, building relationships and providing counsel rather than just processing documents.*"

The system also supports Miguel's professional development. When it identifies contract provisions related to emerging regulatory areas or novel business models, it connects them to relevant legal resources and learning materials. This integration of learning into daily workflows helps Miguel continuously expand his expertise while applying it to client challenges.

Like Sarah at ComPlus, Miguel participates in a continuous feedback loop that improves the AI systems he uses. His interactions with the contract analysis tools generate data about which flags required attention and which didn't, gradually refining the system's ability to identify truly significant issues. Monthly review sessions bring together legal analysts and technology teams to discuss system performance and prioritize improvements, ensuring that technology development remains aligned with legal practice needs.

This implementation exemplifies Human-centric AI through its emphasis on augmenting rather than replacing professional judgment, its transparent presentation of analysis and reasoning, and its integration of human feedback into ongoing system refinement. The technology doesn't attempt to automate legal analysis entirely; instead, it handles routine processing tasks while elevating the human role to focus on judgment, counselling, and relationship building.

Core Principles of Human-Centric AI

The experiences of Sarah and Miguel illustrate how Human-centric AI transforms daily work across different organisational contexts. Underlying these transformations are core principles that guide the design and implementation of AI systems in cognitive enterprises. Both ComPlus and LegalDeal have incorporated these principles into their transformation strategies, though their specific applications vary based on industry context and organisational needs.

Transparency and Explainability

AI systems must provide clear visibility into how they operate and explain their recommendations or decisions in ways that users can understand. This transparency builds trust and enables informed collaboration between humans and AI.

At ComPlus, the Network Operations Centre implements this principle through visualisation tools that show how AI monitoring systems detect potential service disruptions. When the system flags unusual network patterns, it doesn't simply trigger an alert—it presents the specific metrics that deviate from expected ranges, comparable historical incidents, and the reasoning behind its priority assessment. This transparency allows network engineers to evaluate the AI's recommendations critically rather than following them blindly.

LegalDeal applies this principle in its contract analysis system, which provides clause-by-clause explanations of why specific provisions are flagged as potentially problematic. The system explicitly identifies the regulatory requirements, precedent cases, or client specifications that inform its assessment, enabling lawyers to understand and evaluate its reasoning. This transparency is particularly important in legal contexts where practitioners bear professional responsibility for advice provided to clients.

Both implementations recognize that explainability isn't just a technical feature—it's a foundational element of human-AI collaboration. When AI systems operate as black boxes, humans tend to either over-rely on their recommendations without appropriate scrutiny or reject them entirely due to a lack of trust. Transparency creates the conditions for productive partnership, where AI provides insights that humans can evaluate based on their expertise and context knowledge.

Fairness and Equity

AI systems must deliver equitable outcomes across different user groups, avoiding biases that could disadvantage specific populations or perpetuate existing inequities. This principle requires ongoing monitoring and mitigation of potential biases in both training data and algorithmic operations.

ComPlus implements fairness considerations in its customer service operations, where AI systems prioritize and route support requests. The company regularly audits these systems to ensure they don't inadvertently disadvantage specific customer segments based on factors like language proficiency, technical knowledge, or service region. When analyses revealed that rural customers were receiving slower resolution times for similar issues, ComPlus adjusted its algorithms to correct this disparity while maintaining overall efficiency.

LegalDeal addresses fairness in its legal research tools, which attorneys use to find relevant precedents and regulatory guidance. The firm monitors these systems to ensure they don't systematically overlook relevant case law from certain jurisdictions or time periods, which could create blind spots in legal analysis. Regular audits compare AI-generated research results against those produced by experienced legal researchers to identify and address potential biases.

Both organisations recognize that fairness isn't achieved through one-time adjustments but requires continuous monitoring and refinement. They've established cross-functional teams responsible for reviewing AI performance metrics through an equity lens, identifying potential disparities, and implementing appropriate corrections. This ongoing commitment ensures that AI systems promote rather than undermine organisational values related to fairness and inclusion.

Human Agency and Control

AI systems should enhance human capabilities while preserving appropriate human control, particularly for consequential decisions. This principle ensures that automation serves human priorities rather than constraining human agency.

At ComPlus, network management systems implement this principle by distinguishing between routine optimisations that can proceed automatically and significant changes that require human approval. The system might automatically adjust bandwidth allocation to address minor traffic fluctuations, but it will seek engineer approval before implementing changes that could affect service level agreements or critical customer operations. This tiered approach maintains efficiency while preserving human oversight where it matters most.

LegalDeal applies this principle in its document generation system, which assists lawyers in drafting contracts and legal memoranda. While the system can automatically generate initial drafts based on specified parameters, it presents these as suggestions rather than final products, clearly indicating areas that may require attorney customization based on specific client circumstances. Attorneys maintain full editorial control, using the system as a starting point rather than a replacement for their professional judgment.

Both implementations recognize that appropriate human control varies by context. Routine, low-risk activities may be highly automated with minimal human intervention, while high-stakes decisions require meaningful human oversight and ultimate authority. This nuanced approach balances efficiency with responsibility, ensuring that humans remain accountable for consequential outcomes while being relieved of routine processing tasks.

Continuous Learning and Adaptation

Human-centric AI systems must evolve based on user feedback and changing requirements, creating a virtuous cycle of improvement that aligns AI capabilities with human needs.

ComPlus implements this principle through its field service management system, which continuously refines its recommendations based on technician feedback. When technicians like Sarah indicate that a suggested diagnostic approach wasn't effective or that an unflagged issue turned out to be significant, the system incorporates this information into future recommendations. Monthly review sessions bring together field technicians and data scientists to evaluate system performance and prioritize enhancements based on field experiences.

LegalDeal applies continuous learning in its regulatory compliance monitoring, which tracks legislative and judicial developments relevant to client operations. Attorneys provide feedback when the system misses relevant updates or flags changes that don't actually impact client activities. This feedback doesn't simply disappear into a database—it directly influences how the system processes and prioritizes new information, gradually improving its ability to identify truly significant regulatory developments.

Both organisations have established formal processes for collecting, analyzing, and incorporating user feedback into AI system development. These processes ensure that AI tools remain relevant to actual work practices rather than diverging from user needs over time. By treating user experiences as valuable data rather than incidental feedback, they create systems that continuously align with evolving human requirements.

Integrating Human Feedback Loops

The principles described above don't implement themselves—they require structured mechanisms for incorporating human judgment into AI system development and operation. Both ComPlus and LegalDeal have established robust feedback loops that enable continuous refinement of their AI capabilities based on human insights and experiences.

Human-in-the-Loop Mechanisms

The Multi-Agent Orchestrator Platform (MOP) described in Chapter 3 incorporates Human-in-the-Loop (HITL) mechanisms that enable appropriate human oversight and intervention in AI workflows. These mechanisms operate at multiple levels, from individual transactions to system-wide governance.

At the transaction level, HITL mechanisms include validation points where humans review and approve AI outputs before execution. At ComPlus, the customer retention system generates personalised offers for customers at risk of cancellation, but these offers require agent review before being extended to customers. This review ensures that offers align with business policies and customer circumstances while providing agents with learning opportunities about effective retention strategies.

LegalDeal implements similar validation in its compliance advisory workflow. The system analyses client operations against regulatory requirements to identify potential compliance issues, but a qualified attorney reviews these findings before they're communicated to clients. This review ensures that compliance recommendations reflect legal judgment and practical business considerations beyond what the AI system can assess independently.

HITL mechanisms also include escalation pathways that route high-risk or ambiguous cases to appropriate human experts. ComPlus implements this approach in its network security operations, where the AI system handles routine threat detection but escalates unusual or potentially severe security incidents to specialised analysts. The escalation includes relevant context and preliminary analysis, enabling analysts to address the most critical aspects of the situation immediately.

LegalDeal applies escalation in its contract negotiation support system. When the system encounters contractual provisions that fall outside its confidence parameters or that involve emerging legal issues, it routes these specific clauses to senior attorneys with relevant expertise. This targeted escalation ensures that novel legal questions receive appropriate human consideration without requiring attorneys to review routine provisions that the system can reliably assess.

These HITL mechanisms don't operate in isolation—they form part of a comprehensive approach to human-AI collaboration that recognizes different requirements across various operational contexts. Routine, low-risk activities may involve minimal human intervention, while novel or high-stakes situations require more extensive human judgment. This nuanced implementation ensures that human expertise is deployed where it adds the most value rather than being consumed by tasks that AI can handle reliably.

Feedback Amplification and Learning

Beyond transaction-level oversight, both organisations have established processes for aggregating human feedback and incorporating it into system improvements. These processes transform individual interactions into collective learning that enhances AI performance over time.

ComPlus implements this approach through its customer service feedback system. When service agents handle calls after automated interactions, they rate the effectiveness of AI-generated responses and note specific improvements needed. These ratings and comments don't simply accumulate in a database—they drive prioritised updates to conversational models and decision criteria. Monthly review sessions bring together service agents, data scientists, and product managers to evaluate feedback patterns and plan system enhancements.

LegalDeal applies a similar approach in its document review workflow. As attorneys review AI-flagged contract provisions, they indicate whether each flag represents a genuine issue requiring attention or a false positive that consumed unnecessary review time. The system tracks these assessments across thousands of contract reviews, identifying patterns that inform model refinements. Quarterly calibration sessions allow attorneys to review system performance trends and provide collective guidance on priority improvements.

Both organisations have established clear accountability for incorporating human feedback into system development. Dedicated teams track feedback metrics, identify improvement opportunities, and implement model refinements based on human insights. This structured approach ensures that feedback doesn't disappear into a black hole but drives tangible system improvements that align AI capabilities with human needs.

The integration of these feedback mechanisms with the CeAF components described in Chapter 3 creates a coherent architecture for human-AI collaboration. The User Multimodal Interaction Layer provides intuitive interfaces for human input, while the Multi-Agent Orchestrator Platform coordinates the routing of tasks between AI systems and human experts. The AI Governance Layer ensures that feedback processes operate consistently across the organisation, maintaining appropriate oversight of system evolution.

Enhancing Employee and Customer Experiences

While technical mechanisms enable Human-centric AI, its ultimate success depends on the experiences it creates for employees and customers. Both ComPlus and LegalDeal have focused on designing AI implementations that genuinely enhance human experiences rather than simply automating existing processes or maximizing efficiency metrics.

Empowering Employees Through AI Collaboration

For employees like Sarah at ComPlus and Miguel at LegalDeal, Human-centric AI transforms daily work by automating routine tasks while creating opportunities for higher-value activities that leverage uniquely human capabilities.

At ComPlus, customer service representatives have experienced this transformation as AI systems handle routine inquiries and transactions. Rather than processing password resets or balance inquiries, representatives now focus on resolving complex customer issues, identifying appropriate service enhancements, and building relationships through meaningful conversations. The AI doesn't replace these representatives; it elevates their role from transaction processors to customer advocates and problem solvers.

Training and documentation specialists have similarly evolved as AI handles routine content generation and maintenance. Instead of updating basic how-to documents, these professionals now create sophisticated learning experiences that develop employee skills for complex situations where human judgment remains essential. Their expertise doesn't become obsolete—it shifts toward higher-value activities that AI cannot effectively perform.

LegalDeal has experienced parallel transformations across various legal roles. Junior attorneys who previously spent much of their time on document review and basic research now engage in more substantive legal analysis and client interactions. Paralegals who once focused on document organisation and citation checking now manage sophisticated knowledge systems and collaborate with attorneys on complex case preparation. Administrative staff who previously handled routine scheduling and filing now coordinate client relationships and manage project workflows.

Across both organisations, the pattern is consistent: AI handles routine processing tasks that consume significant human time and attention, creating space for people to focus on activities that require creativity, judgment, emotional intelligence, and interpersonal skills. This shift doesn't eliminate jobs; it transforms them into more fulfilling roles that leverage distinctly human capabilities.

This transformation requires more than just technology implementation—it demands thoughtful job redesign, skill development, and cultural change. Both organisations have invested significantly in reskilling programs that help employees develop the capabilities needed for their evolving roles. They've also adjusted performance metrics and reward systems to recognize value creation through judgment and relationship building rather than just transaction volume or processing speed.

The result is a workforce that views AI as a collaborative partner rather than a threatening replacement. When implemented thoughtfully, Human-centric AI doesn't diminish human contributions—it amplifies them by removing routine burdens and creating space for meaningful work that leverages distinctly human capabilities.

Delivering Human-Centred Customer Experiences

For customers, Human-centric AI enables experiences that combine the efficiency and personalisation of automation with the empathy and judgment of human interaction.

ComPlus has implemented this approach in its customer support operations, where AI handles routine inquiries while routing complex or emotionally charged interactions to appropriate human specialists. When a customer contacts support about a service disruption that's affecting their business operations, the AI system recognizes the urgency and routes them to a specialist with relevant expertise, providing that specialist with complete context about the customer's situation, service history, and current issue. The customer doesn't need to repeat information or navigate complex menus—they experience a seamless transition from automated to human support based on their specific needs.

The company also applies Human-centric AI in its service personalisation, using analysis of customer behaviour and preferences to offer relevant options without overwhelming choice or invading privacy. When customers review service plans, the system highlights options that align with their usage patterns and expressed preferences while explaining why these recommendations might be suitable. Customers maintain full control over their choices while benefiting from personalised guidance that simplifies decision-making.

LegalDeal implements Human-centric AI in its client communication, using automated systems to provide timely updates on case status and routine matters while ensuring that substantive legal advice comes from qualified attorneys who understand the client's specific context. When a client inquires about a matter in progress, the system provides basic status information immediately while routing more complex questions to the appropriate legal team with relevant context. This approach respects both the client's time and the importance of informed legal judgment.

The firm also applies Human-centric AI in its legal document delivery, using AI to translate complex legal language into accessible explanations while preserving the precise legal text needed for formal purposes. When providing contracts or compliance guidance to clients, the system generates layered documents that include both formal legal language and plain-language explanations of key provisions and implications. This approach ensures that clients can understand the substance of legal documents without sacrificing the precision required for legal enforceability.

Across both organisations, successful customer experiences combine AI efficiency with human judgment, empathy, and relationship building. Rather than forcing customers to choose between impersonal automation and inefficient manual processes, these implementations create integrated experiences that deploy technology and human expertise in complementary ways based on customer needs and situation complexity.

Ethics and AI Governance

Human-centric AI requires more than good intentions—it depends on robust governance frameworks that ensure the ethical development and deployment of AI systems. Both ComPlus and LegalDeal have established comprehensive governance approaches that address ethical considerations, regulatory compliance, and responsible innovation.

Both organisations have developed explicit ethical frameworks that guide their AI development and deployment, though the specific principles reflect their different industry contexts and stakeholder considerations.

ComPlus has established an AI Ethics Framework centred on five core principles: transparency in automated decisions, fairness across customer segments, data privacy and security, human oversight of consequential actions, and accessibility for customers with diverse needs and capabilities. This framework doesn't exist as an abstract document—it's integrated into the company's development processes through specific guidelines, review procedures, and success metrics for AI initiatives.

The company applies these principles through a dedicated AI Ethics Committee comprising representatives from technology, legal, customer advocacy, and business units. This committee reviews significant AI deployments before implementation, assessing them against established ethical criteria and recommending modifications where needed. The committee also monitors deployed systems for emerging ethical concerns and evolving societal expectations, ensuring that ethical governance remains current and effective.

LegalDeal has developed a parallel framework adapted to its legal services context, with principles including client confidentiality, avoidance of unauthorized practice of law, transparency about AI use in client matters, fairness in service delivery, and maintenance of professional judgment. Given the regulated nature of legal practice, this framework explicitly addresses professional responsibility obligations that apply to technology-assisted legal services.

The firm implements these principles through its Professional Responsibility and Technology Committee, which includes senior attorneys, compliance specialists, and technology leaders. This committee reviews AI applications against both ethical principles and specific legal profession regulations, ensuring that technology adoption maintains compliance with professional obligations. The committee also develops guidelines for appropriate AI use in various practice areas, helping attorneys navigate the boundary between permissible automation and matters requiring direct professional judgment.

Both governance approaches recognize that ethical considerations aren't static—they evolve with technology capabilities, societal expectations, and regulatory developments. Regular reviews ensure that ethical frameworks remain relevant and effective as AI capabilities and applications expand.

Bias Monitoring and Mitigation

Both organisations have implemented specific processes for identifying and addressing potential biases in AI systems, recognising that unchecked bias can undermine fairness and trust.

ComPlus conducts regular bias audits of customer-facing AI systems, analysing performance across different demographic groups, geographic regions, and customer segments. These audits examine key metrics like recommendation accuracy, service resolution time, and approval rates to identify any significant disparities that might indicate bias. When disparities are detected, cross-functional teams investigate root causes and implement appropriate mitigations, whether through data enhancements, model adjustments, or process changes.

The company also implements proactive bias prevention in new AI development through diverse training data, explicit fairness constraints in model objectives, and pre-deployment testing across different user segments. These measures don't eliminate the need for ongoing monitoring, but they reduce the likelihood of significant bias emerging in production systems.

LegalDeal applies similar principles to its legal analysis and document review systems, regularly assessing whether they perform consistently across different client types, industry sectors, and legal jurisdictions. The firm pays particular attention to ensuring that automated legal analysis doesn't systematically disadvantage clients with unique circumstances or novel legal issues that might fall outside typical patterns.

The firm also implements bias prevention through careful curation of training data for legal AI systems, ensuring that precedent cases and regulatory materials represent diverse jurisdictions, time periods, and legal contexts. This approach reduces the risk that automated analysis will reflect historical biases or overlook relevant considerations for non-standard situations.

Both organisations recognize that bias mitigation requires ongoing vigilance rather than one-time solutions. As AI systems evolve and are applied to new contexts, new forms of bias may emerge that weren't evident in initial deployments. Continuous monitoring, combined with diverse perspectives in system development and evaluation, creates the feedback loops necessary to identify and address these emerging concerns.

Regulatory Compliance and Risk Management

Beyond ethical considerations, both organisations have established robust processes for ensuring that AI systems comply with relevant regulations and effectively manage associated risks.

ComPlus operates in a highly regulated telecommunications industry across multiple jurisdictions, each with specific requirements for service delivery, customer privacy, and data protection. The company has integrated these regulatory requirements into its AI governance framework, with explicit compliance checkpoints in the development and deployment process. Regular compliance reviews ensure that AI systems maintain alignment with evolving regulations across all operating regions.

The company has also implemented comprehensive risk management for AI deployments, assessing potential risks related to system performance, data security, business continuity, and customer impact. High-risk applications receive additional scrutiny and testing before deployment, with appropriate controls and contingency plans to mitigate identified risks. This risk-based approach ensures that governance effort aligns with potential impact, applying more rigorous oversight to systems with greater risk profiles.

LegalDeal faces different regulatory considerations related to legal practice regulations, client confidentiality requirements, and jurisdictional variations in legal standards. The firm has developed jurisdiction-specific compliance frameworks that guide AI use in different regions, ensuring that automated systems operate within appropriate boundaries for each legal environment. This approach recognizes that what constitutes appropriate automation may vary significantly based on specific regulatory requirements for legal practice.

The firm also implements risk management tailored to legal service contexts, with particular attention to professional liability, confidentiality breaches, and unauthorized practice risks. AI applications undergo rigorous testing and validation before being applied to client matters, with appropriate limitations and human oversight based on risk assessment. This approach balances innovation with the firm's professional responsibilities and risk management obligations.

Across both organisations, regulatory compliance, and risk management are integrated with broader AI governance rather than operating as separate functions. This integration ensures that compliance considerations inform system design from the beginning rather than being addressed as afterthoughts, reducing the likelihood of costly redesign or deployment delays.

The Path Forward: Evolving Human-AI Partnership

As ComPlus and LegalDeal continue their transformation journeys, their approaches to Human-centric AI will evolve in response to advancing technology capabilities, changing human expectations, and emerging ethical considerations. Both organisations have established roadmaps for this evolution that balance innovation with responsible development.

ComPlus is exploring more sophisticated forms of human-AI collaboration in complex problem-solving scenarios. Rather than viewing automation as an all-or-nothing proposition, the company is developing hybrid workflows where AI systems and human experts work iteratively on challenging issues like network optimisation and capacity planning. These collaborative approaches leverage the complementary strengths of human intuition and AI analytical capabilities, potentially achieving better outcomes than either could accomplish independently.

The company is also investing in enhanced explainability for complex AI systems, recognising that traditional explanation methods may be insufficient for sophisticated models that incorporate multiple data sources and complex reasoning. Advanced visualisation techniques and customized explanations based on user roles and needs are being developed to maintain transparency even as AI capabilities become more sophisticated.

LegalDeal is similarly extending its human-centric AI approach to more complex legal analysis and strategy development. The firm is developing collaborative systems that combine AI-generated legal research and analysis with attorney expertise in novel or precedent-setting matters. These systems don't attempt to automate judgment on unprecedented legal questions; instead, they provide comprehensive information and analysis that help attorneys develop innovative arguments and strategies.

The firm is also exploring expanded applications of Human-centric AI in client counselling, using technology to enhance rather than replace the attorney-client relationship. AI systems that help attorneys identify relevant questions, visualise complex legal scenarios, and model potential outcomes may enable more effective client guidance while maintaining the human connection that defines quality legal service.

Both organisations recognize that the future of human-centric AI lies not in choosing between human and artificial intelligence but in developing increasingly sophisticated partnerships that leverage each other's unique strengths. As AI capabilities advance, the emphasis on human values, judgment, and oversight becomes more important rather than less, ensuring that technology serves human flourishing rather than narrow efficiency metrics.

Conclusion

Human-centric AI represents the philosophical core of the Cognitive Enterprise Architecture Framework, ensuring that technological transformation serves human needs and values rather than subordinating them to automation imperatives. Through the contrasting yet complementary journeys of ComPlus and LegalDeal, we've seen how this approach manifests across different organisational contexts, transforming both employee and customer experiences while maintaining ethical standards and regulatory compliance.

The principles and practices described in this chapter don't exist in isolation—they connect directly to the CeAF components detailed in Chapter 3, informing how those technical capabilities are designed, deployed, and governed. From the User Multimodal Interaction Layer that shapes human-system engagement to the AI Governance Layer that ensures responsible operation, Human-centric AI principles influence every aspect of the cognitive architecture. As organisations implement their own cognitive transformations, the human-centred approach provides both a philosophical foundation and practical guidance. By designing AI systems that empower rather than replace human capabilities, operate transparently rather than opaquely, and respect ethical boundaries rather than ignore them, organisations can create sustainable value that benefits all stakeholders.

In the next chapter, we will examine the assessment methodologies that help organisations understand their current state relative to cognitive enterprise capabilities. This critical step establishes the baseline for transformation planning, helping organisations identify gaps, prioritize initiatives, and create realistic roadmaps toward their cognitive future. Through the experiences of ComPlus and LegalDeal, we'll explore how different organisations approach this assessment process and use the resulting insights to guide their transformation journeys.

Chapter 6: Assessing the Current State – The Starting Point for Transformation

---

Michael Reynolds, ComPlus's Lead Enterprise Architect, stared at the visualisation on his screen with mixed emotions. The sprawling network diagram representing the company's application landscape resembled a complex spider web, with thousands of connections crisscrossing between systems that had accumulated over decades. "*This is why our transformation keeps hitting roadblocks*," he explained to the executive committee. "*We have over 2,000 applications, multiple integration patterns, and data trapped in dozens of siloed systems. Before we can become the cognitive enterprise we envision, we need to understand exactly where we stand today.*"

Across the continent, Elena Martinez, Technology Director at LegalDeal, faced a different but equally challenging assessment. "*Our systems are modern but limited in scope*," she noted during the firm's strategic planning session. "*We've avoided the legacy burden that larger organisations face, but we lack the advanced capabilities needed to scale our services through AI. Understanding these limitations is our first step toward transformation.*"

Beginning with Reality: The Importance of Current State Assessment

In Chapter 5, we explored how Human-centric AI principles guide cognitive transformation at organisations like ComPlus and LegalDeal. However, before implementing these principles, organisations must thoroughly understand their starting point—the foundation upon which transformation will build. This assessment reveals not just technical limitations but also human impacts, organisational readiness, and strategic alignment that will shape the transformation journey.

Current state assessment serves as the critical bridge between aspirational vision and practical implementation. Without this clear-eyed evaluation, organisations risk pursuing transformation initiatives that either fail to address fundamental challenges or overlook critical dependencies between systems, processes, and people. By conducting a thorough assessment, enterprises gain the insights needed to develop realistic roadmaps, prioritize investments, and prepare their workforces for the changes ahead.

For ComPlus and LegalDeal, this assessment process revealed dramatically different starting points despite their shared destination of becoming cognitive enterprises. Their contrasting situations illustrate how the path to cognitive transformation varies based on organisational context, while the assessment framework itself provides a template that any organisation can adapt to its specific circumstances.

The Assessment Framework: Four Dimensions of Readiness

Both organisations applied a comprehensive assessment framework designed to evaluate their readiness for cognitive transformation across four key dimensions: technology landscape, data ecosystem, operational capabilities, and organisational readiness. This framework, aligned with the CeAF components introduced in Chapter 3, provides a structured approach to identifying gaps, prioritising initiatives, and building transformation roadmaps.

Before embarking on their cognitive journeys, successful organisations like ComPlus and LegalDeal conducted thorough readiness assessments across four critical dimensions. Their experiences reveal that understanding your starting position is the most crucial first step to transformation success.

The Four-Dimensional Diagnostic

Dimension	Key Questions	Critical Indicators
TECHNOLOGY LANDSCAPE	How modernised is your application portfolio? What's your technical debt burden? How flexible are your integration capabilities?	Cloud adoption percentage Legacy system dependency API maturity Architecture flexibility
DATA ECOSYSTEM	Is your data accessible across systems? How consistent is your data quality? Can you generate integrated insights?	Data integration levels Quality measurement practices Analytics maturity Knowledge management capabilities

Dimension	Key Questions	Critical Indicators
OPERATIONAL CAPABILITIES	How automated are your core processes? What's your operational efficiency score? How adaptive are your service models?	Process standardisation Automation levels Decision support systems Operational agility metrics
ORGANISATIONAL READINESS	Does your workforce have future-ready skills? Is leadership aligned on transformation goals? How adaptable is your organisational culture?	Digital literacy levels Change resistance indicators Innovation culture metrics Learning agility measures

By applying this framework systematically, both ComPlus and LegalDeal gained a comprehensive understanding of their current state, establishing the foundation for transformation planning. Let's explore what they discovered and how these insights shaped their approach to becoming cognitive enterprises.

ComPlus: Navigating Complexity and Legacy

At ComPlus, the assessment revealed a technology landscape characterized by complexity, fragmentation and significant technical debt—challenges common to large enterprises with decades of technology investments. However, the assessment also uncovered how these technical challenges manifested in human experiences across the organisation, affecting employees, customers, and operations.

The Human Impact of Technology Fragmentation

For James Chen, a customer service supervisor at ComPlus, the fragmented technology landscape translated into daily frustration. "*When a customer calls about a service issue, I often need to navigate through five different systems just to get a complete picture of their account and services,*" James explained during an assessment interview. "*By the time I gather all the information, the customer has already spent several minutes waiting and I still might miss something important because the data isn't consistent across systems.*"

This experience wasn't unique to customer service. Network operations, billing, sales, and virtually every department reported similar challenges stemming from application sprawl, siloed data, and inconsistent integration patterns. What began as a technical assessment quickly revealed a human story about how technology fragmentation undermined employee effectiveness and customer satisfaction.

Technology Landscape Findings

The assessment documented ComPlus's complex technology environment in detail:

Application Portfolio: The company operated over 2,000 applications across its global footprint, ranging from modern cloud-native services to decades-old legacy systems. Many critical business functions relied on ageing platforms that were increasingly difficult to maintain and enhance. While 40% of applications had been modernised to cloud-native architectures, core systems for customer relationship management, billing, and network operations remained on legacy platforms.

Integration Patterns: Years of point-to-point integrations have created a tangled web of dependencies between systems. While recent efforts had implemented API standards for newer applications, the majority of integrations relied on brittle point-to-point connections or ageing middleware platforms. This integration complexity made changes risky and time-consuming, with even minor updates requiring extensive testing across multiple systems.

Technical Debt: Decades of customizations, deferred modernisation, and tactical fixes had accumulated significant technical debt. Many systems could no longer be upgraded to current versions due to extensive modifications, forcing the company to maintain outdated platforms and creating security and compliance risks.

Infrastructure: While ComPlus had invested in modern cloud infrastructure for new capabilities, approximately 65% of its application workloads still ran in traditional data centres. This hybrid environment increased operational complexity and limited the company's ability to scale resources dynamically based on demand.

For Michael Reynolds, these findings confirmed what he had long suspected. "*Our technology landscape evolved through years of mergers, acquisitions, and tactical decisions rather than strategic planning*," he noted. "*Each individual decision made sense at the time, but collectively, they've created a complex environment that's increasingly difficult to maintain, let alone transform.*"

Data Ecosystem Challenges

The data ecosystem assessment revealed equally significant challenges:

Fragmented Data Architecture: Customer, product, and operational data existed in multiple systems with limited integration. The company maintained several data warehouses and data lakes, each serving different business units and use cases. This fragmentation made it difficult to generate comprehensive insights or create the unified data foundation needed for advanced AI applications.

Data Quality and Governance: Inconsistent data definitions, limited metadata management, and manual reconciliation processes undermined data quality and trust. Business users often maintained shadow databases and spreadsheets because they didn't trust official data sources, further fragmenting the information landscape.

Analytics Maturity: While ComPlus had invested in business intelligence and reporting capabilities, most analytics remained retrospective rather than predictive or prescriptive. The limited integration between operational systems and analytics platforms created delays in insight generation, preventing real-time decision-making.

Sarah Wong, a data analyst at ComPlus, described the impact of these challenges: "*I spend about 70% of my time just finding, cleaning, and consolidating data before I can start any meaningful analysis. By the time I deliver insights, the business situation has often already changed, making my work less valuable than it could be. We have incredible data assets, but they're locked in systems that don't talk to each other.*"

Operational Capabilities and Organisational Readiness

The assessment also examined operational capabilities and organisational readiness:

Operational Efficiency: Manual processes and handoffs between systems created inefficiencies across core operations. Network monitoring, customer service, and provisioning all relied heavily on human intervention for tasks that could potentially be automated. Mean time to repair for network issues averaged four hours, while customer service representatives spent approximately 65% of their time on administrative tasks rather than customer interaction.

Workforce Skills: While ComPlus had strong technical expertise in traditional telecommunications technologies, it lacked sufficient capabilities in cloud architecture, data science, and AI engineering. The assessment identified significant gaps in the skills needed to implement and maintain cognitive systems.

Change Readiness: The organisation had a mixed track record with large-scale change initiatives. Previous transformation efforts had often focused on technology implementation without sufficient attention to process redesign and organisational change management, limiting their effectiveness.

Leadership Alignment: Executive leadership strongly supported the cognitive transformation vision, but middle management alignment varied across the organisation. Some departments embraced the vision enthusiastically, while others expressed concerns about disruption to established processes and responsibilities.

These findings painted a comprehensive picture of ComPlus's starting point—an organisation with significant legacy challenges but also considerable assets and opportunities. The assessment provided the foundation for developing a transformation strategy that would address both technical and human dimensions of change.

SWOT Analysis: Balancing Challenges and Opportunities

To synthesize these findings into actionable insights, ComPlus conducted a SWOT analysis examining strengths, weaknesses, opportunities, and threats related to its cognitive transformation:

ComPlus at the Crossroads: Legacy Giant Meets Cognitive Future

The Transformation Challenge Snapshot

STRENGTHS	WEAKNESSES
✓ **Extensive customer base** providing scale for investment	X **Complex legacy systems** limiting agility and innovation
✓ **Strong telecommunications expertise** and engineering talent	X **Fragmented data architecture** undermining insight generation
✓ **Recent cloud infrastructure investments** creating modernisation foundations	X **Critical skills gaps** in AI, ML, and cloud-native development
✓ **Executive commitment** ensuring leadership support for change	X **Manual operational processes** restricting efficiency and scale

The Stakes: Disruption or Dominance?

OPPORTUNITIES	THREATS
⚡ **AI-enabled customer experience** driving retention and revenue	⚠ **Agile competitors** potentially implementing cognitive capabilities faster
⚡ **Predictive maintenance networks** reduce costs while improving reliability	⚠ **Evolving privacy regulations** creating compliance challenges
⚡ **Advanced analytics** identifying new service opportunities	⚠ **Rising customer expectations** outpacing traditional telco adaptation
⚡ **Cognitive automation** streamlining operations and employee experience	⚠ **Highly competitive talent market** for AI and data science professionals

The Critical Tension

ComPlus stands at the intersection of established market power and technological disruption. Their transformation journey isn't just about adopting new technologies—it's about leveraging their considerable strengths to overcome entrenched weaknesses before more agile competitors can capitalize on the same opportunities.

Executive Insight: "*We're not starting from scratch—we're starting from legacy. That's both our biggest challenge and our greatest asset.*" — ComPlus CIO.

This analysis revealed specific intervention points where ComPlus could achieve maximum transformation impact while addressing its most vulnerable areas. Their story demonstrates how even organisations with significant legacy constraints can chart a path toward cognitive capabilities when they honestly assess their starting position.

LegalDeal: Scaling with Limited Resources

While ComPlus grappled with complexity and legacy constraints, LegalDeal faced a different set of challenges. As a medium-sized legal firm with modern but limited technology capabilities, LegalDeal's assessment focused on how to scale operations and enhance service delivery with constrained resources. The assessment revealed both advantages and limitations that would shape the firm's cognitive transformation approach.

The Human Experience of Scaling Challenges

For David Torres, a senior attorney at LegalDeal specializing in commercial contracts, the firm's growth had created increasing pressure on traditional work methods. "*Five years ago, I could personally review every contract and maintain close relationships with all my clients*," he explained during an assessment interview. "*Now, our client base has grown by 40%, but our team hasn't scaled proportionally. I'm constantly choosing between thoroughness and responsiveness because I simply can't keep up with the volume while maintaining the quality our clients expect.*"

This experience resonated across the firm, where attorneys and staff found themselves handling growing workloads with tools designed for a smaller scale of operation. What had once been manageable manual processes now created bottlenecks and quality risks as the organisation expanded.

Technology Landscape Findings

LegalDeal's technology assessment revealed a more modern but less comprehensive environment than ComPlus:

Application Portfolio: Unlike many established legal firms, LegalDeal has avoided significant legacy technology investments. The firm operated primarily with modern SaaS applications for practice management, document management, time tracking, billing and collaboration. These cloud-based systems provided a solid foundation for basic operations but lacked advanced AI capabilities or extensive customization options.

Integration Capabilities: While LegalDeal's core applications offered standard integrations, the firm had limited middleware or API management capabilities. Most integrations relied on vendor-provided connectors or manual processes, creating potential scaling limitations as the firm's needs became more sophisticated.

Technical Agility: The modern SaaS foundation gave LegalDeal significant agility advantages compared to firms with legacy investments. The firm could adopt new capabilities quickly through subscription changes and configuration rather than custom development. However, this same standardisation limited the firm's ability to develop highly specialised capabilities tailored to its practice areas.

Infrastructure: LegalDeal operated almost entirely in the cloud, with minimal on-premises technology. This approach reduced infrastructure management overhead but created potential challenges around data sovereignty and integration with client systems, particularly for clients with strict security requirements.

Elena Martinez, Technology Director at LegalDeal, summarized these findings: "*Our technology foundation is modern and efficient, but it's designed for standardised legal workflows rather than cognitive capabilities. We need to augment our core systems with specialised AI tools and integration capabilities without losing the simplicity and cost advantages of our current approach."*

Data Ecosystem Assessment

The data assessment revealed both strengths and limitations in LegalDeal's current state:

Document-Centric Structure: As a legal practice, LegalDeal's primary information assets were documents rather than structured data. The firm had implemented a modern document management system with basic search and classification capabilities, but these features relied on manual tagging and organisation rather than automated understanding.

Limited Analytics Capabilities: While the firm's practice management system provided operational metrics like utilization, billing realization, and matter profitability, LegalDeal lacked advanced analytics capabilities for pattern recognition, outcome prediction, or process optimisation. Most analysis relied on standard reports and manual spreadsheet manipulation rather than data science approaches.

Knowledge Management Challenges: The firm's collective expertise remained largely in the minds of individual attorneys rather than codified inaccessible knowledge systems. This approach worked when the firm was smaller but became increasingly problematic as the organisation grew and expertise became more distributed.

Sophia Kim, a paralegal at LegalDeal, described the practical impact: *"When I research precedents for a new matter, I first have to figure out which attorney might have worked on something similar, then reach out to them personally. Even with our document system, finding relevant examples is time-consuming because documents aren't consistently tagged with the information that would make them searchable. I know the knowledge exists somewhere in the firm, but accessing it efficiently is a constant challenge."*

Operational Capabilities and Organisational Readiness

The assessment also examined LegalDeal's operational capabilities and organisational readiness:

Operational Efficiency: LegalDeal's operations were relatively streamlined for core activities like time tracking, billing, and document management. However, legal analysis, research, and document drafting remained highly manual and time-intensive. Attorneys reported spending approximately 60% of their time on document review and creation activities that had significant automation potential.

Workforce Skills: The firm had strong legal expertise and reasonable digital literacy, with most staff comfortable using modern SaaS applications. However, it lacked specialised skills in areas like data science, AI implementation, and advanced analytics that would be essential for cognitive transformation.

Change Readiness: As a smaller organisation with a collaborative culture, LegalDeal demonstrated strong change readiness characteristics. The firm had successfully implemented several technology initiatives with good adoption rates, creating a foundation of trust for more ambitious changes.

Leadership Alignment: The firm's leadership, particularly CEO Maria Hernandez, strongly supported cognitive transformation as a strategic priority. This alignment extended throughout the partnership, with broad recognition that technology-enabled scaling was essential for the firm's continued growth and competitiveness.

These findings highlighted LegalDeal's distinctive starting point—a modern but limited technology foundation coupled with strong organisational readiness and clear transformation motivation.

SWOT Analysis: Leveraging Agility for Transformation

LegalDeal's SWOT analysis reflected its unique position as a mid-sized firm with modern systems but limited resources:

The Transformation Equation

STRENGTHS	WEAKNESSES
✓ **Modern SaaS foundation** providing flexibility without technical debt	X **Limited IT resources** constraining implementation capabilities
✓ **Collaborative culture** creating favourable conditions for change	X **Restricted customization options** in standardised SaaS applications
✓ **Specialised contract expertise** ripe for AI augmentation	X **Manual knowledge management** creating scaling bottlenecks
✓ **Manageable organisational scale** making comprehensive transformation feasible	X **Modest technology budget** limiting investment capacity

The Innovation Imperative

OPPORTUNITIES	THREATS
ϟ **AI-assisted document review** dramatically increasing attorney productivity	⚠ **Resource-rich competitors** making significant technology investments
ϟ **Knowledge graph technologies** transforming expertise capture and utilization	⚠ **Alternative legal service providers** commoditizing traditional practice areas
ϟ **AI-enhanced client portals** improving service while reducing overhead	⚠ **Rapidly evolving client expectations** for technology-enabled efficiency
ϟ **Predictive analytics** optimizing matter scoping, pricing, and resources	⚠ **Fierce competition** for legal technology talent

The Strategic Advantage of Agility

Unlike established giants with legacy infrastructure, LegalDeal's transformation journey leverages the nimbleness of a specialised practice with modern technology foundations. Their challenge isn't overcoming technical debt—it's maximizing limited resources to create AI-enhanced capabilities before larger competitors can leverage their superior resources to dominate the innovation landscape.

Client Perspective: "*We chose LegalDeal because they deliver the expertise of a specialised boutique with a digital experience that rivals firms ten times their size.*" — Fortune 500 General Counsel

This analysis revealed that LegalDeal's path to cognitive transformation isn't about matching the massive investments of larger firms but instead focusing on high-impact applications that amplify their specialised expertise and collaborative culture while addressing critical scaling limitations.

Real-World Diagnostic Findings

ComPlus Telecommunications: "*The assessment revealed our greatest asset wasn't our technology—it was our extensive customer data. Unfortunately, that data was trapped in silos that would need to be dismantled before we could realise its value.*" — ComPlus CTO.

LegalDeal: "*Our diagnostic showed we had a modern technology foundation but critical skills gaps in AI implementation. This completely changed our approach—from building internal capabilities to strategic partnerships.*" — LegalDeal Managing Partner.

Applying Assessment Insights to Transformation Planning

For both ComPlus and LegalDeal, the current state assessment provided essential insights that shaped their transformation strategies and implementation approaches. While their starting points differed dramatically, both organisations used the assessment findings to develop targeted initiatives aligned with their capabilities and constraints.

From Assessment to Actionable Priorities

The assessment process didn't just document current limitations—it translated those findings into actionable priorities that would guide transformation planning:

For ComPlus, the assessment highlighted the critical need to address application sprawl and data fragmentation before implementing advanced cognitive capabilities. This insight led the company to prioritize initiatives focused on application rationalization, API standardisation, and unified data architecture as foundations for subsequent AI implementation.

For LegalDeal, the assessment showed that limited resources would constrain the firm's ability to implement comprehensive solutions across all practice areas simultaneously. This insight led the firm to adopt a focused approach, targeting specific high-value processes like contract analysis and knowledge management where cognitive capabilities could deliver immediate productivity improvements.

Looking Ahead: From Assessment to Transformation Blueprint

With comprehensive current state assessments completed, both ComPlus and LegalDeal were positioned to develop transformation blueprints aligned with their specific circumstances. These blueprints would translate assessment insights into structured roadmaps, considering both technical and human dimensions of change.

In the next chapter, we will examine how these organisations developed transformation blueprints based on their assessment findings, prioritising initiatives that balanced strategic ambition with practical constraints. We'll explore how they aligned these blueprints with the CeAF components introduced in Chapter 3, creating cohesive transformation strategies that addressed current limitations while building toward their 2027 visions.

The contrast between ComPlus and LegalDeal will continue to illustrate how cognitive transformation approaches vary based on organisational context while highlighting common principles that apply regardless of size or industry. By following their journeys from assessment to blueprint, we'll develop a deeper understanding of how any organisation can chart its path toward becoming a cognitive enterprise.

Chapter 7: Laying the Foundation – Application Architecture Evolution

The comprehensive assessments conducted by ComPlus and LegalDeal in Chapter 6 revealed distinct starting points for their cognitive transformation journeys. ComPlus faces a complex web of legacy systems and fragmented data landscapes, while LegalDeal operates with modern but limited technology capabilities. Despite these differences, both organisations must establish robust application architectures to support their transformation visions. This foundation will determine their ability to deliver personalised experiences, streamline operations, and harness the power of AI across their enterprises.

This chapter explores how these organisations can evolve their application architectures to support their long-term goals. Using insights from their capability assessments, we will examine how to align application landscapes with business priorities, identify modernisation opportunities and implement architecture patterns that enable cognitive capabilities. Before diving into specific transformation strategies, we'll first explore how application architecture has evolved to address changing business needs and technological advancements.

The Evolution of Application Architecture

Over the past 25 years, application architecture has undergone a remarkable transformation. Organisations have progressed from monolithic, tightly-coupled systems to flexible, distributed architectures capable of supporting AI-driven capabilities. Understanding this evolution provides an important context for the architectural decisions that ComPlus and LegalDeal must make as they build their cognitive foundations.

Monolithic Architecture (Early 2000s)

In the early 2000s, enterprise applications were typically built as large, self-contained units with tightly coupled components. These monolithic architectures had several defining characteristics:

Tight Integration: Business logic, user interfaces, and data access layers were integrated into a single codebase, making changes difficult and risky.

Shared Databases: Multiple systems often access the same database, creating complex dependencies.

Centralized Workflows: Orchestration and business processes were implemented within the application itself.

Limited Scalability: Scaling required duplicating entire applications rather than specific components.

At ComPlus, many core systems still operate on this model. The company's billing platform, for example, consists of millions of lines of code with tightly integrated modules for rating, charging, and invoicing. When engineers need to modify a single feature, like introducing a new discount type, they must test the entire system to ensure nothing breaks—a process that takes weeks and limits the company's ability to introduce new offerings quickly.

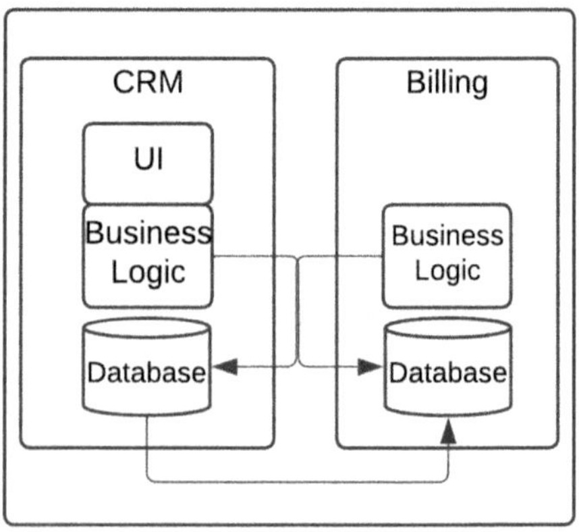

LegalDeal, as a younger firm, largely avoided this phase, having been established after cloud-based SaaS solutions became widely available.

However, some of their legal document management vendors still operate monolithic platforms that limit customization and integration possibilities.

Service-Oriented Architecture (SOA) & Enterprise Service Bus (Mid-2000s)

As businesses sought greater flexibility, Service-Oriented Architecture (SOA) emerged as a more modular approach:

Modular Services: Applications exposed functionalities as services that could be accessed across different platforms.

Enterprise Service Bus (ESB): A central integration platform manages communications between services, often becoming a performance bottleneck.

Business Process Management (BPM): Specialised tools orchestrated workflows across services.

Multi-Channel Support: SOA enabled businesses to support multiple channels like IVR, web portals, and mobile apps.

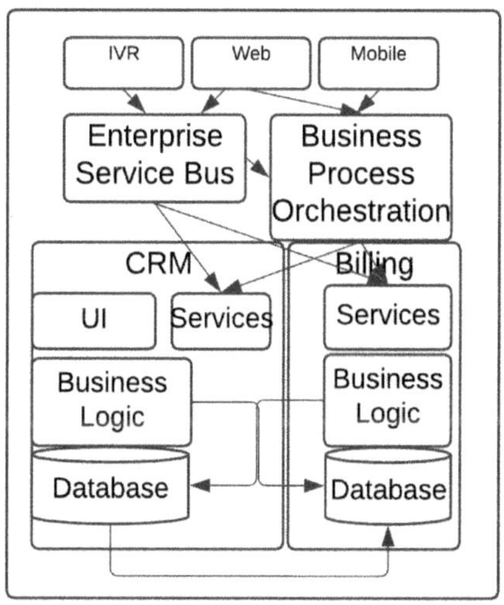

ComPlus implemented SOA extensively during this period, creating hundreds of services connected through several ESBs. While this improved flexibility compared to purely monolithic systems, it created new challenges. The company's network provisioning workflow, for instance, requires orchestration across fifteen different services. When one service is unavailable, the entire workflow fails, creating customer-impacting delays. Additionally, the central ESBs have become performance bottlenecks during peak periods.

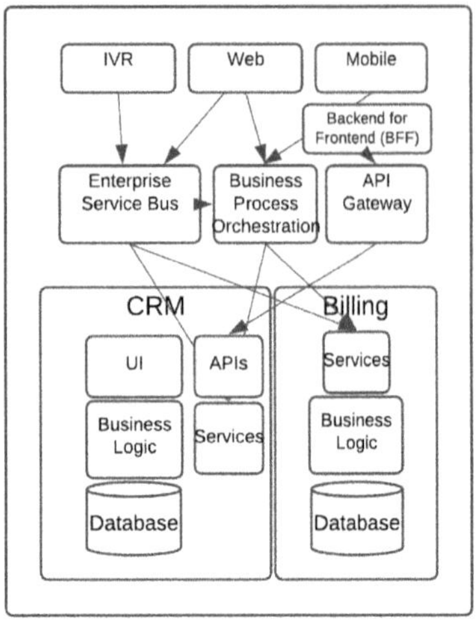

Cloud Computing & API-Driven Architectures (2010s)

The rise of cloud computing and API-first design transformed how organisations built and deployed applications:

Cloud Infrastructure: Reduced reliance on physical hardware and enabled dynamic scaling.

API-First Design: Prioritized well-defined interfaces for communication between applications.

Standardised Protocols: REST, JSON, and other standards simplified integration across platforms.

Mobile-First Development: Applications were designed for mobile access from the beginning.

LegalDeal entered this phase directly, building its operations around cloud-based practice management systems with API capabilities. The firm uses these APIs to integrate document management, billing, and client portal systems, creating a cohesive user experience despite using solutions from different vendors. However, these integrations remain relatively simple, lacking the sophistication needed for AI-powered workflows.

ComPlus has partially embraced this model, with approximately 40% of its applications now cloud-native. The company has established API standards and created an API gateway to expose core services, but legacy systems still present integration challenges.

Microservices Architecture (Mid-2010s Onwards)

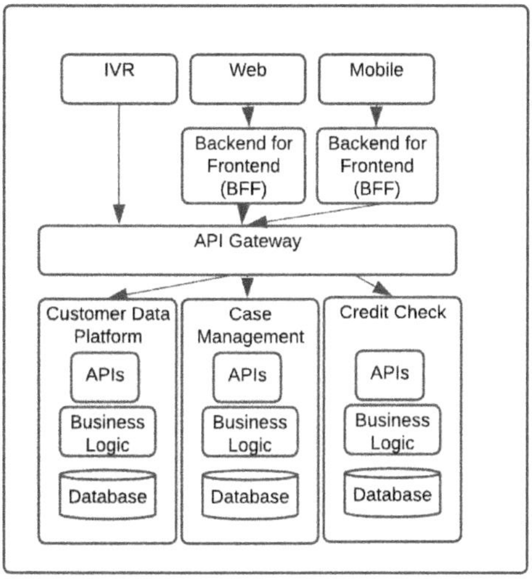

Microservices architecture represented a further evolution toward distributed, specialised components:

Focused Services: Applications were decomposed into small, independent services handling specific business functions.

Service Independence: Each microservice could be developed, deployed, and scaled independently.

Dedicated Databases: Services maintained their own data stores rather than sharing databases.

Event-Driven Communication: Asynchronous messaging enabled loose coupling between services.

ComPlus has begun adopting microservices for new capabilities, particularly in customer-facing applications. Their mobile app backend, for example, consists of twenty microservices handling functions like authentication, profile management and service activation. This approach has enabled faster feature delivery and improved resilience, as failures in one service don't necessarily affect others. However, only a small portion of the company's application landscape follows this pattern.

LegalDeal's SaaS vendors increasingly offer microservices-based platforms, but the firm hasn't yet leveraged the full potential of this architectural style for its custom development.

Emerging Now: Cognitive AI Architecture

Today, we're seeing the emergence of cognitive AI architectures that go beyond traditional application designs. These architectures integrate intelligence directly into the application fabric, enabling systems to reason, learn, and adapt to changing conditions automatically.

The Cognitive Enterprise Architecture Framework (CeAF) introduced in Chapter 3 represents this evolution, with components like the Multi-Agent Orchestrator Platform (MOP) enabling a new paradigm of intelligent, autonomous operations. In these systems, traditional applications are complemented or even replaced by AI agents that perform specific functions with greater adaptability and intelligence.

This evolution isn't just a technical shift – it fundamentally changes how organisations deliver value. While traditional applications execute pre-defined logic, cognitive systems can reason through complex scenarios, make autonomous decisions, and continuously improve based on experience.

The shift from monolithic systems to microservices has paved the way for cognitive AI architectures—intelligent, adaptable, and scalable frameworks that support advanced technologies like machine learning, natural language processing, and autonomous reasoning models. These architectures go beyond traditional applications, evolving into Agentic AI agents—autonomous systems capable of reasoning, learning, and making real-time decisions.

What Is an AI Agent?

An AI agent is a software entity capable of perceiving its environment, making decisions, and taking actions to achieve specific goals, often in collaboration with other agents or systems. Unlike traditional services, agents are not limited to static, pre-defined logic. They combine memory, planning, tool usage, and self-reflection to operate adaptively and autonomously. It includes the following components:

Memory: Agents leverage both short-term and long-term memory to retain context, learn from past interactions, and adapt to new situations.

Tools: Agents can access and orchestrate external tools such as calendars, calculators, code interpreters, search engines, and more to augment their capabilities and execute complex tasks.

Planning: Agents break down user goals into actionable steps using mechanisms like decomposition, chain-of-thought reasoning, and task planning.

Self-Reflection: Through reflection and self-critique, agents evaluate their own performance, adjust strategies, and improve over time.

Action: Agents execute tasks, interact with users, and coordinate with other agents or systems to fulfill objectives.

This architecture enables agents to operate not just as passive responders but as proactive, context-aware collaborators within the enterprise.

Characteristics of AI Agents

Autonomy: Agents can make decisions and act independently, reducing the need for constant human intervention.

Adaptability: By leveraging memory and learning, agents adjust their behavior based on feedback and changing conditions.

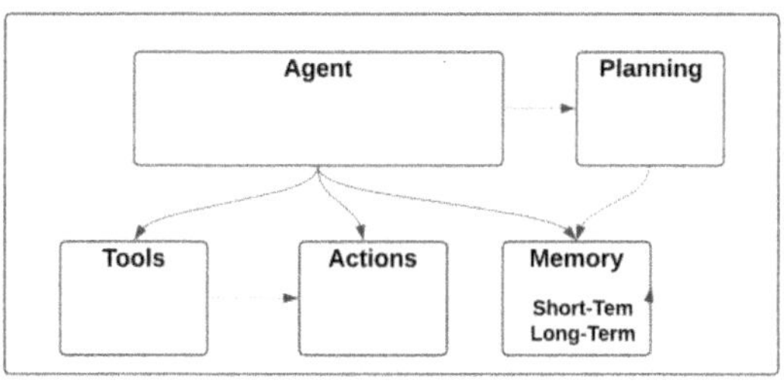

Collaboration: Agents communicate and coordinate with other agents, sharing knowledge and dividing complex tasks into manageable components.

Tool Integration: Agents are equipped with operational tools, allowing them to interact with enterprise systems, retrieve and process data and perform specialised functions.

Continuous Improvement: Through self-reflection and feedback loops, agents refine their strategies and outputs, driving ongoing optimization.

This agent-based paradigm enables organisations to move beyond static automation and embrace dynamic, human-centric intelligence. Agents can proactively anticipate needs, personalise interactions, and continuously improve operations-unlocking new levels of agility, efficiency, and innovation. By embracing agents, organisations lay the foundation for truly cognitive enterprises-where intelligence is woven into every process, decision, and customer experience.

Key Characteristics of Cognitive AI Application Architectures

1. Adaptive Business Processes

Cognitive AI architectures integrate intelligent, dynamic workflows that adapt to real-time changes in data, context, or environment. With embedded machine learning models and reasoning capabilities, these processes continuously evolve, ensuring efficiency and relevance in rapidly changing conditions.

2. Decoupled and Modular Services

These architectures are built on a modular design, exposing business capabilities as independent services. Unlike traditional microservices, cognitive AI architectures extend functionality, allowing AI agents to autonomously interact with services, optimizing workflows without manual intervention.

3. Dynamic Service Orchestration and Composition

Cognitive AI systems use advanced reasoning models and machine learning to dynamically orchestrate service flows. This enables real-time composition of services based on contextual needs. Agentic AI agents enhance this further by autonomously planning and executing workflows, reducing human oversight in complex business processes.

4. Event-Driven Processing

At the core of cognitive AI systems lies event-driven architecture, allowing real-time responsiveness. These systems process continuous data streams, analyse patterns using cognitive models, and make instant decisions—crucial for applications like fraud detection, cybersecurity, and autonomous operations.

5. Composable Applications

Cognitive AI architectures promote agile development by supporting composable applications—where organisations can integrate existing services and external APIs to introduce new capabilities without rebuilding from scratch. AI agents autonomously identify and use relevant services to complete complex tasks efficiently.

6. Learning and Memory

To ensure continuous improvement, cognitive AI architectures incorporate supervised, unsupervised, and reinforcement learning models. These systems accumulate and organize knowledge through the following:

- Semantic memory (world knowledge),
- Episodic memory (experience-based knowledge) and
- Procedural memory (task-specific knowledge).

7. Reasoning and Decision-Making

Beyond traditional automation, cognitive AI systems reason through complex scenarios, leveraging:

- Inference engines for logical deductions,
- Problem-solving algorithms to navigate uncertainties and
- Predictive models for proactive decision-making.

8. Scalability and Modularity

Cognitive AI architectures are highly scalable, enabling deployment across various industries and domains. Each module specializes in a specific function—learning, perception, or decision-making—while maintaining smooth integration.

Neither ComPlus nor LegalDeal has fully implemented cognitive architectures, but both organisations recognize this evolution as key to their transformation visions. ComPlus aims to build intelligent network operations that self-optimize and self-heal, while LegalDeal envisions AI-powered contract analysis and knowledge management systems.

Application Architecture Transformation Approach

Understanding the historical evolution provides context for the transformation journeys that ComPlus and LegalDeal must undertake. Each organisation needs to develop a structured approach to modernise its application landscape while maintaining business continuity. This transformation must address several key dimensions:

Breaking Down Monoliths: Decomposing large, monolithic applications into modular components that can evolve independently.

Establishing Integration Patterns: Creating seamless communication between systems using modern approaches like event-driven architecture.

Implementing Data Architecture: Building data foundations that support real-time analytics and AI capabilities.

Enabling AI Integration: Creating interfaces and structures that allow AI to be embedded within applications.

Let's examine how each organisation can approach these dimensions, starting with breaking monolithic architectures.

Breaking the Monolithic Architecture

The Challenge of Legacy Systems

Legacy systems create significant barriers to innovation, making it difficult for organisations to deliver seamless, personalised experiences and adapt to changing business needs. At ComPlus, the challenge is particularly acute.

The company's customer relationship management system, developed over twenty years ago, illustrates this problem vividly. When a customer calls the service centre, representatives must access five different screens to get a complete view of the customer's services, billing history, and previous interactions. This fragmentation not only frustrates customers who have to repeat information but also prevents the company from implementing the real-time personalisation needed for its cognitive transformation.

Michael Reynolds, Lead Enterprise Architect at ComPlus, explains the technical implications: "*Our monolithic systems weren't designed for the speed and flexibility we need today. Making even simple changes requires extensive testing and redeployment of entire applications, creating risk and slowing our ability to innovate.*"

While LegalDeal doesn't face the same legacy burden, the firm encounters limitations with the monolithic SaaS platforms it uses. When the firm wanted to create a specialised workflow for handling regulatory compliance cases, it found its practice management system couldn't be customized to support the unique documentation and approval steps required. This limitation constrains their ability to implement AI-enhanced legal workflows that could drive efficiency and growth.

Establishing Architecture Principles

Breaking away from monolithic systems requires a strong architectural foundation that supports modular, AI-driven services. Both ComPlus and LegalDeal need to establish clear architectural principles to guide their transformation efforts.

Architecture Principle: Service Granularity

The first principle focuses on defining the appropriate scope and boundaries for services. Traditional approaches to service design must evolve to support cognitive capabilities that can operate as intelligent, context-aware entities.

For ComPlus, this means redefining how they structure network management capabilities. Rather than building a single, comprehensive network management application, they need to develop specialised services for functions like fault detection, performance monitoring,, and configuration management. These focused services can then evolve independently and integrate with AI capabilities that optimize specific aspects of network operations.

At LegalDeal, service granularity applies to how they structure their document management workflows. By separating document intake, classification, analysis, and storage into distinct services, they can incrementally enhance each capability with AI while maintaining the overall workflow.

Implementation Guidelines:

1. **Define Functional Scope**: Each service should focus on a specific business capability with clear boundaries. For example, ComPlus might create a dedicated "Service Activation" service rather than embedding this function within a larger customer management system.
2. **Ensure Loose Coupling**: Services should interact through well-defined interfaces rather than direct database access or tight integration. This enables independent evolution and reduces the risk of changes in one service affecting others.
3. **Balance Size and Complexity**: Services should be small enough to be managed by a single team but large enough to deliver meaningful business value. Excessively fine-grained services can create unnecessary complexity.

At ComPlus, applying these guidelines has started to yield results. The company has successfully extracted customer profile management from its monolithic CRM system, creating a dedicated service that provides a unified view of customer information. This service now supports both legacy applications and new digital channels, improving data consistency while enabling incremental modernisation.

LegalDeal has taken a similar approach to document management, creating a specialised service for contract analysis that works alongside its existing practice management system. This modular approach allows them to enhance specific capabilities without disrupting their core operations.

Architecture Principle: API-First Design

API-First Design represents a fundamental shift in how organisations build applications. Rather than treating APIs as an afterthought, this principle prioritizes defining clear, consistent interfaces before implementing underlying functionality. This approach is particularly important for cognitive enterprises, as it enables seamless integration between systems and provides the foundation for AI-enhanced workflows.

API-First Design in Practice

For ComPlus, API-First Design addresses a critical challenge: enabling innovative customer experiences without waiting for complete backend modernisation. The company has over 200 legacy systems that can't be replaced immediately, but customers expect digital experiences comparable to those of leading technology companies.

By implementing an API layer that presents unified, well-designed interfaces to frontend applications, ComPlus can hide the complexity of backend systems while gradually modernising them. Their mobile app teams can work with these consistent APIs rather than integrating directly with diverse backend systems, accelerating development and improving user experience.

At LegalDeal, API-First Design enables the firm to combine specialised legal AI tools with its practice management platform. By defining standard APIs for document handling, client information, and matter management, they can integrate best-of-breed AI solutions for contract analysis or legal research without creating data silos.

Implementation Guidelines:

1. **Start with API Specifications**: Begin by defining clear API specifications using tools like OpenAPI (Swagger) before implementing the actual services. This ensures that interfaces are consistent, well-documented, and aligned with business needs.
2. **Adopt Industry Standards**: Leverage industry standards like REST, GraphQL, or SOAP, depending on specific requirements. ComPlus, for example, uses TM Forum Open APIs for telecommunications-specific functions while adopting REST for customer-facing services.
3. **Implement Consistent Patterns**: Establish patterns for common operations like pagination, filtering, error handling, and authentication across all APIs. This consistency simplifies integration and reduces development effort.
4. **Provide Comprehensive Documentation**: Include detailed documentation, example requests, responses, and use cases for each API to facilitate adoption both internally and by partners.
5. **Build for Versioning**: Design APIs with versioning in mind to enable evolution without breaking existing integrations. This is particularly important during transformation when multiple systems may consume the same APIs.

When ComPlus implemented API-First Design for customer management, they saw immediate benefits. Development teams could build new customer experiences without waiting for backend modernisation, accelerating time-to-market for digital initiatives. Meanwhile, backend teams could refactor legacy systems incrementally without disrupting frontend applications, reducing risk and enabling continuous improvement.

Architecture Principle: Real-Time Data Exchange

Modern cognitive enterprises require seamless, real-time data flow between systems to enable intelligent decision-making and personalised experiences. Traditional batch processes and point-to-point integrations can't deliver the immediacy needed for AI-driven operations. This principle focuses on establishing patterns that enable event-driven, real-time interactions across the application landscape.

Architecture Principle: Event-Driven Architecture

Event-Driven Architecture (EDA) represents a fundamental shift from request-response patterns to a model where systems communicate through events. When something significant happens—a customer places an order, a network anomaly is detected, or a document is uploaded—the system publishes an event that other systems can consume and act upon.

For ComPlus, implementing EDA addresses a critical operational challenge. When a service disruption occurs, multiple systems need to respond: network management must identify the cause, customer service needs to be alerted, affected customers should be notified, and technical teams must be dispatched if necessary. Previously, these workflows required manual coordination and multiple system updates, creating delays and inconsistencies.

By implementing an event-driven approach, ComPlus has transformed this process. When their monitoring system detects an outage, it publishes a "Service disruption" event to an event bus. Different systems subscribe to this event stream: the customer notification system automatically alerts affected customers via their preferred channels, the workforce management system dispatches technicians, and the customer service dashboard displays real-time status information. This coordinated response happens without the systems being directly connected, enabling ComPlus to modify or replace individual components without disrupting the overall workflow.

At LegalDeal, EDA enables more responsive client service. When a client uploads a new contract for review, the document management system publishes a "DocumentUploaded" event. The contract analysis service automatically begins processing the document, while the matter management system updates the case status and notifies the assigned attorney. This coordination happens seamlessly, even though these functions are provided by different systems.

Implementation Technologies:

1. **Event Streaming Platforms**: Technologies like Apache Kafka or Amazon Kinesis enable high-volume, scalable event distribution. ComPlus uses Kafka to handle millions of network events daily, ensuring reliable delivery even during service disruptions.
2. **Change Data Capture (CDC)**: CDC tools capture database changes and convert them into events, enabling legacy systems to participate in event-driven workflows without modification. This has been particularly valuable for ComPlus in integrating older systems that lack modern APIs.
3. **Message Queues**: Platforms like RabbitMQ or AWS SQS provide reliable message delivery for asynchronous processing. LegalDeal uses message queues to distribute document processing tasks, ensuring that resource-intensive operations don't impact interactive response times.
4. **API Gateways**: Modern API gateways support WebHooks and event subscriptions, enabling real-time notifications for external systems. Both organisations use API gateways to secure and manage event-based integrations with partner systems.

By implementing these technologies, both ComPlus and LegalDeal have established foundations for real-time data exchange that support their cognitive transformation goals. ComPlus now processes network events in real-time, enabling faster response to service issues and providing the data velocity needed for predictive maintenance. LegalDeal has reduced document processing delays, enabling more responsive client service and creating the foundation for AI-enhanced workflows.

Architecture Principle: AI-Ready Database Design

Traditional database designs optimize for transaction processing or analytical queries but often fall short in supporting the dynamic, real-time needs of AI-driven applications. AI-Ready Database Design focuses on creating data foundations that enable both operational efficiency and intelligent capabilities.

Hybrid Database Strategy

Neither a purely relational nor a purely NoSQL approach can address all the data requirements of a cognitive enterprise. Instead, organisations need a hybrid strategy that leverages different database technologies for specific use cases.

ComPlus illustrates this approach with its customer data platform. The company maintains customer master data in a relational database (PostgreSQL) to ensure transactional integrity for core operations like billing and service provisioning. However, they store customer interaction histories and behavioural data in a document database (MongoDB) that can accommodate varying data structures and scale horizontally. For real-time personalisation, they maintain frequently accessed customer preferences and session data in an in-memory database (Redis), enabling sub-millisecond response times for customer-facing applications.

LegalDeal similarly employs a hybrid strategy for document management. They store document metadata in a relational database for efficient searching and organisation, while the documents themselves are managed in a specialised document store. When clients need real-time collaboration on legal documents, the system uses in-memory caching to ensure responsive editing experiences.

Implementation Guidelines:

1. **Match Database Types to Use Cases**: Select database technologies based on specific requirements rather than adopting a one-size-fits-all approach. For instance, ComPlus uses time-series databases for network performance data, graph databases for relationship analysis, and relational databases for transactional systems.
2. **Implement Caching Layers**: Use in-memory databases like Redis or Memcached to cache frequently accessed data, reducing latency for real-time operations. This is particularly important for AI-driven personalisation, which requires an immediate response.

3. **Enable Data Synchronization**: Establish patterns for keeping data consistent across different database systems, using technologies like Change Data Capture (CDC) or event sourcing. This ensures that each database has the data it needs without requiring direct connections between systems.
4. **Design for Analytics**: Structure data to support both operational needs and analytical processing, enabling AI models to access the information they need without complex transformations. This might involve maintaining denormalized views specifically for analytical purposes.

By implementing these patterns, both organisations have established database foundations that support their cognitive transformation goals. ComPlus can now analyse customer behaviour in real-time to provide personalised recommendations while maintaining the transactional integrity needed for core operations. LegalDeal has improved document retrieval times while enabling more sophisticated analysis of legal content, supporting their AI-enhanced knowledge management vision.

Architecture Principle: Domain-Driven Design for Application Organisation

While the previous principles address technical aspects of application architecture, Domain-Driven Design (DDD) provides a methodology for organizing systems around business concepts. This approach is particularly valuable for cognitive enterprises, as it ensures that technical implementations align with business domains and enable meaningful AI augmentation.

Core DDD Concepts

Domain-Driven Design: It centres on several key concepts that help organize complex application landscapes:

Bounded Contexts: Explicitly defined boundaries within which specific models and terms have consistent meanings. For example, the term "customer" might have different attributes and behaviours in a billing context versus a service management context.

Ubiquitous Language: A shared language between business and technical teams that ensures everyone understands domain concepts consistently. This common language is reflected in code, documentation, and communication.

Strategic Design: The process of identifying core domains that provide competitive advantage, supporting domains that enable the business, and generic domains that can be commoditized or outsourced.

At ComPlus, applying DDD has helped address the fragmentation resulting from years of siloed development. The company identified "Customer Experience" as a core domain critical to its competitive strategy, while "Network Infrastructure" emerged as another core domain due to its fundamental importance to service delivery. Supporting domains included "Partner Management" and "Product Catalog," while "Human Resources" and "Finance" were classified as generic domains that could leverage standard industry solutions.

This classification guided investment decisions: ComPlus prioritized custom development and AI enhancement for the core domains while adopting standard solutions for generic domains. For supporting domains, they balanced customization and standardisation based on specific business needs.

LegalDeal applied a similar approach on a smaller scale, identifying "Legal Advisory" and "Knowledge Management" as core domains central to their value proposition. "Client Relationship Management" emerged as a supporting domain, while "Accounting" and "HR" were treated as generic domains where standard solutions were sufficient.

Implementation Approach:

1. **Conduct Domain Workshops**: Bring together business and technical teams to identify and define domains, establish bounded contexts, and develop the ubiquitous language. Both ComPlus and LegalDeal held structured workshops with key stakeholders to establish their domain models.
2. **Create Context Maps**: Document the relationships between different bounded contexts, including upstream/downstream

dependencies and integration patterns. These maps help teams understand how changes in one context might affect others.

3. **Align Teams with Domains**: Structure development teams around business domains rather than technical layers, enabling end-to-end ownership and faster decision-making. ComPlus reorganized its development teams to align with core domains, improving coordination and business alignment.
4. **Implement Strategic Portfolio Management**: Use the domain classification to guide investment decisions, focusing resources on areas that provide competitive differentiation. LegalDeal applied this approach to prioritize investments in its document analysis capabilities, which is a core differentiator for their practice.

By applying Domain-Driven Design, both organisations established clearer boundaries between systems, reduced duplication of functionality, and aligned technical implementations with business priorities. This foundation enables more focused AI implementation, as cognitive capabilities can be targeted to specific domains where they deliver the most value.

Architecture Principle: AI Embedded in Your Applications

From Separate Systems to Integrated Intelligence

Traditional enterprises maintain a clear separation: operational systems run the business while analytical systems study it. This division creates delays between insight and action. Modern cognitive enterprises are breaking down this wall by embedding AI directly into their applications, enabling real-time intelligent decisions exactly where and when they're needed.

What Does AI Embedded in Applications Look Like?

Traditional Approach	Embedded AI Approach	Business Impact
AI models run in separate environments from business applications	AI capabilities built directly into application components	Immediate intelligence without system-switching delays
Analysis happens after business events occur	Real-time analysis during business processes	Problems prevented instead of diagnosed afterwards
Insights require human intervention to implement	Automated actions triggered by model outputs	Faster response times and consistent execution
Models managed separately from applications	Unified lifecycle management	Reduced maintenance overhead and better alignment

How to Make This Work in Your Enterprise

1. Build Intelligence Into the Right Places

Rather than creating massive, all-encompassing AI systems, focused intelligence should be embedded into specific business functions where it adds the most value. When ComPlus needed to prevent network outages, they didn't build a separate analytical platform—they placed anomaly detection directly into their existing network monitoring microservices. This targeted approach delivered a 70% reduction in service disruptions while requiring minimal change to existing operations.

2. Design for Real-Time Decisions

The value of embedded AI comes from closing the gap between insight and action:

- Optimize models for speed, even if it means slight reductions in theoretical accuracy
- Implement streaming data processing instead of batch operations
- Create clear action paths for every model output (alerts, automated processes, guided recommendations)
- Include confidence scores so applications can determine when human judgment is needed

3. Manage the Full AI Lifecycle

Embedded AI requires disciplined management to remain effective over time:

- Implement observability systems that track both technical performance and business outcomes
- Automate retraining workflows to maintain accuracy as conditions change
- Create feedback loops that capture application interactions to continuously improve models
- Design for gradual model updates without disrupting operations

Where Operational and Analytical Systems Converge

Traditional boundaries between transactional and analytical systems are disappearing as:

- **Real-time data frameworks** eliminate the lag between business events and analytical insights
- **Edge computing** pushes intelligence closer to where data originates
- **Cloud-native architectures** make formerly complex AI capabilities available as composable services

- **Integrated platforms** combine operational and analytical workloads in unified environments

This convergence enables new capabilities like instant fraud detection during transactions, dynamic product recommendations during browsing sessions, and predictive maintenance that prevents equipment failures before they affect customers.

Why Does This Architectural Principle Matter?

Embedding AI directly into your applications isn't just a technical choice—it fundamentally changes how your business operates by:

1. Eliminating the delay between insight and action
2. Scaling intelligence across your enterprise without complexity
3. Creating continuous improvement cycles as models learn from real-world interactions
4. Making AI capabilities feel like natural extensions of existing workflows

By following this principle, organisations can achieve efficiency in automation while maintaining flexibility and insight into human judgment—exactly the balance that defines successful cognitive enterprises.

Case Study:

Embedding Intelligence: ComPlus Inventory Management Transformation

From Static Supply Chain to Cognitive Inventory Management

Among ComPlus's most transformative initiatives was the complete reimagining of its equipment inventory management system. Before their cognitive transformation, ComPlus managed a vast inventory of customer premises equipment (CPE)—including routers, modems, set-top boxes, and mobile devices—using traditional enterprise resource planning systems that operated on static reorder points and predetermined safety stock levels.

The legacy inventory system epitomized the limitations constraining the business. Regional warehouse managers would manually analyse spreadsheets to determine ordering needs, typically following quarterly forecasts that remained unchanged regardless of actual consumption patterns. When new service promotions unexpectedly succeeded, equipment shortages would occur, leading to customer installation delays of up to three weeks. Conversely, when devices underperformed in the market, warehouses would accumulate excess inventory, tying up millions in capital and ultimately leading to obsolescence write-offs.

Traditional Inventory Management Limitations

The original system suffered from several critical deficiencies:

Disconnected Forecasting: Marketing would create sales forecasts, but these are rarely integrated with inventory systems in real-time. When a promotional campaign performed 40% better than expected, the inventory system had no mechanism to automatically adjust ordering patterns.

Reactive Replenishment: Warehouse staff discovered stockouts only during physical counts or when field technicians reported shortages, often after customers were already promised installation dates.

Fixed Pricing Models: Device prices remained constant regardless of supply constraints or demand shifts, missing opportunities to balance supply and demand through pricing signals.

Siloed Data: Installation schedules, marketing campaigns, network expansion plans, and supplier delivery timelines existed in separate systems with no integrated view for holistic planning.

The Cognitive Inventory Transformation:

By applying the CeAF framework, ComPlus embedded multiple AI models directly into their inventory management workflow, transforming it from a static system into an intelligent, adaptive platform that responds dynamically to changing conditions.

The transformed system incorporates several intelligent capabilities:

Predictive Demand Forecasting: Machine learning models now continuously analyse historical consumption patterns, current orders, social media sentiment about products, weather forecasts (which affect installation schedules), and even competitor promotions to predict equipment needs with 93% accuracy.

Dynamic Safety Stock Calculation: Rather than fixed inventory levels, AI algorithms adjust safety stock requirements daily based on supplier reliability, delivery time variations, and demand volatility, optimizing capital allocation while maintaining service levels.

Real-Time Replenishment Triggers: The system automatically initiates purchase orders when inventory projections indicate potential shortages, routing them through an approval workflow only when they exceed predefined thresholds or appear anomalous.

Intelligent Allocation: When supply constraints occur, the system dynamically allocates available inventory across regions based on prioritized customer segments, revenue potential, and contractual obligations rather than first-come-first-served.

Dynamic Pricing Models: Similar to Uber's surge pricing, the system recommends temporary price adjustments when demand-supply imbalances occur. During supply shortages for premium routers, the system might suggest a 15% price increase for non-contract customers while maintaining prices for strategic accounts.

Business Impact

This cognitive transformation delivered substantial business results:

Inventory holding costs decreased by €32M annually while improving equipment availability by 28%

Customer installation wait times dropped from an average of 7 days to less than 48 hours

Obsolescence write-offs decreased by 64% as the system proactively identified slow-moving items for promotional campaigns before they became obsolete.

Dynamic pricing during supply constraints increased margins by 12% while effectively managing demand.

A technical operations director at ComPlus noted: "*What's remarkable isn't just the cost savings, but how the system has fundamentally changed our relationship with suppliers and customers. We're no longer constantly firefighting inventory problems—we're strategically managing our supply chain as a competitive advantage.*"

Human-AI Partnership

Consistent with ComPlus's human-centric approach, the system doesn't replace inventory managers but transforms their roles. These professionals now focus on supplier relationship management, strategic inventory positioning, and exception handling rather than routine ordering and allocation decisions. The AI handles pattern recognition and repetitive calculations, while humans apply judgment to unusual situations and strategic decisions that require contextual understanding.

This inventory management transformation exemplifies how embedding AI directly into core business processes creates intelligence at the point of operation rather than as a separate analytical function, delivering both immediate operational benefits and strategic advantages through enhanced agility and responsiveness.

Applying Architecture Principles to ComPlus and LegalDeal

The architecture principles we've explored provide a framework for application transformation, but their application varies based on organisational context. Let's examine how ComPlus and LegalDeal are applying these principles to address their specific challenges and opportunities.

ComPlus: Modernisation at Scale

ComPlus faces the challenge of modernising hundreds of applications while maintaining service continuity for millions of customers. Their approach combines incremental transformation of existing systems with strategic investments in new capabilities.

For customer-facing operations, ComPlus is implementing an API layer that presents unified interfaces to digital channels while gradually modernising backend systems. This approach enables immediate improvement in customer experience without waiting for complete backend transformation. When a customer interacts with the mobile app or website, they experience a consistent interface even though the underlying systems remain fragmented.

In network operations, ComPlus is adopting event-driven architecture to enable real-time monitoring and autonomous optimisation. Network equipment now publishes events about status changes and performance metrics to a central event bus, enabling various applications to consume and act on this information without point-to-point integration. This foundation supports the company's vision for self-healing networks and predictive maintenance.

For data management, ComPlus is implementing a hybrid database strategy that combines transactional systems of record with real-time operational data stores and analytical repositories. This approach balances integrity requirements with the need for speed and flexibility, enabling AI-driven insights without compromising core operations.

Domain-Driven Design helps ComPlus organize this complex landscape, providing clear boundaries between systems and guiding investment decisions. By identifying core domains like customer experience and network operations, they can focus modernisation efforts where they deliver the most value.

LegalDeal: Building on Modern Foundations

While LegalDeal doesn't face the same legacy challenges as ComPlus, it needs to enhance its modern but limited systems to support advanced cognitive capabilities. Their approach focuses on extending existing platforms through APIs and integrations while building specific AI-enhanced capabilities for core legal functions.

For document management, LegalDeal is implementing specialised services for contract analysis and knowledge extraction that integrate with their existing document management platform. These services use AI to identify key provisions, assess risks, and extract insights, enhancing the firm's ability to handle complex legal matters efficiently.

In client engagement, LegalDeal is adopting an API-first design to create a unified client portal that integrates matter management, document sharing, and communication functions. This approach enables a seamless client experience while leveraging specialised capabilities from different systems.

For knowledge management, LegalDeal is implementing a hybrid database approach that combines structured matter information with unstructured document content and relationship data. This foundation supports their vision for AI-enhanced legal research and knowledge sharing across the firm.

Domain-Driven Design helps LegalDeal maintain clarity as they enhance their systems, ensuring that new capabilities align with their core legal advisory and knowledge management domains. This focus enables efficient use of limited resources, targeting investments where they deliver the most value for clients and attorneys.

From Legacy to Cognitive: A Phased Transformation Approach

Both ComPlus and LegalDeal recognize that transformation to a cognitive enterprise architecture requires a phased approach that balances immediate improvements with long-term goals. Their implementation strategies reflect this understanding, combining tactical enhancements with strategic investments in foundational capabilities.

Phase 1: Foundation Building

The initial phase focuses on establishing the architectural foundations needed for cognitive capabilities:

API Management: Implementing API gateways and management platforms that enable controlled access to existing systems while supporting new digital channels.

Event Infrastructure: Deploying event streaming platforms and establishing patterns for event-driven communication between systems.

Data Platforms & Products: Building unified data platforms that enable comprehensive analysis across previously siloed information and build a set of critical data products that deliver the most business value.

ComPlus has completed much of this foundation work, deploying an enterprise API management platform, establishing a Kafka-based event infrastructure, and implementing a unified data lake that combines customer, network, and operational information. These investments haven't yet delivered major visible changes but provide the essential groundwork for cognitive capabilities.

LegalDeal has similarly established foundational elements, implementing API integration capabilities, document processing workflows, and enhanced data management. While smaller in scale than

ComPlus's efforts, these investments provide the necessary foundation for their transformation.

Phase 2: Domain-Specific Modernisation

With foundations in place, both organisations are now focusing on modernising specific domains to enable cognitive capabilities:

Customer Experience: ComPlus is decomposing its monolithic customer management systems into microservices that support personalised, omnichannel experiences. This modernisation enables AI-driven personalisation and proactive customer service.

Network Operations: ComPlus is enhancing its network management capabilities with real-time analytics and automation, creating the foundation for self-optimizing networks.

Document Processing: LegalDeal is implementing AI-enhanced document analysis that automatically extracts key provisions, identifies risks, and connects related information across matters.

Knowledge Management: LegalDeal is developing a knowledge graph that connects legal concepts, precedents, and firm expertise, enabling more effective knowledge sharing and reuse.

These domain-specific initiatives deliver immediate business value while advancing the overall transformation vision. By focusing on core domains first, both organisations ensure that their investments address priority business needs while building momentum for broader transformation.

Phase 3: Cognitive Integration

The final phase focuses on integrating cognitive capabilities across domains to enable truly intelligent operations:

Autonomous Workflows: Implementing AI-driven workflows that dynamically adapt based on context and outcomes.

Predictive Operations: Developing capabilities that anticipate issues and opportunities rather than simply responding to events.

Continuous Learning: Establishing feedback loops that enable systems to improve based on outcomes and experiences.

While neither organisation has fully reached this phase, both have begun implementing initial cognitive capabilities in specific areas. ComPlus has deployed predictive maintenance for network equipment, while LegalDeal has implemented AI-assisted legal research. These targeted implementations provide learning opportunities and demonstrate value while the broader transformation continues.

Beyond Microservices: Comparing Traditional Approaches with Agentic AI

While microservices represent a significant advancement in application architecture, the Cognitive Enterprise Architecture Framework introduces a more profound evolution through the Multi-Agent Orchestrator Platform (MOP) and agentic AI. This section compares traditional microservices approaches with the agentic AI paradigm enabled by the MOP, using a concrete example from the telecommunications domain to illustrate the differences.

Case Study: Order Fulfilment

This comprehensive review of application architecture evolution culminates in a practical demonstration of how these principles can be applied to solve real business challenges. To illustrate the transformative potential of modern architectural approaches, we examine a critical use case from ComPlus's operations—streamlining the telecom order fulfilment process. This case study demonstrates how the architectural principles discussed throughout this chapter can be practically implemented to achieve tangible business outcomes.

A User Story for Telecom Order Fulfilment

Telecommunication providers like ComPlus face significant challenges in streamlining their order fulfilment processes. These processes often involve multiple departments, systems, and touchpoints, creating opportunities for errors, delays, and customer dissatisfaction. The following user story encapsulates the business requirements for enhancing telecom order fulfilment:

Business Requirements and User Needs

Telecom operations managers and logistics coordinators need streamlined order fulfilment processes that ensure seamless provisioning, delivery, and activation of telecom services and equipment. An effective solution must reduce delays and errors, guarantee timely delivery and activation, deliver a "first-time-right" experience to enhance customer satisfaction, and optimize resource utilization for operational efficiency.

The acceptance criteria for such a solution encompass the entire order fulfilment journey, from initial validation through completion. This includes verifying customer details, confirming inventory availability, scheduling installations, preparing and dispatching equipment, activating services, providing customer training when applicable, securing customer sign-off, and collecting feedback for continuous improvement.

The business value derived from such a solution is multifaceted. It enhances customer experience through timely delivery and transparent communication, increases operational efficiency by automating key steps, reduces costs associated with rework and delays, supports scalability for managing increasing order volumes, and generates actionable insights into fulfilment performance metrics for ongoing optimisation.

Architectural Approaches for Order Fulfilment

Building on the architectural principles discussed throughout this chapter, we can approach this challenge through three distinct architectural paradigms, each representing a stage in the evolution of application architecture.

Microservices-Based Solution for Order Fulfilment

The microservices approach represents a significant advancement over monolithic systems, as detailed earlier in our architectural evolution discussion. For the order fulfilment use case, this approach decomposes the process into discrete, purpose-built microservices that manage specific phases of the fulfilment lifecycle.

Design Components and Workflow

In this architecture, the order fulfilment process is divided into specialised services, each responsible for a distinct aspect of the workflow. These services include Order Validation Service, Inventory Management Service, Scheduling Service, Delivery Management Service, Service Activation Service, and Customer Notification Service. Each service operates independently with its own data store, communicating through well-defined APIs.

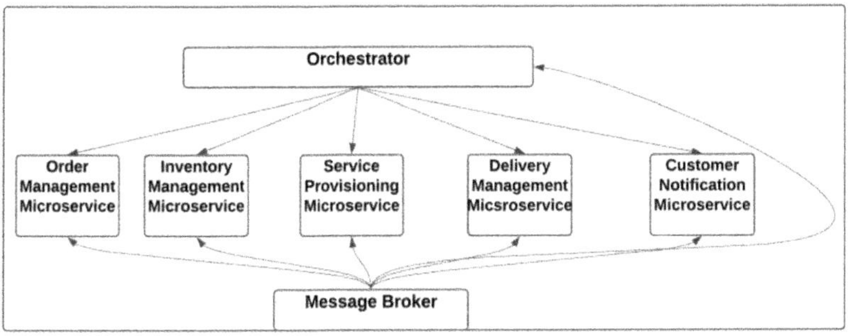

The workflow coordination is handled through a workflow orchestrator that sequences the execution of services based on predefined process flows. A message broker facilitates asynchronous, event-driven communication between services, enabling loose coupling and improved resilience. For instance, when inventory status changes, the Inventory Management Service publishes an event that other services can subscribe to and react accordingly.

While this architecture offers significant improvements over monolithic systems in terms of modularity and scalability, it still relies on static, predefined workflows that may require development efforts to accommodate new order types or changing business requirements.

Agentic AI-Based Architecture with CeAF

Moving beyond traditional microservices, the Cognitive Enterprise Architecture Framework (CeAF) with Agentic AI represents the next evolutionary stage, aligning with our discussion on Cognitive AI Architecture earlier in this chapter. This approach transforms the order fulfilment process by replacing static microservices with intelligent, autonomous agents orchestrated through the Multi-Agent Orchestrator Platform (MOP).

Intelligent Agents and Dynamic Orchestration

In this architecture, domain-specific intelligent agents handle different aspects of order fulfilment. These include Order Verification Agent, Inventory Management Agent, Delivery Coordination Agent, Service

Provisioning Agent, and Customer Notification Agent. Unlike traditional microservices, these agents possess reasoning capabilities, enabling them to make context-aware decisions and adapt to changing conditions.

The MOP coordinates agent activities, maintaining a shared context that enables collaborative workflows. The Context Manager ensures all agents have access to relevant information, while the Event Bus facilitates real-time communication between agents through events or using protocols like A2A (Agent to Agent), which we explain later. This architecture implements the event-driven patterns discussed in our "Design For Real-Time Data Exchange" section, enabling responsive, real-time processing of order fulfilment tasks.

Enhanced Solution with Reasoning-Capable Orchestration

Building upon the CeAF and MOP foundation, the most advanced architectural approach introduces a reasoning-capable orchestrator that further enhances the system's adaptability and intelligence. This approach exemplifies the principles of AI-ready architecture discussed earlier, particularly in terms of dynamic task decomposition and autonomous decision-making.

Dynamic Task Decomposition and Collaborative Execution

The reasoning-capable orchestrator employs advanced reasoning models, such as large language models (LLMs) or domain-specific AI algorithms, to dynamically analyse incoming orders and determine their structure. It then breaks down complex tasks into smaller sub-tasks based on dependencies, complexity, and agent capabilities, assigning them to specialised agents.

The workflow begins with order placement through an API or online portal, followed by dynamic task decomposition by the reasoning orchestrator. Sub-tasks are assigned to relevant agents who execute them independently while updating the shared context. The orchestrator consolidates outputs from all agents to produce a comprehensive order fulfilment result, which is then communicated to the customer.

This approach exemplifies the real-time data exchange principles discussed earlier, with agents collaborating by sharing results through a shared context managed by the Context Manager. The architecture's adaptability for order variability demonstrates how AI-ready systems can handle diverse workflows without requiring code changes, aligning with our discussion on adaptive business processes in Cognitive AI architectures.

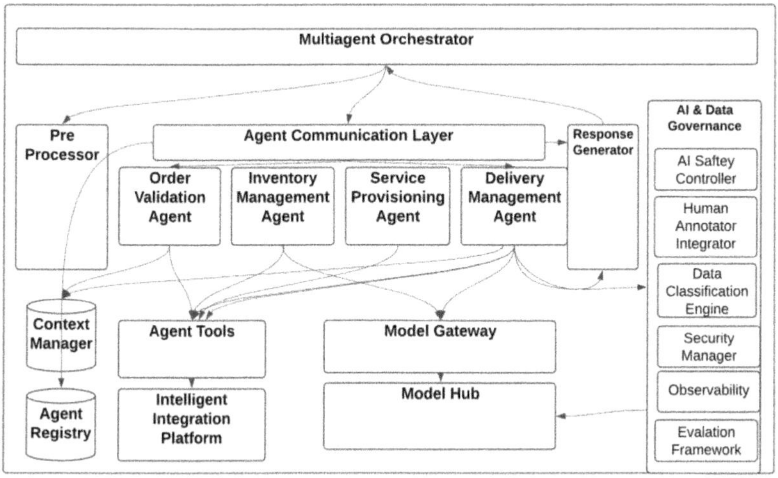

Comparative Analysis of Architectural Approaches

To provide practical guidance on selecting the appropriate architectural approach, let us examine the key differences between traditional microservices and AI agents, specifically in the context of inventory management within the order fulfilment process.

Microservices vs. AI Agents: Key Distinctions

The fundamental differences between these approaches manifest in several critical dimensions. In task execution, microservices rely on predefined tasks executed based on static workflows, while AI agents dynamically decompose tasks into subtasks executed collaboratively. Decision-making in microservices is rule-based and static, whereas AI agents employ AI-driven, dynamic decision-making using predictive models and reasoning capabilities.

In terms of adaptability, microservices require development efforts to accommodate new workflows or logic, while AI agents adapt dynamically without code changes through shared context and reasoning models. Context awareness also differs significantly—microservices have limited awareness, focusing only on specific tasks, while AI agents maintain holistic awareness with decisions informed by global context and inter-agent collaboration.

Perhaps most importantly, microservices have no built-in learning capabilities and depend on external systems for analytics or machine learning. In contrast, AI agents feature continuous real-time learning with feedback loops, improving performance over time—a critical distinction for organisations seeking long-term operational excellence.

Solution Comparison: Strategic Considerations

When comparing the microservices-based and Agentic AI-based solutions holistically, several strategic considerations emerge. The Agentic AI solution offers superior flexibility and adaptability, handling diverse workflows and order types dynamically without requiring code changes. While microservices offer faster implementation cycles compared to monolithic systems, the Agentic AI solution significantly reduces time-to-market by enabling updates through reasoning models instead of traditional development.

Both solutions offer scalability, but the Agentic AI approach provides autonomous scaling and enhanced fault tolerance through self-healing agents and real-time context sharing. The microservices solution relies on established practices and technologies, making skilled talent easier to find, while the Agentic AI solution requires advanced expertise in cognitive systems and AI modelling.

Cost considerations reveal that the Agentic AI solution incurs higher initial costs due to fine-tuning or training AI models and inference costs. However, it offers long-term cost savings through reduced operational overhead and increased automation. Customer experience is notably enhanced in the Agentic AI solution through predictive insights, proactive updates, and real-time adaptability.

Choosing the Right Architecture for Your Organisation

Based on this comparative analysis, organisations should select their architectural approach based on their specific context and strategic priorities. The microservices-based solution is appropriate for organisations dealing with simpler, well-defined workflows, requiring faster implementation without high upfront costs and having teams with expertise in microservices but limited experience with cognitive systems.

Conversely, the Agentic AI-based solution (CeAF & MOP) is ideal for organisations managing complex workflows requiring dynamic adaptability, aiming for long-term scalability, automation, and future-proofing and willing to invest in upskilling their team or hiring talent with expertise in cognitive system design and AI modelling.

Conclusion: Building the Foundation for Cognitive Enterprise

The architectural principles and patterns explored throughout this chapter provide a comprehensive framework for organisations like ComPlus and LegalDeal to transform their application landscapes. By adopting modern architectural approaches such as microservices, API-

First design, Domain-Driven Design, and eventually Cognitive AI architectures with Agentic AI, these organisations can build scalable, intelligent, and adaptive systems that align with their strategic business objectives.

The telecom order fulfilment case study demonstrates how these architectural principles can be practically applied to solve real business challenges, with different approaches offering varying levels of intelligence, adaptability, and operational efficiency. The evolution from traditional microservices to cognitive AI architectures with reasoning-capable orchestration represents a journey towards increasingly autonomous, intelligent systems capable of handling complex business processes with minimal human intervention.

As organisations embark on this transformation journey, they must balance immediate operational needs with long-term strategic goals, considering factors such as existing architecture, available talent, budget constraints, and the complexity of their business processes. By aligning their architectural choices with business priorities and strategically adopting cognitive capabilities, organisations can establish a solid foundation for becoming true cognitive enterprises.

In the next chapter, we will explore how data serves as the foundation for cognitive systems, examining modern data paradigms such as Data Fabric and how they enable advanced analytics, real-time decision-making, and machine learning-driven automation. The integration of robust application architecture with advanced data capabilities will provide a comprehensive framework for organisations striving to harness the full potential of the cognitive enterprise.

Chapter 8: The Data Foundation for Cognitive Enterprise

Before diving into their cognitive journeys, both ComPlus and LegalDeal recognized a crucial truth: without a solid data foundation, even the most advanced AI systems would fail to deliver value. Like building a house on sand, implementing cognitive capabilities on fragmented, inconsistent, or inaccessible data would lead to unstable results and limited benefits. This chapter explores how organisations can evolve their data architectures to support cognitive transformation, with a special focus on modern approaches like Data Fabric and Data Mesh that enable intelligence at scale, along with the critical role of ontologies in creating a common semantic understanding across the enterprise.

The data landscape has shifted dramatically over the past decade. Organisations once struggled with rigid, siloed systems that couldn't adapt to changing business needs. Today, cognitive enterprises are embracing flexible, integrated data architectures that provide real-time insights while maintaining governance and trust. These modern data foundations don't just store information—they actively contextualize it, enrich it with meaning, and make it accessible for both human decision-makers and AI systems to leverage effectively.

For telecommunications giant ComPlus and legal services firm LegalDeal, building this foundation is essential to achieving their 2027 visions. ComPlus needs to unify customer data across 25 countries to enable hyper-personalised experiences, while LegalDeal must transform unstructured legal knowledge into searchable, actionable insights. Let's explore how they can establish data architectures that will power their cognitive transformations.

The Evolution of Data Architectures

Like application architectures discussed in the previous chapter, data architectures have evolved significantly to meet changing business needs and technological possibilities. Understanding this evolution helps us appreciate why approaches like Data Fabric and Data Mesh have become essential for modern enterprises.

1. Traditional Data Warehouses (Early 2000s)

Traditional data warehouses emerged as centralized repositories designed to consolidate structured data for reporting and analysis. These systems relied on predefined schemas and batch processing to support business intelligence efforts.

Characteristics:

- Centralized architecture with Extract, Transform, Load (ETL) processes
- Relational database models with star or snowflake schemas
- Optimized for structured data and predefined reports
- ACID compliance for transaction reliability

Challenges:

- Rigid schemas made adapting to new business requirements slow and costly
- High infrastructure and maintenance expenses
- Limited ability to handle unstructured data
- Difficult to scale efficiently as data volumes grow

For a company like ComPlus, traditional warehouses would struggle to handle the diverse data types from their IoT devices, customer interactions, and network operations. LegalDeal would find these systems inadequate for managing unstructured legal documents and case knowledge.

2. Data Lakes (2010s)

As organisations began generating more diverse data, data lakes emerged to store raw, unprocessed information across various formats. Unlike warehouses, data lakes embraced a "schema-on-read" approach for greater flexibility.

Characteristics:

- Stores raw data without predefined schemas
- Accommodates structured, semi-structured, and unstructured data
- Uses distributed file systems like Hadoop for cost-effective storage
- Enables direct access to raw data for machine learning training

Challenges:

- Often became "data swamps" where information was difficult to find or use
- Lacked robust governance and metadata management
- Query performance was typically slower than that of data warehouses
- Required specialised skills to extract value

ComPlus might have used data lakes to store network logs and customer interactions but would struggle to connect this information meaningfully or govern it effectively across 25 countries. LegalDeal would find valuable legal documents buried in the lake without proper context or accessibility.

3. Modern Data Lakehouses (Late 2010s)

To address the limitations of both warehouses and lakes, data lakehouses emerged to combine the best of both worlds—the structure and performance of warehouses with the flexibility and scalability of lakes.

Characteristics:

- Unifies storage with structured querying capabilities
- Supports ACID transactions while maintaining schema flexibility
- Optimizes for diverse workloads (batch, streaming, ML)
- Uses open table formats like Delta Lake or Apache Iceberg

Advantages:

- Reduces data duplication across systems
- Enables both historical analysis and real-time processing
- Provides better performance than data lakes for structured queries
- Supports direct ML model training on raw data

While lakehouses represented significant progress, they still didn't fully address the needs of cognitive enterprises requiring contextual understanding, real-time insights, and seamless integration across domains.

4. Cognitive Data Architectures (Present and Future)

In the cognitive enterprise, data is not merely an asset-it is the foundation for intelligence, adaptability and innovation. Yet, for most organisations, data remains fragmented, inaccessible, or unreliable, undermining the promise of AI and advanced analytics. The Data Products and Platform layer of the Cognitive Enterprise Architecture Framework (CeAF) addresses this challenge head-on, providing the structural and operational backbone that transforms raw information into actionable insights and trusted business value.

The Data Products and Platform layer serves as the connective tissue between data sources, business processes, and AI-driven outcomes. It unifies disparate data, embeds governance, and enables the creation of reusable, high-quality data products that fuel every layer of the cognitive enterprise.

Today's cognitive enterprises need data architectures that go beyond storage and retrieval—they require systems that actively enable intelligence, context, and adaptive learning. Modern cognitive data architectures integrate advanced capabilities like Data Fabric, Data Mesh, semantic layers, ontologies, and real-time processing to support AI-driven operations.

Characteristics:

- Contextual understanding through knowledge graphs and ontologies
- Real-time decision support via streaming analytics
- Integrated governance and active metadata management
- Support for both human and AI-driven workflows
- Flexibility across hybrid and multi-cloud environments

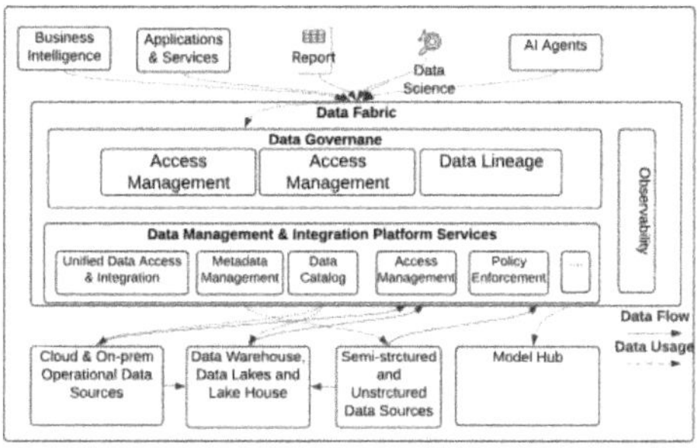

For ComPlus and LegalDeal, cognitive data architectures provide the foundation needed to transform their operations and deliver new capabilities to customers, employees, and stakeholders.

Key Data Capabilities for Cognitive Enterprises

Building on this evolution, let's explore the key data capabilities that enable cognitive transformation for enterprises like ComPlus and LegalDeal.

1. Data Fabric: Unified Data Access Across Ecosystems

Data Fabric represents one of the most significant advancements in modern data architecture—providing a unified, intelligent layer that connects disparate data sources across environments. Rather than forcing organisations to consolidate all data into a single repository, Data Fabric creates an integrated "fabric" over existing systems, ensuring seamless access while automating governance, security, and analytics.

What Is a Data Fabric?

Think of Data Fabric as a smart network overlay connecting all your data sources—from cloud services to on-premises databases, from real-time streams to historical archives. It's not a physical data repository but rather an architectural approach that uses a combination of technologies to make data accessible, usable, and governable regardless of where it resides.

Key Components of a Data Fabric

1.1 Data Governance and Security

A Data Fabric embeds governance directly into data flows, automating policy enforcement across environments without creating friction for users. This is crucial for organisations like ComPlus that operate across multiple regulatory jurisdictions.

Capabilities:

- Role-based access control (RBAC)
- Automated compliance with regulations like GDPR
- Real-time policy enforcement
- Encryption and masking of sensitive data

1.2 Data Management & Integration Platform Services

1.2.1 Unfied Data Access:

A Data Fabric connects diverse data sources through APIs, virtualization, and pipeline automation. Unlike traditional point-to-point integrations that ComPlus struggled with, a Data Fabric creates a flexible mesh of connections that adapt to changing needs.

Capabilities:

- Real-time and batch integration pipelines
- Event-driven architectures for capturing data changes
- Support for Change Data Capture (CDC)
- ETL/ELT frameworks for data transformation

For ComPlus, this means seamlessly connecting customer data from CRM systems with network performance metrics from IoT devices across 25 countries, all without creating duplicate copies or integration bottlenecks.

1.2.2 Active Metadata Management

Metadata serves as the backbone of a Data Fabric, providing context about what data exists, where it came from, how it's been transformed, and who can access it. Modern Data Fabrics use active metadata—continuously analysed and enriched by machine learning—to automate governance and enhance discoverability.

Capabilities:

- Centralized metadata catalogues with business context
- Automated data lineage tracking
- AI-powered data classification and tagging
- Knowledge graph integration for relationship mapping

For LegalDeal, active metadata helps track sensitive client information throughout document workflows, ensuring compliance with regulations like GDPR while making case knowledge discoverable for attorneys.

1.2.3 Data Catalogue

A Data Catalogue acts as the enterprise's searchable inventory of available data assets. It indexes datasets, tables, files, and streams, making them easily discoverable for analysts, data scientists, and business users. Modern data catalogues often leverage AI to automate tagging, classification, and recommendations, accelerating data discovery and self-service analytics.

Capabilties:

- Indexes all available datasets, tables, and data products for easy discovery
- Offers search, filtering, and recommendation features
- Enables self-service analytics by making data assets visible and accessible

- Integrates with metadata and access management for trusted data usage

1.2.4 Policy Enforcement

Policy enforcement within a data fabric ensures that organisational rules, regulatory requirements, and data governance policies are automatically and consistently applied to all data assets across the enterprise. This capability monitors data usage and enforces controls such as data masking, retention, and privacy-helping organisations like ComPlus and LegalDeal maintain compliance, protect sensitive information, and reduce the risk of policy violations.

Capabilities:

- Automates enforcement of data governance, privacy, and retention policies
- Applies data masking, encryption, and quality rules at ingestion and access points
- Ensures regulatory compliance (e.g., GDPR)
- Provides audit trails and policy violation alerts

How Data Fabric Transforms ComPlus

ComPlus operates in a complex environment with multiple legacy systems, cloud platforms, and growing data volumes. Their current challenges include:

- Fragmented customer data across 25 countries
- Slow access to insights due to data silos
- Inconsistent governance across regions
- Limited ability to support AI initiatives

By implementing a Data Fabric approach, ComPlus can:

1. **Break down customer data silos**
   Instead of executing a costly migration to consolidate all systems, Data Fabric creates a virtual layer that unifies customer profiles across CRM, billing, support, and IoT

systems. When a customer calls about a network issue, agents instantly see a complete profile without switching between applications.

2. **Enable real-time network operations**
   By connecting network telemetry data with customer profiles and historical performance metrics, ComPlus can predict and prevent service disruptions. For example, when latency spikes are detected on broadband routers, the system can automatically correlate this with customer impact and prioritize resolution based on service level agreements.
3. **Ensure consistent governance**
   Data Fabric automates privacy and compliance policies across all environments. When handling customer data in Europe, GDPR rules are automatically applied, while different regulations might apply in other regions—all managed through centralized policies rather than duplicate implementations.
4. **Power AI-Driven customer experiences**
   With unified data access, ComPlus can train AI models on comprehensive customer histories to offer hyper-personalised recommendations. The Next Best Action system can suggest relevant offers based on usage patterns, support history, and predicted needs without requiring manual data integration.

2. Data Mesh: Empowering domain ownership for scale

While Data Fabric focuses on the technological integration of data, Data Mesh addresses organisational aspects—specifically, how data is owned, managed, and shared across teams. This approach shifts from centralized data management to domain-oriented ownership, treating data as a product managed by the teams closest to its creation and use.

What Is Data Mesh?

Data Mesh is an organisational and architectural paradigm that distributes data ownership to domain teams while maintaining global governance standards. It recognizes that central data teams often become bottlenecks as organisations scale and instead empowers individual business domains to manage their own data as "products" with clear interfaces and service levels.

Key Principles of Data Mesh

1. **Domain-Oriented Data Ownership**

Business domains (e.g., Network Operations, Customer Support, Finance) own and manage their datasets independently, reducing dependencies on central data teams.

2. **Data as a Product**

Domains treat their datasets as products with defined interfaces, documentation, and quality standards, making them easily consumable by other teams.

3. **Self-Service Data Infrastructure**

A central platform team provides tools and capabilities that enable domain teams to create and manage their data products without requiring specialised expertise.

4. **Federated Governance**

While domains maintain autonomy, federated governance ensures consistent standards for security, compliance, and interoperability across the organisation.

How Data Management and Integration Platform Powers Data Product Delivery?

The data management & integration platform described earlier serves as the backbone that enables decentralized data ownership while maintaining centralized support for scalability, interoperability, and governance. It provides the foundational capabilities required to operationalize data as a product and ensure seamless integration across domains.

Key Capabilities of the Data Platform

1. Data Discovery and Cataloging
    - Enables users to locate and understand data products through metadata management and lineage tracking.
    - Supports self-service by providing visibility into available datasets, their quality and usage policies.
2. Data Integration and Interoperability
    - Facilitates event-driven pipelines for real-time data ingestion and processing from diverse sources like CRM, billing, or IoT systems.
    - Provides APIs and connectors for seamless integration between domains.
3. Scalable Storage and Processing
    - Implements hybrid storage models (e.g., in-memory caches for operational needs and columnar warehouses for analytics).
    - Ensures low-latency access for real-time applications while supporting complex analytical workloads.
4. Governance and Security
    - Embeds governance policies into data products, ensuring compliance with regulations like GDPR.
    - Provides role-based access controls, encryption, and audit trails to maintain security and trust.
5. Automation and Observability
    - Automates workflows for data quality checks, schema validation, and model retraining pipelines.
    - Offers monitoring tools to track data usage, performance metrics and potential anomalies.

6. Self-Service Enablement
    - Empowers domain teams with tools to create, manage, and share data products independently while adhering to platform-wide standards.
    - Supports templated workflows for faster deployment of new data pipelines or products.

How Data Mesh Complements Data Fabric

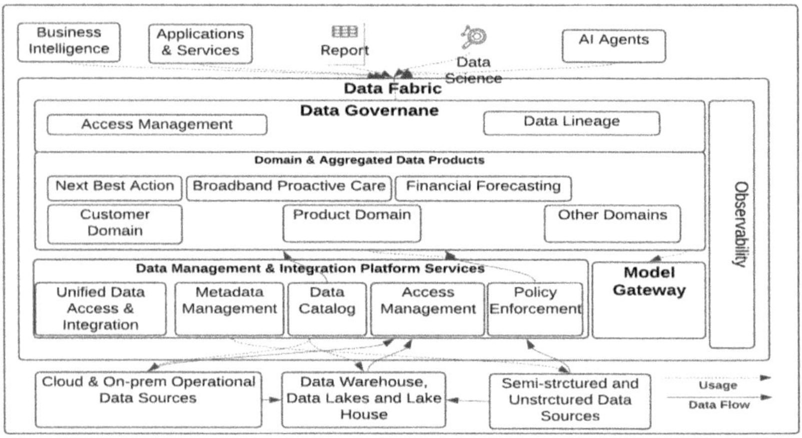

Data Fabric and Data Mesh are complementary approaches that address different aspects of enterprise data challenges:

- **Data Fabric** provides the technological foundation—integration, metadata, and governance capabilities that span the entire organisation
- **Data Mesh** provides the organisational model—how teams collaborate, who owns what data, and how they share it

Together, powered by data platform, they create a powerful combination for cognitive enterprises:

Aspect	Data Fabric	Data Mesh	Combined Benefit
Focus	Technology integration	Organisational structure	Complete organisational & technical solution
Strength	Unified access and governance	Domain autonomy and scalability	Agile and governed data ecosystem
Implementation	Platform capabilities	Team structures and practices	Sustainable, scalable data architecture

Data Mesh in Action at ComPlus

ComPlus can implement Data Mesh principles alongside Data Fabric to address their scale challenges:

1. **Domain Teams as Data Owners**

The Network Operations team becomes responsible for telemetry data from broadband routers, ensuring it's available, accurate, and properly documented for other teams to use. Similarly, the Customer team owns interaction data, while Marketing owns campaign and customer journey information.

2. **Data Products for Cross-Domain Consumption**

Each domain publishes data products such as "Customer 360 Profiles", "Network Performance Metrics," or "Service Usage Analytics"-with documented APIs, quality metrics, and service level agreements (SLAs). In addition to these domain-specific products, organisations can also deliver aggregated data products, such as "Next Best Action," by combining data from different domains like CRM, Billing, and Network.

3. **Federated Governance Model**

While domains maintain autonomy, a central governance council ensures consistent standards for privacy, security, and metadata across ComPlus's operations in 25 countries.

By combining Data Fabric technology with Data Mesh organisational principles, ComPlus can scale its data operations effectively while maintaining the agility needed for innovation.

Data Mesh Benefits for LegalDeal

Even a mid-sized firm like LegalDeal can benefit from Data Mesh principles, though at a smaller scale:

1. **Practice-Area Data Ownership**

Different legal practice areas (Corporate Law, Litigation, Intellectual Property) can own their specific domain data, ensuring specialised knowledge is properly managed by experts in that field.

2. **Client Data Products**

Each practice area creates standardised client data products that can be securely shared across the firm when appropriate, with strict adherence to client confidentiality requirements.

3. **Simplified Compliance**

Standardised approaches to data management across practice areas make regulatory compliance easier to implement and audit.

For LegalDeal, Data Mesh principles help address their knowledge management challenges while maintaining the autonomy different practice areas need.

3. Ontologies: Creating a Common Business Language

Ontologies serve as a critical foundation for both Data Fabric and Data Mesh approaches by providing a formal representation of shared domain knowledge. Unlike simple taxonomies or data dictionaries, ontologies define rich, formal relationships, constraints, and rules between entities that enable semantic interoperability and reasoning across systems.

What Are Ontologies in Data Management?

An ontology is a formal, explicit specification of a shared conceptualization—essentially, a structured representation of knowledge within a domain. It defines classes of entities, their attributes, the relationships between them, and the rules governing their behaviour. In the context of data management, ontologies provide the semantic foundation that ensures consistent understanding across systems, teams, and applications.

How Ontologies Support Cognitive Data Architectures

1. **Semantic Integration**: Ontologies enable seamless data integration by providing a common vocabulary and semantic model that transcends individual systems or domains. This is especially valuable for organisations like ComPlus that have complex, distributed data environments.
2. **AI and Machine Learning Enhancement**: By providing structured knowledge and explicit relationships, ontologies help train AI models more effectively and enable reasoning capabilities that would be difficult to achieve with raw data alone.
3. **Context-Aware Applications**: Applications can leverage ontologies to understand the business context of data, enabling more intelligent responses and better decision support.
4. **Governance Standardisation**: Ontologies help standardize terminology and relationships across the enterprise, making governance policies more consistent and easier to implement.

Ontologies in Data Fabric and Data Mesh

Ontologies play different but complementary roles in Data Fabric and Data Mesh architectures:

In Data Fabric:

- Serve as the semantic glue that connects disparate data sources across the enterprise
- Enable automated discovery and integration of new data sources by mapping them to the enterprise ontology
- Support cross-domain queries and analytics by providing a common semantic understanding
- Facilitate data lineage and impact analysis by explicitly modelling dependencies

In Data Mesh:

- Allow domain teams to create specialised ontologies that reflect their unique knowledge
- Provide a federation layer that maps between domain ontologies to enable cross-domain understanding
- Define clear semantics for data product interfaces, ensuring consistent interpretation
- Support federated governance by standardizing compliance and security concepts

Ontologies in Action: ComPlus and LegalDeal

For ComPlus:

A telecommunications domain ontology would formalize concepts like "Network Element," "Service," "Customer," and "Subscription Plan" along with their relationships:

- **Network Understanding**: The ontology would define a "Broadband Router" as a type of "Network Element" that "connects to" other elements and "provides" specific "Services" to "Customers."
- **Impact Analysis**: When network issues arise, the ontology enables automated reasoning about which customers and services are affected
- **Cross-Country Integration**: Despite differences in terminology across 25 countries, the ontology provides

mappings that ensure a "Subscriber" in one region is recognized as equivalent to a "Customer" in another
- **AI Enhancement**: Virtual assistants can leverage the ontology to understand complex customer queries about service configurations or billing details

This telecommunications ontology becomes particularly powerful when combined with Data Fabric and Data Mesh approaches. The Data Fabric uses the ontology to dynamically discover and integrate relevant data sources, while domain teams in the Data Mesh use it to ensure their data products are semantically consistent.

For LegalDeal:

A legal domain ontology would define concepts like "Case," "Statute," "Precedent," and "Jurisdiction" with their complex interrelationships:

- **Document Classification**: The ontology enables automatic classification of legal documents based on the concepts they contain and their relationships
- **Compliance Mapping**: Regulations and compliance requirements are explicitly mapped to specific document types and clauses
- **Semantic Search**: Attorneys can search for precedents using conceptual queries rather than keywords, finding relevant cases based on legal principles rather than specific terminology
- **Knowledge Transfer**: New attorneys can navigate complex legal relationships through ontology, accelerating their understanding of practice areas

By implementing a comprehensive legal ontology, LegalDeal creates a foundation for cognitive capabilities that would be impossible with traditional keyword-based systems. Their Data Fabric leverages this ontology to provide unified access to case knowledge across practice areas, while their Data Mesh approach allows each legal domain to extend the ontology with specialised concepts.

5. Semantic Data Management: Adding Meaning to Information

Building on ontologies, semantic data management creates a comprehensive layer of meaning through additional technologies like knowledge graphs that capture connections between entities. While ontologies provide the formal structure and rules for understanding data, knowledge graphs implement these connections as navigable graphs that AI systems can traverse and query.

Ontologies in Data Architecture Approaches

Architecture	Role of Ontologies	Key Benefits	Challenges
Data Fabric	Semantic glue connecting disparate sources Enables automated discovery/integration Supports cross-domain queries Facilitates lineage and impact analysis	Enterprise-wide data access Reduced integration time Automated data discovery	Complex initial implementation Requires enterprise-wide consensus
Data Mesh	Domain-specific semantic models Federation layer between domains Semantic standardisation for data products Supports federated governance	Domain ownership Specialised knowledge capture Distributed implementation	Cross-domain coordination Potential semantic conflicts

6. Knowledge Graphs for Contextual Understanding

A knowledge graph represents entities (like customers, products, or network components) and their relationships as a connected graph structure, enabling AI systems to "reason" about connections and dependencies.

For ComPlus:

- Links customers with their devices, service plans, and support history
- Maps network infrastructure to identify dependencies during outages
- Connects customer issues with relevant troubleshooting procedures

For LegalDeal:

- Relates legal concepts to specific clauses and precedents
- Maps relationships between cases, regulations, and client matters
- Links attorneys to expertise areas and case histories

By implementing knowledge graphs based on their domain ontologies, both organisations enable AI systems to understand the context—not just retrieve information—which is essential for cognitive capabilities.

From Ontologies to Knowledge Graphs: The Cognitive Data Foundation

Feature	Ontologies	Knowledge Graphs	Combined Capability
Primary Function	Define formal structure, relationships, and rules	Implement connections as navigable paths	Structured meaning with traversable relationships
AI Enablement	Provides semantic framework and rules	Enables contextual navigation and discovery	Cognitive reasoning about entities and relationships

ComPlus Application	Defines telecommunications domain concepts and rules	Links customers, devices, service plans, network infrastructure	Enables service impact analysis and predictive maintenance
LegalDeal Application	Defines legal concepts, document types, and practice areas	Maps relationships between cases, regulations, and expertise	Powers intelligent document analysis and precedent discovery

7. Real-Time Processing Engines: Enabling Immediate Action

Cognitive enterprises can't rely on batch processing when opportunities and threats emerge in real time. Real-time processing engines analyse streaming data as it's generated, enabling immediate insights and actions.

For ComPlus, real-time processing means:

- Detecting network anomalies before they affect service
- Personalising customer interactions during ongoing engagements
- Preventing fraud through immediate transaction analysis

For LegalDeal, it enables:

- Immediate compliance checks during document review
- Real-time risk assessments during client consultations
- Automatic citation of relevant cases during legal research

These capabilities transform passive data systems into active enablers of business agility.

8. Vector Databases: Managing AI-Ready Information

Traditional databases weren't designed for the high-dimensional data required by modern AI systems. Vector databases store and query embeddings—numerical representations of content that capture semantic meaning—enabling powerful capabilities like semantic search and recommendation systems.

For ComPlus, vector databases support:

- Finding similar customer service cases to expedite resolution
- Matching customer descriptions of issues with technical documentation
- Detecting unusual network patterns that might indicate security threats

For LegalDeal, they enable:

- Semantic search across case law and legal documents
- Identifying similar contract clauses and their implications
- Finding precedents based on situation similarity rather than keyword matching

Vector databases form the backbone of many cognitive capabilities by making unstructured content AI-accessible.

Building Trust Through Governance

As organisations adopt AI-driven architectures, they must ensure that data systems remain trustworthy, compliant, and ethical. Modern data governance extends beyond traditional controls to address the unique challenges of cognitive systems.

Data Lineage and Traceability

Organisations need to track data from its source through all transformations to its ultimate use, especially for decisions made by AI systems. This traceability is essential for both regulatory compliance and building stakeholder trust.

For ComPlus, data lineage tracking ensures:

- Customer data handling complies with regulations across 25 countries
- AI-driven decisions about network priorities can be audited and explained
- The source of data used in customer recommendations is transparent

For LegalDeal, it means:

- Client confidentiality is maintained throughout document workflows
- Sources for legal advice can be traced and verified
- Recommendations from AI systems are backed by identifiable precedents

Ethical AI and Responsible Data Use

Beyond compliance with regulations like GDPR, cognitive enterprises must establish frameworks for ethical AI use. This includes mechanisms to prevent bias, ensure fairness, and provide transparency in AI-driven decisions.

ComPlus implements ethical safeguards by:

- Testing AI models for bias before deployment
- Providing explainability for automated decisions affecting customers
- Establishing human oversight for high-impact AI applications

LegalDeal ensures ethical use through:

- Clear disclosure when AI assists with legal analysis
- Regular audits of AI systems for fairness and accuracy
- Training programs for attorneys on responsible AI use

Putting It All Together: The Cognitive Data Platform

The capabilities described above don't exist in isolation—they work together as an integrated cognitive data platform that supports intelligence at scale. This platform combines Data Fabric and Data Mesh approaches with ontologies, semantic understanding, real-time processing, and embedded governance to create a foundation for cognitive transformation.

For ComPlus, the cognitive data platform enables their vision of:

- Hyper-personalised customer experiences across all touchpoints
- Self-healing networks that predict and prevent service disruptions
- AI-augmented employee experiences that boost productivity

For LegalDeal, it supports their goals of:

- AI-enhanced legal services that improve outcomes for clients
- Knowledge management that preserves and amplifies expertise
- Streamlined compliance processes that reduce risk

The Cognitive Data Platform forms the foundation for transformative initiatives across various industries, highlighting its capability to unify advanced data architectures with cognitive technologies. In the upcoming case study, we will delve into how ComPlus successfully implemented Data Mesh principles in practice to deliver "Next Best Action" as a data product.

Case Study: Next Best Action as a Data Product

In today's hyper-competitive telecommunications landscape, delivering personalised customer experiences at scale has become a critical differentiator. For ComPlus, this challenge is magnified by its diverse customer base, multiple interaction channels and varied regional market dynamics. The company recognized that its traditional approach to customer engagement—with separate systems for operational interactions and analytical insights—was creating fragmented customer experiences and preventing them from fully leveraging their vast data assets. This case study explores how ComPlus transformed its customer engagement capabilities by implementing a Next Best Action (NBA) data product that seamlessly integrates both operational and analytical capabilities.

The Business Challenge: Fragmented Customer Interactions

Before implementing their Next Best Action data product, ComPlus faced several critical challenges that limited their ability to deliver personalised customer experiences and optimize commercial outcomes across their global footprint.

Operational Disconnects

On the operational front, ComPlus struggled with inconsistent customer interactions across channels and countries. Contact centre agents lacked real-time guidance during customer conversations, resulting in missed opportunities for relevant recommendations. Digital channels operated independently from voice channels, creating disjointed customer journeys where the context from one interaction was lost in subsequent touchpoints. This fragmentation frustrated customers who increasingly expected ComPlus to understand their needs and preferences regardless of how or where they engaged with the company.

Analytical Limitations

From an analytical perspective, ComPlus had accumulated vast amounts of customer data but struggled to convert this into actionable insights that could drive better customer interactions. Marketing teams relied on batch-processed campaigns based on static customer segments rather than responding to dynamic customer needs. Performance analysis happened weeks after campaigns concluded, making it impossible to adapt strategies in real-time. While ComPlus had invested in sophisticated analytics capabilities, these remained disconnected from frontline operations, creating a gap between insight and action.

The Next Best Action Data Product Solution

After analyzing these challenges, ComPlus identified the need for a comprehensive Next Best Action data product that would unify operational decision-making and analytical insights within a single domain-owned product approach.

Core Components and Features

The Next Best Action data product encompassed several key components that bridged operational and analytical capabilities:

Customer Context Hub

The foundation of the data product was a unified customer context hub that consolidated information from multiple sources, including:

- Historical interaction data from all channels (call centre, digital, retail, field)
- Product ownership and usage patterns from billing systems
- Network experience data from performance monitoring systems
- Customer lifetime value and churn risk scores from predictive models
- Preference and consent data from privacy management systems

This hub created a single source of truth for customer context, accessible in real-time during interactions while also supporting deeper analytical processes.

Real-Time Decision Engine

The operational core of the data product was a sophisticated decision engine that determined the most appropriate next action for each customer interaction:

- API-based decision services with sub-100ms response times for real-time channels
- Action selection based on customer context, business rules, and ML models
- Support for multiple action types (offers, service actions, educational content)
- Channel-specific delivery parameters for consistent experiences
- Embedded compliance and eligibility rules to ensure appropriate actions

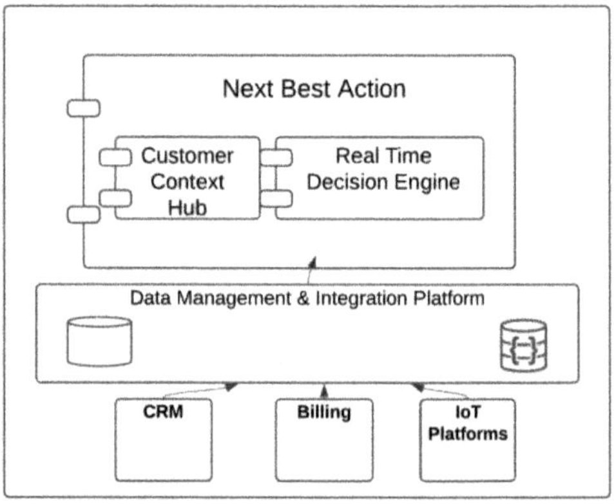

This engine enabled frontline systems to access Next Best Action recommendations during live customer interactions across all channels.

Analytical Learning System

Alongside the operational capabilities, the data product incorporated a continuous learning system:

- A/B testing framework to evaluate different action strategies
- Conversion tracking across all channels and interaction types
- Performance analytics with drill-down capabilities by segment, region, and offer
- ML model retraining pipelines based on the latest interaction outcomes
- Simulation capabilities to forecast outcomes of strategy changes

This analytical component ensured that the Next Best Action system continuously improved based on real-world performance data.

Implementation Through Data Mesh Principles

ComPlus implemented the Next Best Action data product following data mesh principles, fundamentally changing how customer engagement was managed throughout the organisation.

Domain Ownership

The Customer Experience domain took full ownership of the data product, with a dedicated cross-functional team responsible for its quality, reliability, and evolution. This team included:

- Data engineers who built and maintained data pipelines
- Data scientists who developed and refined analytical models
- API developers who created operational interfaces
- Business analysts who defined action strategies and business rules
- Domain experts who understood customer experience requirements

This ownership model ensured that both operational and analytical aspects of the data product remained aligned with business needs rather than being split across different teams.

Data as a Product Mindset

The team approached development with a product mindset, defining clear service-level objectives for both operational and analytical components:

- 99.99% availability targets for real-time decision services
- Sub-100ms response times for all operational interfaces
- Daily model retraining schedules for continuous improvement
- Comprehensive documentation for all interfaces and analytical models
- Feedback mechanisms for internal consumers across the organisation

This product approach ensured the data product remained valuable for both operational and analytical consumers throughout the organisation.

Technical Architecture

The NBA data product leveraged a modern, integrated architecture to support both real-time operational needs and sophisticated analytical capabilities:

Event-Driven Pipeline

An event-driven architecture captured all customer interactions and system events via data platform:

- Event streams for all customer touchpoints (calls, website visits, app usage)
- Real-time processing using stream processing technologies
- Event enrichment with contextual data for complete interaction records
- Persistent event storage for historical analysis and model training

This unified event foundation ensured consistency between operational and analytical views of customer interactions.

Hybrid Storage Model

To meet both operational and analytical requirements, the data product implemented a hybrid storage approach:

- Low-latency in-memory store for operational customer context
- Columnar data warehouse for analytical processing and reporting
- Real-time replication between operational and analytical stores
- Consistent access patterns through abstraction layers

This hybrid approach delivered millisecond response times for operational queries while enabling complex analytical workloads on the same underlying data.

Business Value Delivered

The Next Best Action data product transformed ComPlus's business capabilities by unifying operational and analytical functions, delivering significant value:

Enhanced Customer Experience

By providing contextually relevant actions during every interaction, the data product enabled:

- 31% improvement in customer satisfaction scores
- 42% reduction in customer effort scores
- 27% increase in Net Promoter Score
- Consistent experiences across all 25 countries and multiple channels

Operational Efficiency

The unified approach significantly improved operational efficiency:

- 23% reduction in average handling time for contact centre interactions
- 18% improvement in first-contact resolution rates
- 35% increase in digital self-service completion rates
- Reduced training time for frontline staff through simplified guidance

Revenue Growth

The Next Best Action data product directly contributed to revenue growth:

- 28% increase in acceptance rates for personalised offers
- 21% improvement in cross-selling and upsell conversion rates
- 17% reduction in customer churn through proactive retention actions
- 31% increase in digital channel sales through contextual recommendations

A Continuous Evolution

The success of ComPlus's Next Best Action data product demonstrates the power of unifying operational and analytical capabilities within a single, domain-owned product. By breaking down the traditional barriers between real-time operations and deep analytics, ComPlus created a system that continuously improves through a virtuous cycle: operational interactions generate data that fuels analytical insights, which in turn enhance operational decisions.

The approach has transformed how ComPlus thinks about data architecture, moving from siloed operational and analytical systems toward domain-oriented data products that serve diverse needs through common semantic foundations. As they continue their cognitive enterprise journey, this integrated approach positions them to rapidly develop AI-powered capabilities that leverage both real-time operational data and rich analytical insights.

Operating Model Impacts of Data Mesh: People, Process and Organisation

Adopting a data mesh fundamentally transforms the enterprise operating model by decentralising data ownership and bridging the gap between operational and analytical domains. This paradigm shift has significant implications for people, processes, and organisational structure:

People

- Data mesh empowers cross-functional domain teams to own, manage, and serve their data as a product, fostering a culture of accountability and data literacy.
- Roles such as data product owners, domain data engineers and federated governance leads become central, requiring upskilling and closer collaboration between business and IT.
- For ComPlus, this means network, customer, and product teams take direct responsibility for the quality and availability of their respective data products. At LegalDeal, legal practice groups curate and govern their own knowledge assets, accelerating innovation and responsiveness.

Process

- Data mesh replaces centralised data pipelines with standardised, domain-driven processes for data publishing, discovery, and consumption.
- Federated governance ensures compliance and interoperability without stifling domain autonomy.
- Operational and analytical data converge, enabling near real-time insights and continuous feedback loops. This allows ComPlus to embed customer analytics into operational support and LegalDeal to integrate contract intelligence directly into service delivery.

Organisation

- The organisational structure evolves from centralised data teams to distributed, domain-aligned squads, each responsible for their own data products and services.

- Coordination mechanisms-such as data product marketplaces and shared platform services-support consistency and reusability across domains.
- Both ComPlus and LegalDeal benefit from faster delivery cycles, improved data quality, and greater agility in responding to business needs.

Alignment with Application Architecture Principles

Embedding intelligence into applications through APIs, microservices, and event-driven designs naturally aligns with data mesh principles:

- Domain-oriented application teams can directly consume and contribute to data products, embedding AI and analytics into operational workflows.
- Intelligent applications become both producers and consumers of data products, supporting closed feedback loops and adaptive business processes.
- This synergy enables ComPlus to deliver proactive network care and personalised customer experiences, while LegalDeal automates contract analysis and integrates AI-driven insights into client-facing tools.

By unifying operational and analytical worlds, data mesh and modern application architecture together enable a truly cognitive enterprise where intelligence is woven into every process, decision, and interaction.

Conclusion

We explored the foundational principles and components required to transition from traditional data management systems to a cognitive data architecture. This transformation represents a paradigm shift where data becomes an active enabler of intelligence, adaptability, and innovation rather than a passive resource. By embedding intelligence into every layer of the data ecosystem—through unified customer profiles, real-time decision-making, and continuous learning systems—organisations can unlock unprecedented value. However, this journey is not just about technology; it demands a strategic alignment of processes, governance, and organisational culture.

For ComPlus and LegalDeal, the transformation to a cognitive data architecture is not merely a technical upgrade but a fundamental reimagining of how they operate. As we conclude this chapter, it's clear that success lies in adopting a structured, phased approach that balances ambition with pragmatism.

Looking Ahead

Building the data foundation is a critical step in cognitive transformation, but it's just the beginning. In the next chapter, we'll explore how ComPlus and LegalDeal can build upon this foundation to create innovative data products and services that deliver tangible business value.

The journey to becoming a cognitive enterprise requires rethinking not just technology but also organisational structures, processes, and cultures. By embracing modern approaches like Data Fabric and Data Mesh, supported by rich semantic technologies like ontologies and knowledge graphs, companies like ComPlus and LegalDeal are establishing the foundation they need to thrive in an AI-powered future—where data isn't just stored and analysed, but actively contributes to business intelligence and growth.

Chapter 9: Digital Enablers with Embedded AI

As organisations embark on their cognitive transformation journey, they require robust, flexible systems that bridge the gap between traditional infrastructure and modern intelligent experiences. Digital enablers serve as these critical systems of engagement, sitting atop legacy systems while delivering dynamic, personalised interactions demanded by today's customers, partners, and employees. Unlike traditional systems of record that focus on capturing and storing information, digital enablers prioritize active engagement, real-time intelligence, and contextual experiences that drive business value. When enhanced with artificial intelligence, these enablers transform from passive interaction layers into intelligent ecosystems that anticipate needs, adapt to changing contexts, and deliver personalised experiences at scale.

For enterprises like ComPlus and LegalDeal, digital enablers represent the practical implementation of cognitive capabilities in their everyday operations. By embedding AI into platforms such as Customer 360, knowledge management systems, and content management solutions, these organisations leverage their existing data assets while delivering transformative experiences that drive customer loyalty, operational efficiency, and competitive advantage.

The Evolution from Systems of Record to Systems of Engagement

The journey toward cognitive enterprise capabilities has been marked by a fundamental shift in how business systems are designed and deployed. To understand the transformative impact of digital enablers, we must first examine the evolution from traditional systems of record to modern systems of engagement.

Systems of Record: The Traditional Foundation

For decades, enterprises have relied on systems of record as their operational backbone. These systems—such as Enterprise Resource Planning (ERP), Customer Relationship Management (CRM), and financial ledgers—were designed primarily to capture, store and manage transactional data. While effective for their intended purpose, these systems prioritized data integrity and operational consistency over user experience and engagement. They typically feature:

Rigid, transaction-focused architectures that emphasize data storage and retrieval rather than interaction.

Batch-oriented processing with predefined workflows and limited flexibility for real-time adaptation.

Siloed structures create data islands across different business functions, hindering a unified view of customers or operations.

Both ComPlus and LegalDeal maintain extensive systems of record that excel at record-keeping but struggle to deliver the responsive, contextual experiences modern stakeholders expect.

Systems of Engagement: The Interactive Layer

The digital era brought a paradigm shift in how enterprises interact with their stakeholders. Systems of engagement emerged as a new category of applications designed specifically to facilitate interactions, collaboration, and personalised experiences. Unlike their record-keeping predecessors, these systems prioritize:

User-centric design with intuitive interfaces tailored to specific audience needs and preferences.

Real-time interactivity that enables dynamic, contextual responses to user actions and requests.

Omnichannel accessibility across devices, platforms, and touchpoints to deliver consistent experiences.

While systems of engagement represent a significant advancement, their true potential remains constrained by limited intelligence and adaptability.

Digital Enablers: Intelligent Systems of Engagement

Digital enablers represent the next evolution in enterprise systems—intelligent platforms that combine the interactive capabilities of systems of engagement with the cognitive abilities of AI. These enablers sit atop existing systems of record, extracting value from legacy data while delivering transformative experiences through:

Embedded AI capabilities such as natural language processing, predictive analytics, and machine learning enable intelligent, context-aware interactions.

API-driven architectures that facilitate seamless integration with both legacy systems and modern microservices.

Event-driven frameworks that support real-time data synchronization and responsive user experiences.

For enterprises like ComPlus and LegalDeal, digital enablers serve as the bridge between their established operational systems and the cognitive capabilities they need to thrive in an increasingly competitive landscape.

Core Digital Enablers for Cognitive Enterprise

Digital enablers encompass a range of platforms and solutions, each designed to address specific aspects of the modern enterprise experience. When enhanced with AI capabilities, these enablers transform from static interaction layers into intelligent, adaptive systems that drive business innovation and customer engagement.

Customer 360 Platforms: Unified Context for Personalised Engagement

Customer 360 platforms serve as centralized repositories that consolidate customer data from disparate sources into comprehensive, unified profiles. For cognitive enterprises, these platforms go beyond simple data aggregation to create dynamic, AI-enhanced views that enable contextual understanding and personalised engagement.

Modern Customer 360 platforms feature several key capabilities that make them essential to cognitive transformation:

Data Unification: Aggregates customer information from multiple systems of record, including CRM databases, transaction histories, interaction logs, and preference data.

Real-Time Synchronization: Employs Change Data Capture (CDC) mechanisms to ensure that customer profiles reflect the most current information across all touchpoints.

Identity Resolution: Uses AI algorithms to reconcile customer identities across channels and systems, creating a single, accurate view of each customer.

Predictive Analytics: Applies machine learning models to anticipate customer needs, identify churn risks, and recommend next-best actions.

For ComPlus, a Customer 360 platform addresses the challenge of fragmented customer data across multiple legacy systems, enabling service representatives to view comprehensive customer information during support calls, personalise self-service portals, and develop targeted marketing campaigns.

For LegalDeal, a unified client profile consolidates case histories, billing records, and communication logs, allowing attorneys to access comprehensive client information, prioritize work based on client preferences, and identify opportunities for additional services.

Knowledge Management Systems: Intelligent Insight Distribution

Knowledge Management Systems serve as central repositories for organisational expertise, best practices, and information assets. In cognitive enterprises, these systems evolve from passive document stores into intelligent platforms that actively capture, organize, and distribute knowledge to support decision-making and operational excellence.

AI transforms knowledge management systems through:

Automatic Knowledge Extraction: NLP models identify and extract key insights from unstructured sources like emails, conversations, and documents.

Content Summarization: Machine learning models generate concise summaries of complex documents to improve accessibility.

Intelligent Routing: AI engines direct questions to appropriate knowledge sources or human experts based on context and content.

ComPlus implements an AI-enhanced knowledge management system to support technical operations and customer service, providing field technicians with troubleshooting guides tailored to specific equipment and common issues.

LegalDeal's knowledge management system serves as a central repository for legal expertise and precedents, where attorneys access relevant case precedents through semantic search capabilities and paralegals receive AI-generated summaries of complex legal documents.

Content Management Systems: Dynamic Experience Delivery

Content Management Systems have evolved from simple website management tools into sophisticated platforms for creating, managing, and delivering digital experiences across multiple channels. In cognitive enterprises, these systems leverage AI to dynamically optimize content delivery based on user context, preferences, and behaviour.

AI transforms content management systems through:

Automated Content Tagging: Machine learning models automatically categorize and tag content to improve searchability and contextualization.

Personalised Content Selection: AI algorithms determine which content assets are most relevant to specific users based on their profiles and behaviours.

Adaptive Content Generation: NLP systems generate or modify content to match specific audience needs or engagement patterns.

ComPlus leverages an AI-enhanced content management system to deliver personalised experiences across its digital touchpoints, adapting product information based on visitor industry and browsing patterns.

LegalDeal employs a cognitive content management system to deliver tailored information to clients and prospects, presenting practice area information with case studies relevant to each visitor's industry and legal needs.

Customer Engagement Platforms: Orchestrating Intelligent Interactions

Customer Engagement Platforms serve as the orchestration layer for customer interactions across channels, ensuring consistent, contextual experiences throughout the customer journey. In cognitive enterprises, these platforms leverage AI to optimize engagement strategies and deliver hyper-personalised interactions at scale.

AI transforms customer engagement platforms through:

Next-Best-Action Determination: Machine learning models analyse customer context to recommend optimal engagement strategies.

Channel Optimisation: AI algorithms identify the most effective communication channels for specific customers and messages.

Content Customization: NLP models adapt message content based on customer preferences, behaviour patterns, and emotional context.

ComPlus implements an AI-enhanced customer engagement platform to coordinate interactions across its diverse touchpoints, dynamically adjusting offers based on customer service history and usage patterns.

LegalDeal leverages a cognitive customer engagement platform to coordinate client and prospect communications, personalising business development outreach based on the prospect industry, legal needs, and engagement history.

Digital Enablers in Action: Delivering Business Value

Digital enablers with embedded AI deliver tangible business value by transforming how organisations engage with customers, optimize operations and drive innovation. For cognitive enterprises like ComPlus and LegalDeal, these enablers serve as catalysts for achieving strategic priorities while building competitive advantage.

Customer-Centric Experiences

Digital enablers place customers at the centre of the business, enabling hyper-personalised experiences that drive loyalty and satisfaction. By leveraging unified customer data and embedded AI capabilities, organisations can create contextual, relevant interactions that address individual needs and preferences.

For ComPlus, this means delivering telecommunications services tailored to each customer's usage patterns, preferences, and history. Their AI-powered Customer 360 platform enables service representatives to view complete customer profiles during interactions and provide personalised recommendations.

For LegalDeal, customer-centricity translates to client-focused legal services informed by a comprehensive understanding of each client's situation, enabling attorneys to access complete client histories before meetings and provide proactive alerts about regulatory changes.

Operational Efficiency

By automating routine tasks and enabling intelligent workflows, digital enablers reduce costs, minimize errors, and free up resources for strategic initiatives. AI-embedded platforms can identify patterns, predict outcomes and suggest optimisations that drive operational excellence.

ComPlus leverages digital enablers to streamline network operations and customer service through knowledge management systems that automatically suggest troubleshooting steps and self-service capabilities that reduce call centre volume.

LegalDeal employs digital enablers to enhance productivity through document automation systems that generate standardised legal documents with customized elements and AI-assisted review processes that identify potential issues in legal documents.

Data-Driven Decision Making

Digital enablers provide real-time insights and predictive analytics that empower decision-makers to act with confidence. By surfacing relevant information at the right time, these platforms transform raw data into actionable intelligence that drives strategic outcomes.

ComPlus uses digital enablers to inform decisions through customer engagement platforms that analyse interaction patterns to identify emerging service issues and churn prediction models that enable proactive retention initiatives.

LegalDeal leverages digital enablers for evidence-based decision-making through case outcome analytics that identify factors influencing success rates and resource allocation tools that optimize staffing based on case complexity.

Competitive Differentiation

AI-powered digital enablers position organisations as industry leaders by delivering exceptional experiences and leveraging innovative technology. These platforms enable capabilities that set organisations apart in increasingly competitive markets.

ComPlus achieves differentiation through personalised service recommendations that anticipate customer needs and proactive service monitoring that identifies potential issues before customers are affected.

LegalDeal distinguishes itself through AI-assisted legal research that uncovers relevant precedents and predictive case analytics that provide clients with realistic timelines and outcome probabilities.

Case Study: Customer 360 Service for ComPlus

ComPlus, a leading telecommunications provider, faced significant challenges in delivering consistent, personalised customer experiences across its diverse touchpoints. Customer data was fragmented across multiple legacy systems, resulting in disjointed customer interactions, inefficient service delivery, and missed opportunities for personalisation.

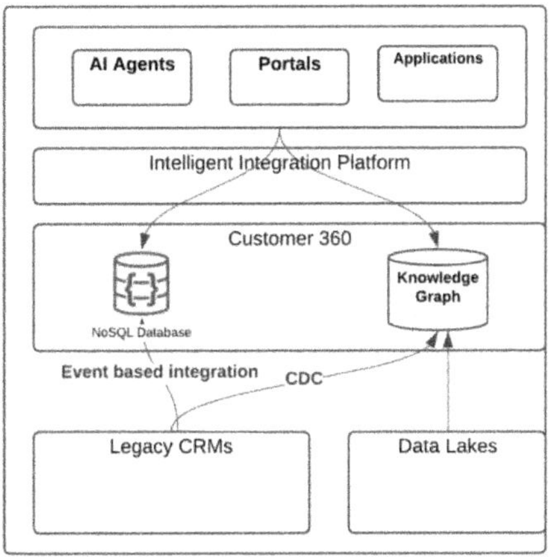

Business Challenge and Vision

As competition intensified, ComPlus recognized that delivering exceptional customer experiences had become a critical differentiator. The company envisioned a centralized, real-time customer data platform that would unify customer information and power personalised interactions across all channels, enabling:

Hyper-personalised interactions by empowering service agents, AI-driven chatbots, and self-service portals with comprehensive customer profiles.

Proactive customer engagement by providing actionable insights about upcoming contract renewals, service opportunities, or potential issues.

Seamless multichannel experiences by synchronizing customer interactions across mobile apps, customer portals, and agent interfaces.

Solution Architecture

The Customer 360 Service was designed as a high-performance, read-only platform that consolidated customer data from multiple source systems while ensuring scalability, security, and real-time access. The architecture included:

Data Synchronization Layer: Implemented event-driven data ingestion using Change Data Capture (CDC) mechanisms to capture updates from source systems in real-time.

Customer 360 Service: Exposing REST/GraphQL APIs, enabled by a hybrid database architecture combining a knowledge graph to model relationships and NoSQL databases optimized for high-performance lookups.

Integration Layer: Connected the Customer 360 Service with consuming applications, including customer portals, agent interfaces, and AI agents.

Integration with AI Capabilities

The Customer 360 Service served as a key data source for AI-driven capabilities, enabling:

Retrieval-Augmented Generation (RAG): AI agents could embed knowledge graph queries into their workflows, enriching interactions with contextual customer information.

Next-Best-Action Recommendations: AI engines analysed customer profiles to suggest optimal next steps for service agents and automated systems.

Churn Prediction: Machine learning models identified patterns indicative of potential customer churn, enabling proactive retention efforts.

Business Outcomes

The implementation of the Customer 360 Service delivered significant business value:

Improved Customer Satisfaction: Customer satisfaction scores increased by 27% as interactions became more personalised and efficient.

Enhanced First Contact Resolution: First-contact resolution rates improved by 34% as agents gained access to comprehensive customer information.

Reduced Average Handling Time: Service interactions were completed 22% faster due to the elimination of system switching and duplicate data entry.

Increased Self-Service Adoption: Customer adoption of self-service channels increased by 45% as these portals delivered more personalised experiences.

Case Study: Knowledge Management System for LegalDeal

LegalDeal struggled with efficiently capturing, managing, and distributing the firm's collective expertise. Critical knowledge was siloed within individual attorneys' experiences, document folders, email archives, and disconnected research databases, creating challenges for collaboration, training, and service delivery.

Business Challenge and Vision

As LegalDeal expanded its practice areas and client base, the firm recognized that a systematic approach to knowledge management was essential for maintaining service quality and operational efficiency. The leadership team envisioned an AI-enhanced knowledge management system that would:

Centralize the firm's collective expertise, precedents, and best practices in a searchable, accessible platform.

Accelerate research and preparation processes through intelligent search and recommendation capabilities.

Ensure consistent application of legal approaches across similar cases and matters.

Solution Architecture

LegalDeal implemented an AI-enhanced Knowledge Management System built on modern architectural principles:

Content Aggregation Layer: Automatically collected and indexed content from multiple sources, including document management systems, email archives, and research databases.

Process Flow:

1. Source systems expose content through the API Gateway
2. The Document Crawler regularly accesses this content on schedule
3. The Event Bus captures real-time updates to ensure synchronization

4. The Content Indexer processes retrieved documents
5. The Metadata Generator enriches documents with basic metadata
6. All content is stored in the Document Store for further processing

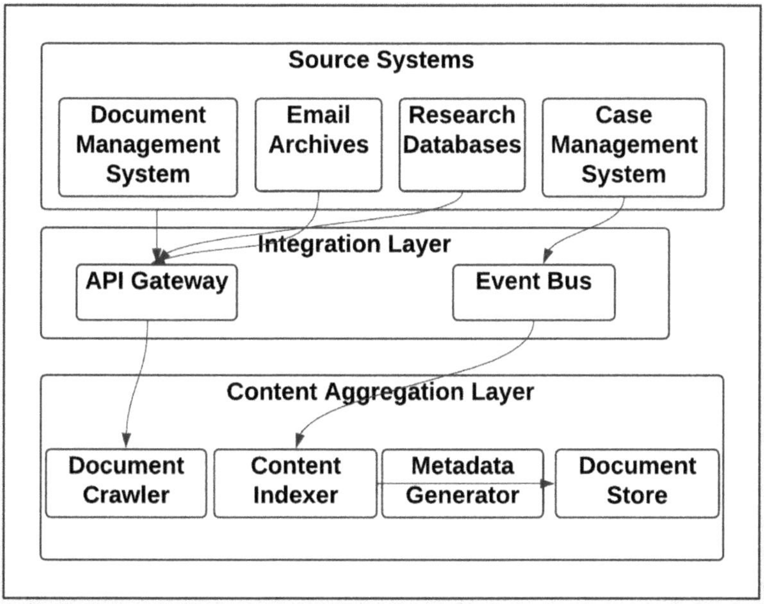

Semantic Processing Engine: Employed natural language processing and machine learning to extract key concepts, categorize and tag documents, and generate metadata to enhance searchability.

Process Flow:

1. Raw documents from the Document Store enter the NLP Pipeline
2. The NLP Pipeline extracts structured information from unstructured text
3. Entity Recognition identifies legal entities and their relationships
4. Document Classifier assigns categories and practice areas to documents
5. Topic Modelling discovers common themes across document collections
6. The Knowledge Graph stores the semantic relationships between entities
7. The Vector Database stores document embeddings for semantic search

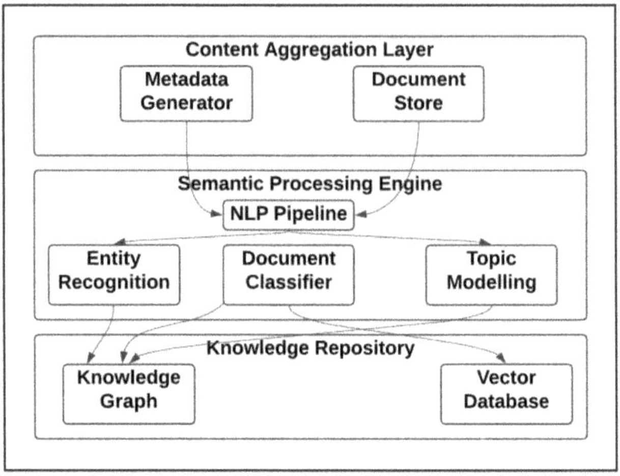

The next step demonstrates how attorneys interact with the system to find relevant information and precedents.

Process Flow:

1. Attorney submits a query through the Portal
2. Query Understanding analyses the intent and context of the search
3. Semantic Search executes parallel searches against the Knowledge Graph and Vector Database
4. Relevance Ranking combines and prioritizes results based on multiple factors
5. Results Formatter retrieves original documents and prepares them for display
6. Portal presents the attorney with relevant documents, precedents, and related knowledge

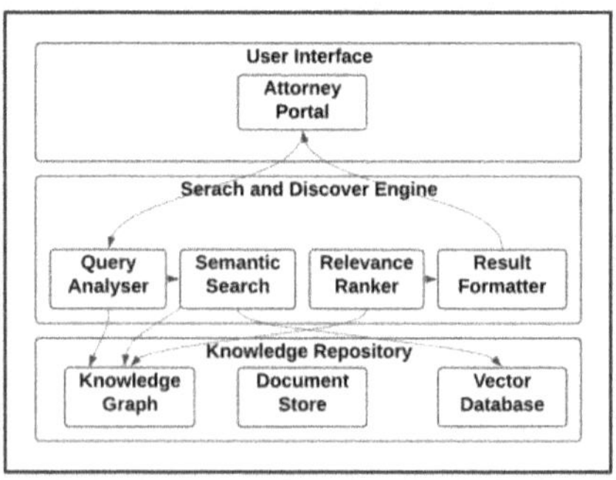

Search and Discovery Engine: Implemented vector-based search capabilities that understood the semantic meaning of queries rather than relying solely on keywords.

The final step illustrates how AI capabilities enhance the knowledge management experience with automated insights and recommendations.

Process Flow:

1. Case parameters from active matters feed into the Precedent Matching engine.
2. Precedent Matching identifies relevant historical cases from the Knowledge Graph.
3. Document Summarization creates concise overviews of complex legal documents.
4. Knowledge Extraction identifies key points and principles from documents.
5. Insight Generation analyses patterns to produce actionable recommendations.
6. The Attorney Portal presents these AI-generated enhancements alongside search results.

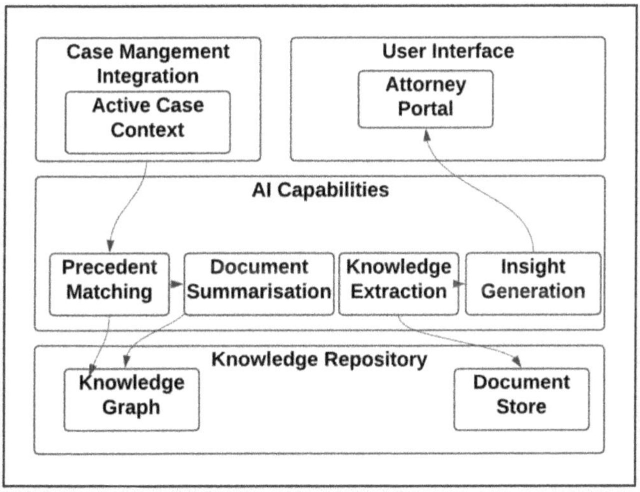

Business Outcomes

The implementation of the AI-enhanced Knowledge Management System delivered significant business value:

Reduced Research Time: Attorneys reported a 40% reduction in time spent researching precedents and legal approaches.

Improved Quality: Document quality and consistency improved, with a 30% reduction in review cycles for standard legal documents.

Enhanced Client Satisfaction: Client satisfaction scores increased by 25% as the firm delivered more consistent, well-informed services.

Accelerated Onboarding: New associate productivity ramped up 35% faster due to structured access to firm knowledge and precedents.

The above case studies of ComPlus and LegalDeal highlight a pivotal shift in how organisations must approach solution architecture in the era of AI-driven transformation. The boundaries between machine learning workloads and operational engineering are increasingly dissolving, as AI capabilities are now directly embedded into operational systems to deliver real-time intelligence and automation. For ComPlus, the integration of AI into their Customer 360 Service enabled hyper-personalised customer experiences and proactive engagement, while LegalDeal's AI-enhanced Knowledge Management System streamlined legal research and amplified expertise. These examples underscore the need for organisations to rethink their structures, processes, and technologies. To truly evolve into cognitive enterprises, they must embrace a holistic approach that unifies data, AI, and operational workflows while fostering cross-functional collaboration. Starting now is essential to ensure they are equipped to thrive in this new paradigm of integrated intelligence.

Integrating Digital Enablers with Legacy Infrastructure

For organisations like ComPlus and LegalDeal, implementing digital enablers requires thoughtful integration with existing legacy systems. These enterprises have significant investments in core operational systems that cannot be replaced overnight, yet they need the agility and intelligence that digital enablers provide.

API-First Integration Approach

An API-first approach provides a flexible, scalable method for connecting digital enablers with legacy systems without requiring extensive modifications to either environment. This strategy focuses on creating well-defined interfaces that enable controlled, secure data exchange while maintaining system independence.

Event-Driven Integration

Event-driven architectures enable real-time data synchronization between digital enablers and legacy systems by treating data changes as events that can be published, subscribed to, and processed independently. This approach minimizes direct coupling between systems while ensuring data consistency.

Progressive Modernisation

Rather than attempting wholesale replacement of legacy systems, progressive modernisation decomposes monolithic applications into smaller components that can be individually upgraded or replaced. This approach enables organisations to gradually integrate digital enablers while managing risk and maintaining operational continuity.

ComPlus used the strangler pattern to gradually transition customer self-service functionality from its legacy portal to a new AI-enhanced customer engagement platform, minimising disruption to customer experience during the transition.

Conclusion: Digital Enablers as the Foundation for Cognitive Enterprise

Digital enablers with embedded AI capabilities serve as the foundation for cognitive enterprise transformation, bridging the gap between legacy infrastructure and intelligent, adaptive experiences. By implementing platforms such as Customer 360, knowledge management systems, content management solutions, and customer engagement frameworks, organisations can leverage their existing investments while delivering the personalised, contextual interactions that modern stakeholders expect.

For telecommunications providers like ComPlus, these enablers transform fragmented customer data into unified profiles that power consistent experiences across channels. They enable proactive service management, personalised recommendations, and efficient issue resolution that drive customer loyalty and operational excellence.

Legal service firms like LegalDeal benefit equally from digital enablers, using AI-enhanced knowledge management systems to capture and distribute collective expertise. These platforms accelerate research, improve document quality, and ensure consistent application of best practices across the firm.

As we look to the future, digital enablers will continue to evolve, becoming more autonomous, collaborative, and ambient in their operation. Multi-agent systems will enable more sophisticated problem-solving, while human-AI teaming models will redefine how work is performed throughout the enterprise. Organisations that embrace these trends will be well-positioned to maintain competitive advantage and drive continued innovation in their respective industries.

The journey toward cognitive enterprise capabilities is an ongoing evolution rather than a destination. By establishing robust digital enablers as a foundation, organisations create the flexibility, intelligence, and scalability needed to adapt to changing market conditions and emerging opportunities.

The merging of operational and analytical worlds is reshaping how organisations work, demanding changes not just in technology but in how teams are structured and skilled. As AI becomes seamlessly embedded into everyday systems, the traditional divide between data science and operational engineering is disappearing. This means teams need to work more closely together, breaking down silos and fostering collaboration across departments. Organisations will need to rethink their structures, moving towards more agile, cross-functional setups that make it easier to integrate AI insights into daily operations. At the same time, employees will need new skills—like understanding real-time analytics and deploying machine learning models—while leaders must focus on creating a culture that encourages innovation and adaptability. By embracing this shift in both mindset and structure, businesses can empower their people to thrive in this new era and position themselves to become truly cognitive enterprises.

Looking Ahead

As organisations move closer to becoming cognitive enterprises, the ability to seamlessly connect systems, data, and AI capabilities is becoming a cornerstone of success. The blending of operational and analytical worlds demands a platform that can unify these elements, enabling real-time insights and intelligent automation. This is where an Intelligent Integration Platform becomes essential. These platforms bring everything together, enabling capabilities like Model Context Protocol (MCP), which ensures AI models operate within the right context, delivering accurate and actionable insights. By supporting real-time data synchronization, automating workflows, and embedding intelligence into operations, these platforms help businesses break down silos and work smarter. In the next chapter, we'll explore how intelligent integration platforms enable organisations to unify their data and processes, paving the way for smarter decisions, greater agility, and the seamless integration of AI into everyday business activities.

Chapter 10: The Intelligent Integration Platform – Connecting Systems and AI

As Maria Rodriguez, ComPlus's newly appointed Integration Director, reviewed the system architecture diagrams spread across her desk, she smiled at how far they had come. "*Two years ago, we had 47 separate point-to-point integrations between our systems, creating a maintenance nightmare,*" she explained to her team. "*Today, our Intelligent Integration Platform connects everything seamlessly. When a customer calls about service issues, our agents instantly access a complete view that pulls data from our CRM, billing, network monitoring, and field service systems—all through a single interface.*"

At LegalDeal, Chief Technology Officer James Chen demonstrated their transformation to a visiting client. "Before implementing our integration platform, attorneys spent hours manually gathering information from multiple databases for each case," he noted. "*Now, our systems communicate seamlessly. When researching a regulatory compliance issue, our platform automatically pulls relevant precedents, applicable regulations, and client-specific considerations into a unified workspace. What previously took days now happens in minutes.*"

Building on Digital Foundations

In Chapter 9, we explored how Digital Enablers provide the tools and capabilities that bridge traditional systems with cognitive AI innovations, creating unified experiences across channels. However, these Digital Enablers cannot function in isolation—they require a robust integration layer that connects systems, orchestrates data flows, and enables communication across the enterprise. This is where the Intelligent Integration Platform becomes essential.

The Intelligent Integration Platform serves as the nervous system of a cognitive enterprise, connecting disparate applications, data sources, and AI systems into a cohesive ecosystem. It eliminates silos, automates workflows, and ensures that information flows seamlessly to where it's needed when it's needed. By providing standardised ways for systems to communicate, this platform creates the foundation upon which cognitive capabilities can flourish.

For both ComPlus and LegalDeal, the Intelligent Integration Platform represents a critical step in their transformation journeys. It connects their traditional systems of record with modern cognitive capabilities, enabling new levels of operational efficiency, customer experience, and business agility. This chapter explores how these organisations have implemented their integration platforms and the value they've delivered.

The Evolution of Enterprise Integration

Enterprise integration has evolved significantly over the past decades, transitioning from simple point-to-point connections to sophisticated platforms that leverage AI and cloud-native technologies. Understanding this evolution provides important context for the approaches that ComPlus and LegalDeal have adopted.

Point-to-Point Integration (Early 2000s)

The earliest integration approach involved direct connections between systems:

- **Direct Connections**: Systems were connected through custom-coded interfaces specific to each pair of applications.
- **Tight Coupling**: Changes to one system often require modifications to multiple integration points, creating maintenance challenges.
- **Limited Scalability**: As the number of systems grew, the number of connections increased exponentially, creating an unsustainable "spaghetti" architecture.

ComPlus experienced these challenges acutely during its early digital initiatives. With hundreds of systems across their global operations, point-to-point integration created a maintenance burden that consumed more than 40% of their IT budget and significantly slowed innovation.

Enterprise Service Bus (Mid-2000s)

To address the limitations of point-to-point integration, organisations adopted more centralized approaches:

- **Centralized Message Broker**: An ESB served as a central hub through which all system communications flowed.
- **Message Transformation**: The ESB handled data format conversion between systems, reducing the need for custom adapters.
- **Service Orchestration**: Simple workflows could be orchestrated across multiple systems through the ESB.

ComPlus implemented an ESB during this period, reducing the number of direct connections and improving manageability. However, their ESB became a bottleneck as transaction volumes grew, and its monolithic architecture limited flexibility and scalability.

LegalDeal, being a younger organisation, largely bypassed this phase, though some of its acquired software included ESB-style integration components.

API-First Integration (2010s)

As organisations embraced cloud computing and microservices, API-centric integration emerged as a more flexible approach:

- **Standardised Interfaces**: APIs provide consistent, well-documented interfaces for system interaction.
- **Decentralized Architecture**: Each system exposed its own APIs, eliminating the central bottleneck of an ESB.
- **Developer Focus**: API management platforms provided developer portals, security controls and monitoring capabilities.

Both ComPlus and LegalDeal adopted API-first approaches during this period. ComPlus established an API management program that enabled more flexible integration while improving security and governance.

LegalDeal implemented API gateways to connect their modern SaaS applications, creating a more unified technology ecosystem.

Event-Driven Architecture (Late 2010s)

As real-time responsiveness became increasingly important, event-driven architectures gained prominence:

- **Event Streams**: Systems publish events to streams that other systems can subscribe to, enabling real-time data flows.
- **Loose Coupling**: Publishers and subscribers operated independently, improving resilience and scalability.
- **Temporal Decoupling**: Systems didn't need to be available simultaneously, as events could persist and be processed later.

ComPlus implemented event streaming platforms to support real-time use cases like network monitoring and customer experience optimisation. LegalDeal adopted event-driven approaches for workflow automation and document processing, improving responsiveness and efficiency.

Intelligent Integration Platforms (Present)

Today, we're seeing the emergence of Intelligent Integration Platforms that incorporate AI, low-code capabilities and cloud-native technologies:

- **AI-Enhanced Integration**: Machine learning optimizes routing, transformation, and orchestration decisions.
- **Low-Code/No-Code Tools**: Visual designers and AI assistants enable non-technical users to create integrations.
- **Hybrid Integration**: Platforms support both cloud and on-premises systems, spanning traditional and modern architectures.
- **Intelligent Automation**: AI-powered workflows combine integration with automation and intelligence.

Both ComPlus and LegalDeal are implementing these modern capabilities, though their specific approaches reflect their different contexts and needs. ComPlus is focusing on modernising its extensive legacy integration landscape while supporting new cognitive capabilities. LegalDeal is enhancing its relatively modern integration architecture with AI capabilities to improve automation and intelligence.

Key Components of the Intelligent Integration Platform

The Intelligent Integration Platform consists of several interconnected components that work together to enable seamless integration across the enterprise. While implementations vary, five core components remain consistent across most modern platforms.

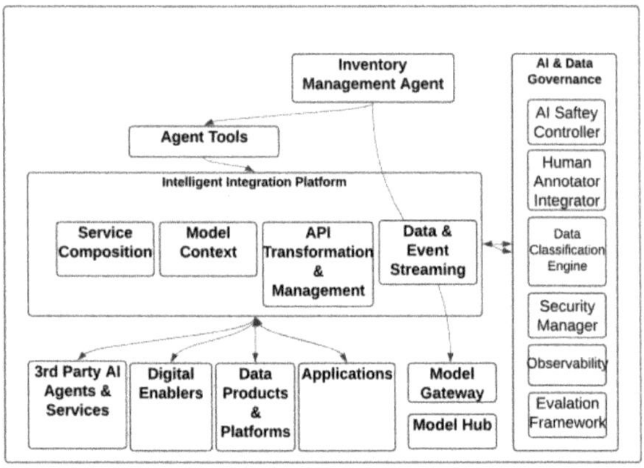

1. *API Management*

API Management provides the tools and capabilities needed to design, secure, publish, and analyse APIs across the organisation:

- **API Design and Documentation**: Tools for creating well-designed, consistent APIs with comprehensive documentation.
- **Security and Access Control**: Mechanisms for authenticating and authorizing API access, including OAuth, API keys, and role-based controls.
- **Traffic Management**: Capabilities for rate limiting, quotas, and traffic shaping to ensure reliable API performance.

- **Analytics and Monitoring**: Tools for tracking API usage, performance, and errors to support optimisation.
- **Performance Monitoring**: Real-time dashboards track API performance, alerting teams to potential issues before they impact users.

Integration Architect Sarah Johnson describes the impact: "*Our API management platform transformed how we approach integration. Instead of one-off connections, we now have a catalogue of over 400 standardised APIs that can be reused across projects. When we needed to integrate our new AI-driven customer service platform, 80% of the required APIs already existed, reducing implementation time by months.*"

LegalDeal Implementation

LegalDeal implemented a lighter API management approach focused on their specific needs:

- **Cloud-Native Gateway**: A cloud-based API gateway provides security and management capabilities without extensive infrastructure.
- **Partner Integration Portal**: A specialised portal enables secure integration with client systems and legal service providers.
- **Compliance Controls**: API security policies enforce regulatory requirements for data protection and client confidentiality.
- **Usage Analytics**: Dashboards track API usage patterns, helping identify opportunities for optimisation and enhancement.

2. *Event Processing*

Event processing capabilities enable real-time data flows and event-driven interactions between systems:

- **Event Capture**: Mechanisms for capturing events from source systems, including change data capture, log monitoring, and API webhooks.

- **Event Streaming**: Platforms for distributing events to multiple consumers in real-time with guaranteed delivery.
- **Event Processing**: Tools for filtering, enriching, and transforming events as they flow through the system.
- **Event Storage**: Capabilities for persisting events for replay, audit, or historical analysis.

ComPlus implemented a sophisticated event processing architecture:

- **Enterprise Event Mesh**: A distributed event streaming platform that handles millions of events daily, from network status changes to customer interactions.
- **Real-Time Analytics**: Stream processing capabilities that analyse events in-flight, identifying patterns and triggering automated responses.
- **Change Data Capture**: Mechanisms that automatically detect changes in databases and convert them into events for downstream processing.
- **Event Schema Registry**: A central repository that manages event schemas, ensuring consistent interpretation across systems.

LegalDeal implemented event processing focused on document workflows and client communications:

- **Document Event System**: A platform that captures events related to document creation, modification, and processing.
- **Matter Workflow Automation**: Event-driven workflows that coordinate tasks across practice management, document review, and client communication systems.
- **Compliance Monitoring**: Real-time tracking of regulatory changes that might affect client matters, triggering appropriate notifications and actions.
- **Client Communication Events**: A system that coordinates client communications across channels, ensuring consistent and timely engagement.

3. Integration Flow Automation

Integration Flow Automation provides tools for orchestrating complex workflows across systems:

- **Visual Flow Design**: Low-code/no-code tools for designing visually integrated workflows.
- **Data Transformation**: Capabilities for mapping and transforming data between different formats and structures.
- **Error Handling**: Mechanisms for detecting and responding to errors in integration flows.
- **Monitoring and Management**: Tools for tracking flow execution, performance, and issues.

ComPlus implemented comprehensive flow automation capabilities:

- **Low-Code Integration Platform**: A visual platform that enables both technical and business users to create integration flows.
- **Pre-Built Connectors**: A library of connectors for common systems, reducing the need for custom integration code.
- **AI-Assisted Mapping**: Machine learning algorithms that suggest appropriate data mappings between systems.
- **Flow Analytics**: Dashboards that track flow performance, identifying bottlenecks and optimisation opportunities.

Business Analyst Maria Rodriguez notes: "*Our integration platform has democratized integration development. I can create flows that connect our customer data with marketing systems without writing code. Last month, I built an integration that synchronizes customer preference data across three systems in just two days—a task that would have taken weeks with traditional approaches.*"

LegalDeal Implementation

LegalDeal focused on lightweight, targeted flow automation:

- **Cloud-Based Integration**: A SaaS platform that provides integration capabilities without infrastructure management.
- **Legal-Specific Templates**: Pre-built integration templates for common legal workflows and systems.
- **Secure Data Handling**: Features that ensure sensitive client data is handled appropriately throughout integration flows.
- **Audit Trails**: Comprehensive logging of all integration activities for compliance and security purposes.

4. AI-Powered Capabilities

Modern integration platforms increasingly incorporate AI capabilities that enhance automation, intelligence, and user experience:

- **Integration Recommendation**: AI systems that suggest appropriate integration patterns and approaches.
- **Anomaly Detection**: Machine learning models that identify unusual patterns or potential issues in integration flows.
- **Natural Language Interfaces**: Capabilities that enable users to describe integration needs in natural language.
- **Automated Data Mapping**: AI that suggests appropriate data mappings between different systems and formats.

The Model Context Protocol(MCP): A New Paradigm for Cognitive Integration

As cognitive enterprises evolve, traditional integration approaches face limitations in supporting context-aware, AI-driven interactions. The Model Context Protocol (MCP) represents a significant advancement in integration capability, providing a standardised framework for sharing context between systems and AI components.

What is the Model Context Protocol?

The Model Context Protocol is an approach for AI systems to access, update and interact with enterprise data and services in a context-aware manner. Unlike traditional integration methods that focus on data movement, MCP emphasizes context sharing—ensuring that AI systems have the comprehensive understanding needed for intelligent decision-making.

As cognitive enterprises scale, traditional API-based integrations struggle to support the dynamic, context-rich interactions required by AI systems. The Model Context Protocol (MCP) addresses this challenge by redefining how intelligent systems access and utilise enterprise data. Unlike rigid point-to-point integrations, MCP creates a living dialogue between AI agents and organisational knowledge, enabling real-time reasoning grounded in operational reality.

For ComPlus and LegalDeal, MCP has become the connective tissue of their cognitive architectures—allowing AI systems to understand rather than merely access enterprise data. This shift from transactional data exchange to contextual intelligence has been pivotal in overcoming the "integration bottleneck" that plagues many AI initiatives.

Key features of MCP include:

Unified Context Access: A consistent method for accessing relevant context across diverse systems and data sources.

Real-Time Updates: Mechanisms for ensuring AI systems operate with current, relevant information.

Standardised Interaction: Common patterns for how AI systems request information and perform actions.

Technical Architecture of MCP

MCP operates on a client-host-server model optimized for secure, context-aware AI interactions:

How MCP Enhances Integration

The Model Context Protocol enhances traditional integration approaches in several important ways:

Context Aggregation

MCP aggregates relevant context from multiple systems into unified views that AI systems can easily consume. This aggregation reduces the complexity of integration and improves AI performance by providing more comprehensive information.

ComPlus uses MCP to create unified customer contexts that combine information from CRM, billing, service management, and interaction history systems. When an AI-powered customer service system assists a customer, it accesses this unified context through MCP, ensuring it has

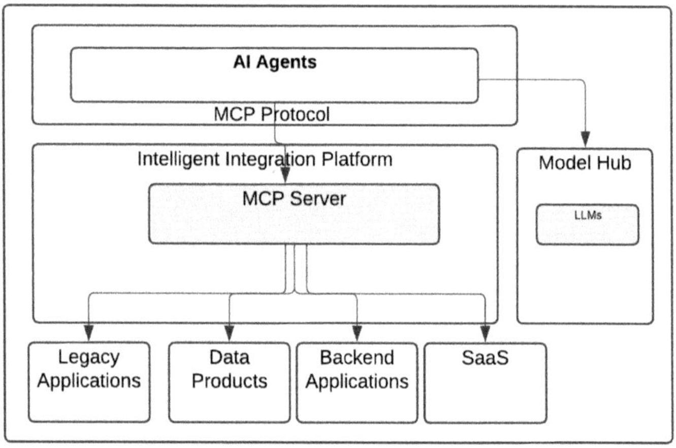

all relevant information without complex integration logic.

Intelligent Interaction

MCP enables more sophisticated interactions between AI systems and enterprise applications by providing rich context and supporting dynamic, intent-based operations. This intelligence improves the quality and relevance of AI-driven processes.

LegalDeal uses MCP to enhance document analysis workflows. When an AI system reviews a contract, MCP provides access to relevant precedents, client-specific requirements, and jurisdictional regulations.

This comprehensive context enables more accurate and relevant analysis than would be possible with traditional integration approaches.

Simplified Development

MCP reduces integration complexity for AI developers by providing a consistent, well-documented protocol for accessing enterprise systems. This simplification accelerates development and improves reliability.

At ComPlus, AI development teams use MCP to access enterprise systems without needing to understand the complex details of each backend system. This abstraction has reduced development time for new AI capabilities by 40% while improving consistency and reliability.

Integration with the Multi-Agent Orchestrator Platform

The Model Context Protocol works seamlessly with the Multi-Agent Orchestrator Platform (MOP) introduced in earlier chapters, enabling agents to access enterprise context efficiently. This integration creates powerful synergies between the integration layer and agent capabilities.

Key integration points include:

Context Sharing: MCP provides unified context to MOP agents, ensuring they have comprehensive information for decision-making.

Action Execution: MOP agents use MCP to interact with enterprise systems, execute actions, and update information.

Dynamic Orchestration: MCP provides the contextual information MOP needs to orchestrate complex workflows involving multiple agents and systems.

Security Enforcement: MCP and MOP work together to enforce security policies, ensuring appropriate data access and action authorization.

Governance Alignment: MCP's audit trails integrate with MOP's Observability Framework, creating unified compliance reports.

ComPlus has implemented this integration to enhance its customer service operations. When a customer contacts the company, MOP orchestrates the interaction while MCP provides comprehensive customer context. If the customer has a technical issue, the TechnicalSupportAgent receives relevant service history, device information, and network status through MCP, enabling more effective assistance.

LegalDeal uses this integration to streamline legal research. When an attorney needs information on a specific legal issue, MOP orchestrates the research process while MCP provides access to relevant precedents, regulations, and client-specific considerations. This integration ensures comprehensive, contextually appropriate research results.

The Model Context Protocol represents more than technical innovation—it embodies the cognitive enterprise's core promise of contextual intelligence at scale. By transforming integration from a technical challenge into a strategic capability, MCP enables organisations like ComPlus and LegalDeal to operationalize their hardest-won asset: institutional knowledge. In doing so, it closes the last mile between AI potential and business impact.

Implementing the Intelligent Integration Platform: Approaches and Lessons

Both ComPlus and LegalDeal have implemented Intelligent Integration Platforms tailored to their specific needs and contexts. Their experiences offer valuable insights for organisations undertaking similar transformations.

ComPlus: Modernising a Complex Integration Landscape

As a large telecommunications provider with hundreds of systems accumulated over decades, ComPlus faced significant integration challenges. Their transformation approach focused on progressive modernisation while supporting both legacy and modern systems.

Key Implementation Phases

ComPlus implemented their platform in three phases:

Phase 1: Foundation Building (2021-2022)

- Implemented API management capabilities for new and modernised systems
- Established event streaming infrastructure for real-time data flows
- Developed integration patterns and standards for consistent implementation
- Built initial data virtualization capabilities for customer and service data

This phase delivered basic integration capabilities while establishing the foundation for more advanced features.

Phase 2: Legacy Integration (2022-2023)

- Connected legacy systems through adapters and gateways
- Implemented data virtualization for critical business domains
- Enhanced event processing with real-time analytics
- Expanded API capabilities with developer portals and lifecycle management

This phase extended integration capabilities to legacy systems, enabling unified workflows across old and new applications.

Phase 3: Intelligent Enhancement (2023-Present)

- Implemented AI-powered integration capabilities

- Deployed the Model Context Protocol for context-aware integration
- Integrated with the Multi-Agent Orchestrator Platform
- Expanded low-code/no-code capabilities for business-led integration

This ongoing phase is adding intelligence and automation to the integration platform, enabling more sophisticated cognitive capabilities.

Lessons Learned

ComPlus's implementation has yielded several important lessons:

Incremental Value Delivery: Rather than attempting a complete transformation at once, ComPlus focused on delivering incremental value through targeted implementation. This approach maintained momentum and demonstrated tangible benefits throughout the journey.

Pattern-Based Integration: The company established standard integration patterns for common scenarios, ensuring consistency and reducing development time. These patterns provided templates for integration teams to follow, accelerating implementation while maintaining quality.

Federated Governance: ComPlus implemented a governance model that balanced central oversight with team autonomy. Central teams established standards and managed shared infrastructure, while individual teams had flexibility in implementing specific integrations.

Skills Development: The company invested heavily in developing integration skills across both technical and business teams. This investment created a broader pool of integration expertise, reducing bottlenecks and accelerating implementation.

Best Practices for Implementing an Intelligent Integration Platform

Based on the experiences of ComPlus and LegalDeal, several best practices emerge for organisations implementing Intelligent Integration Platforms:

Start with a Clear Strategy

Develop a comprehensive integration strategy that aligns with your overall business and technology goals. This strategy should consider:

- Business priorities and use cases
- Existing system landscape and modernisation plans
- Skill availability and development needs
- Governance and operating model requirements

A clear strategy helps ensure that integration investments deliver maximum value and support your broader transformation goals.

Adopt a Hybrid Architecture

Implement a flexible architecture that supports both traditional and modern integration patterns, enabling you to leverage existing investments while building new capabilities. This hybrid approach should include:

- API management for service-oriented integration
- Event processing for real-time data flows
- Data virtualization for unified information access
- Service mesh for microservice communication (where applicable)

This multi-pattern approach ensures you can support diverse integration needs effectively.

Prioritize Security and Governance

Implement robust security and governance from the beginning, ensuring that your integration platform protects sensitive data and complies with regulatory requirements. Key considerations include:

- Authentication and authorization controls
- Data protection and privacy
- Audit and compliance monitoring
- Policy enforcement

Strong security and governance build trust with both internal and external stakeholders while reducing risks.

Balance Centralization and Federation

Find the right balance between centralized control and federated implementation, enabling consistency where needed while supporting team autonomy. This balance typically involves:

- Centralized infrastructure and shared services
- Common standards and patterns
- Federated implementation by domain teams
- Consistent monitoring and management

This balanced approach supports both governance requirements and team agility.

Invest in Skills and Culture

Develop integration skills across both technical and business teams, creating a broader pool of expertise and fostering a culture of integration excellence. This investment should include:

- Technical training on integration tools and technologies
- Integration pattern education for developers
- Basic integration understanding for business users
- Communities of practice for knowledge sharing

Broad skill development reduces bottlenecks and accelerates integration implementation.

Focus on Business Outcomes

Align integration initiatives with specific business outcomes, ensuring that investments deliver tangible value. This alignment involves:

- Mapping integration capabilities to business use cases
- Establishing clear success metrics
- Prioritising high-value integration scenarios
- Demonstrating and communicating business impact

Outcome focus ensures that integration efforts contribute directly to your organisation's strategic objectives.

Future Directions for Intelligent Integration

As integration technology continues to evolve, several emerging trends will shape the future of Intelligent Integration Platforms:

1. Generative AI Integration

Generative AI models are increasingly being applied to integration challenges, enabling capabilities such as:

- **Natural Language Integration Design**: Systems that can design integration flows based on conversational descriptions of requirements.
- **Automated Code Generation**: AI that generates integration code, reducing development time and effort.
- **Dynamic Adapters**: Systems that can automatically create adapters for new applications and data sources.
- **Context-Aware Transformation**: AI models that understand data semantics and can perform intelligent transformation between formats.

2. Edge Integration

As computing moves increasingly to the edge, integration capabilities are following, enabling:

- **Local Data Processing**: Integration flows that process data locally before sending results to central systems.
- **Disconnected Operation**: Integration capabilities that can function offline and synchronize when connectivity is restored.
- **Edge-to-Edge Integration**: Direct integration between edge devices without central coordination.
- **IoT Integration**: Specialised capabilities for integrating with IoT devices and gateways.

3. Autonomous Integration

Integration platforms are becoming increasingly autonomous, with capabilities such as:

- **Self-Optimizing Flows**: Integration flows that automatically adjust to changing conditions and requirements.
- **Self-Healing Integration**: Systems that detect and resolve integration issues without human intervention.
- **Automated Discovery**: Capabilities that automatically discover and map integration opportunities.
- **Continuous Adaptation**: Integration flows that evolve based on usage patterns and feedback.

4. Cross-Enterprise Integration

Integration is increasingly spanning organisational boundaries, enabling:

- **B2B Integration Networks**: Secure networks that connect multiple organisations for seamless business processes.
- **Ecosystem Integration**: Platforms that integrate across partner ecosystems, enabling collaborative workflows.

- **Supply Chain Integration**: End-to-end integration across supply chains for improved visibility and efficiency.
- **Industry Hubs**: Specialised integration hubs for specific industries or functions, e.g., Network API initiatives in the telecommunication industry.

ComPlus is participating in a telecommunications industry integration hub that enables the standardisation of APIs across the industry. LegalDeal is implementing ecosystem integration with client systems and legal research providers, enabling more collaborative legal workflows.

Conclusion: Integration as the Foundation for Cognitive Capabilities

The Intelligent Integration Platform serves as the essential foundation for cognitive enterprise capabilities, connecting systems, data, and processes into a cohesive ecosystem. By providing seamless connectivity and intelligent data flows, this platform enables organisations to leverage their existing investments while building new cognitive capabilities.

For ComPlus and LegalDeal, implementing intelligent integration has delivered significant business value:

- Reduced time-to-market for new capabilities by eliminating integration bottlenecks
- Improved customer and client experiences through unified, real-time information
- Enhanced operational efficiency by automating cross-system workflows
- Enabled new cognitive capabilities by providing the connectivity they require

As these organisations continue their transformation journeys, their integration platforms will evolve to support increasingly sophisticated cognitive capabilities, including AI-driven decision-making, autonomous operations, and ecosystem collaboration.

Looking Ahead

Building on the foundation of the Intelligent Integration Platform, the next step in becoming a cognitive enterprise is to ensure that AI models and intelligent systems are effectively managed, scaled, and orchestrated. In the next chapter, we will explore how the Multiagent Orchestrator Platform (MOP) facilitates the seamless deployment, monitoring, and coordination of multiple AI models and agents across complex environments. By leveraging MOP, organisations can ensure that their AI capabilities remain adaptive, efficient, and aligned with business goals—unlocking the full potential of intelligent systems in real-world operations.

Chapter 11: The Multi-Agent Orchestrator Platform – Building the Cognitive Brain

---

Introduction: The Cognitive Enterprise's Central Nervous System

At ComPlus's Network Operations Centre, Director Elena Rodriguez demonstrates their new system to a group of visiting executives. "*Watch what happens when we simulate a fibre cut in this neighbourhood*," she says, typing a few commands into her console. Within seconds, multiple AI agents spring into action on the large wall display – a NetworkDiagnosticsAgent identifies the affected area, a ServiceImpactAgent determines which customers will experience disruptions, a ResourceAllocationAgent dispatches the nearest field technicians and a CustomerCommunicationAgent begins composing personalised notifications. "*Two years ago, this coordination would have required four separate teams and taken over 40 minutes*," she explains. "*Today, our Multi-Agent Orchestrator Platform manages the entire workflow autonomously in under 90 seconds.*"

At LegalDeal's headquarters, Lead Innovation Attorney Michael Chen shows a similar demonstration to a prospective client. "*When new financial regulations were announced last week, our system immediately detected the changes,*" he explains, navigating through their dashboard. "*Our RegulatoryMonitorAgent identified which client contracts were affected; our ClauseAnalysisAgent determined necessary revisions, and our ComplianceAgent generated implementation timelines for each client – all before our legal team arrived at the office that morning.*" The client, visibly impressed, asks how quickly they had implemented such sophisticated automation. "*This is the culmination of our three-year cognitive transformation journey*," Chen responds. "*What you're seeing is the practical application of everything we've built into our Cognitive Enterprise Architecture.*"

The MOP: Cornerstone of Cognitive Enterprise Architecture

In our journey through the Cognitive Enterprise Architecture Framework (CeAF) introduced in Chapter 3, we've explored multiple critical layers – from data foundations and application architecture to digital enablers and intelligent integration. The Multi-Agent Orchestrator Platform (MOP) now emerges as the brain that brings these components together into a cohesive, intelligent system.

MOP represents a key intelligence layer within the CeAF, connecting the user experience layer with the underlying data, application, and integration layers. It orchestrates complex workflows by breaking down user intents into manageable tasks, assigning these to specialised AI agents, and ensuring seamless collaboration across the enterprise. Unlike traditional workflow engines that follow rigid, predefined paths, MOP dynamically adapts to changing conditions, leverages contextual information and enables truly intelligent automation that reflects the Human-centric AI principles established in Chapter 5.

At its core, MOP interprets user intent and breaks down complex tasks into smaller, manageable subtasks. These subtasks are assigned to specialised agents—ranging from domain-specific to micro-level agents—ensuring efficient execution while adhering to compliance standards. For example, MOP can resolve customer issues in real-time, automate regulatory workflows, or deliver personalised customer experiences by synthesizing insights from diverse data.

In the broader CeAF ecosystem, MOP acts as a bridge between traditional enterprise tools like CRM platforms and modern AI capabilities. It orchestrates interactions between AI models, data repositories, and digital tools such as CRM 360 Service or Knowledge Management systems. This ensures businesses can fully leverage AI for automation and value creation.

The Evolution of Agentic AI and Orchestration

Agentic AI refers to autonomous systems capable of perceiving, reasoning, and acting intelligently. Its evolution has been pivotal in enabling today's multi-agent ecosystems that address complex real-world challenges through collaboration and adaptability. These advancements directly enhance MOP's ability to manage workflows using intelligent agents.

The journey of AI agents and orchestration systems has progressed through several key phases:

Early Machine Learning (1950s–1990s): Early AI relied on static rules and basic supervised learning for narrowly defined tasks. Expert systems could answer predefined questions but lacked flexibility for dynamic scenarios.

Probabilistic and Reinforcement Learning (the 1990s–2000s): Probabilistic models like Bayesian networks introduced decision-making under uncertainty, while reinforcement learning enabled systems to adapt through trial and error.

Deep Learning Revolution (2010s): Deep neural networks brought breakthroughs in image recognition and natural language processing. This era also saw deep reinforcement learning excel at complex tasks such as mastering games like Go.

Multimodal Integration and Generative AI (2020–2023): Advances in multimodal AI allowed systems to process diverse inputs like text, images, and audio simultaneously. Generative AI expanded capabilities further by enabling creative problem-solving.

Autonomous Agents and Multi-Agent Systems (2023–Present): Modern AI focuses on self-directed agents that break down tasks into subtasks, refine solutions iteratively and collaborate within ecosystems. Examples include Auto-GPT and BabyAGI.

The evolution of orchestration systems has followed a similar trajectory:

Rule-Based Workflow Engines (1990s-2000s): Early workflow systems relied on explicitly defined rules and pathways with predictable, deterministic outcomes. These systems excelled at standardisation but provided limited adaptability.

Service-Oriented Orchestration (2000s-2010s): As service-oriented architectures gained prominence, orchestration evolved to coordinate services across applications. These systems provided greater flexibility but still relied on predefined process models.

Cognitive Orchestration with AI (2020s-Present): The current generation of orchestration leverages AI to understand intent, make context-aware decisions, and dynamically adapt workflows. This approach enables personalised experiences, intelligent automation, and continuous optimisation.

This combined evolution has transformed how enterprises manage complex processes, shifting from static, rules-driven approaches to dynamic, intelligence-driven orchestration – the essence of the cognitive enterprise.

The successful design and implementation of a **Multi-Agent Orchestrator Platform (MOP)** requires a structured approach that balances scalability, security, modularity, observability, and resilience. By adhering to best practices across architectural, operational, and data management dimensions, organisations can ensure that MOP operates efficiently, adapts to dynamic business needs, and integrates seamlessly into enterprise ecosystems. These best practices form the foundation for a robust, future-proof platform and serve as a general guideline, with further component-specific practices detailed in their respective sections.

Below is an elaboration of best practices for implementing MOP, categorized into **architectural design, data management, security and operational efficiency** dimensions.

1. **Architectural Design Best Practices**

*1.1. **Modular and Scalable Design***

A modular and scalable architecture ensures that MOP can adapt to increasing workloads, integrate new functionalities, and maintain performance as the system grows.

- **Description**:
    - Design MOP as a set of loosely coupled components to allow independent development, testing, and deployment.
    - Enable scalability to dynamically handle increasing task volumes and agent interactions.
- **Practices**:
    - Use **microservices architecture** to decouple agents and platform functionalities, allowing independent scaling and fault isolation.
    - Implement **horizontal scaling**, enabling components to scale out dynamically based on workload demands.
    - Utilize **load balancers** to distribute tasks evenly across agents or services, preventing overloading of specific components.

1.2. Event-Driven Architecture

Event-driven architecture enables real-time responsiveness and flexibility by allowing MOP to react dynamically to business triggers such as customer interactions, system alerts, or external events.

- **Description**:
    - Use asynchronous event-driven communication to ensure low latency and high responsiveness in workflows.
- **Practices**:
    - Leverage **message brokers** such as Apache Kafka, RabbitMQ, or AWS EventBridge for asynchronous messaging between agents and components.
    - Ensure **event idempotency** to avoid duplicate processing, particularly in cases of retries or replayed events.
    - Design **event prioritization mechanisms** to ensure critical workflows are handled first (e.g., system outages over routine tasks).

1.3. Context Management

Effective context management is essential for maintaining task continuity across multi-step workflows and ensuring consistent decision-making among agents.

- **Description**:
  - Centralize and distribute context to ensure all agents involved in a workflow can access relevant information seamlessly.
- **Practices**:
  - Use a **Context Store** to persist in a shared workflow-specific context, making it accessible to all agents.
  - Ensure **low-latency access** to context data for real-time workflows.
  - Version context data to enable historical audits and insights for long-running processes.

1.4. Resilience and Fault Tolerance

Resilience ensures that MOP remains operational even when components fail, minimising service disruptions and maintaining workflow execution.

- **Description**:
  - Implement mechanisms to detect, contain, and recover from failures to ensure consistent system performance.
- **Practices**:
  - Circuit breakers are used to prevent cascading failures by halting interactions with failing components.
  - Implement **retry mechanisms** with exponential backoff to handle transient errors gracefully.
  - Design workflows with **fallback mechanisms** to ensure tasks are rerouted or escalated in case of agent unavailability.

1.5. Caching for Performance Optimisation

Caching is critical for reducing latency and improving system responsiveness, especially in workflows that involve repeated access to the same data.

- **Description**:
    - Use caching to accelerate access to frequently used data and minimize the load on primary data stores.
- **Practices**:
    - Implement **distributed caching** solutions such as Redis or Memcached to store frequently accessed data close to agents.
    - Use **expiration policies** to ensure cached data remains fresh and relevant.
    - Cache intermediate results in multi-step workflows to avoid redundant computations.

1.6. Infrastructure Abstraction

Abstracting infrastructure ensures MOP can operate seamlessly across different environments, such as on-premises data centres, private clouds, or public cloud platforms.

- **Description**:
    - Use abstraction to simplify deployment, portability, and integration across diverse infrastructure environments.
- **Practices**:
    - Use container orchestration platforms like **Kubernetes** to abstract infrastructure and manage deployments.
    - Implement **Infrastructure as Code (IaC)** solutions such as Terraform or CloudFormation to automate and standardize infrastructure provisioning.
    - Adopt **cloud-native services** for scalability and reliability.

2. **Data Management Best Practices**

2.1. ***Data Governance***

Strong data governance ensures data security, compliance, and integrity, particularly in workflows that handle sensitive or regulated information.

- **Description**:
  - Enforce policies to manage data access, ensure compliance, and maintain data quality.
- **Practices**:
  - Implement **role-based access control (RBAC)** to restrict data access based on agent roles.
  - Anonymize sensitive data during processing and log all access for audit purposes.
  - Ensure compliance with regulations like **GDPR** or industry-specific mandates.

2.2. ***Real-Time Data Processing***

Real-time data processing capabilities are essential for workflows requiring immediate insights, such as fault detection or customer interaction management.

- **Description**:
  - Enable near real-time ingestion and processing of data streams to support dynamic workflows.
- **Practices**:
  - Use frameworks like **Apache Flink** or **Spark Streaming** to process telemetry and event data in real time.
  - Prioritize critical data streams to ensure low latency for time-sensitive workflows.

3. **Operational Best Practices**

*3.1. **Observability and Monitoring***

Observability ensures that the health and performance of MOP and its components can be monitored and optimized in real time.

- **Description**:
  - Implement tools and practices to monitor workflows, agents, and system performance proactively.
- **Practices**:
  - Use distributed tracing tools like **Jaeger** or **OpenTelemetry** to trace agent interactions and workflow execution.
  - Implement real-time dashboards for visibility into task completion rates, agent performance, and error rates.

*3.2. **Experimentation and A/B Testing***

Experimentation enables continuous improvement by testing new workflows, agent behaviours, and orchestration strategies.

- **Description**:
  - Use A/B testing to evaluate the effectiveness of changes and optimize system performance.
- **Practices**:
  - Divide workflows into testing and control groups to measure the impact of new configurations or algorithms.
  - Collect feedback from both system metrics and end-users to assess performance.

4. Security and Reliability Best Practices

*4.1. **AI Safety and Control***

- **Description**: Implement safeguards to prevent unsafe or biased AI behaviour.
- **Practices**:

    - Validate AI model outputs using fallback mechanisms (e.g., human review).
    - Monitor model drift and retrain periodically.

4.2. Resilience and Fault Tolerance

- **Description**: Design the MOP to handle failures gracefully.
- **Practices**:
    - Implement circuit breakers to isolate failing components.
    - Use retries with exponential backoff for transient errors.
- **Example**:
    - ComPlus retries network topology updates if a telemetry feed fails temporarily.

4.3. Zero Trust Security

- **Description**: Ensure least-privilege access for all MOP components.
- **Practices**:
    - Authenticate and authorize all inter-agent communication.
    - Encrypt data in transit and at rest.

Benefits of Following Best Practices

Adhering to these best practices ensures that MOP is:

1. **Scalable**: Capable of handling increasing workloads and integrating new functionalities.
2. **Efficient**: Optimized workflows minimize latency and system resource consumption.
3. **Resilient**: Fault-tolerant mechanisms maintain system stability during failures.
4. **Secure**: Strong governance and access controls protect sensitive data and workflows.
5. **Observable**: Real-time monitoring and tracing provide visibility into system behaviour.

6. **Adaptable**: Modular design and infrastructure abstraction enable MOP to evolve with changing business needs.

Next Steps

These best practices provide a solid foundation for implementing MOP effectively. In subsequent sections, we will delve into component-specific best practices, such as those for the Orchestrator, Classifier, Pre-Processor, and Agent Registry, to further refine and tailor these principles to optimize the performance and functionality of each component.

Let us now dive deeper into the building blocks of MOP and uncover how it transforms enterprise operations.

Core Components of the Multi-Agent Orchestrator Platform

The Multi-Agent Orchestrator Platform consists of several interconnected components that work together to enable intelligent orchestration across the enterprise. Let's explore the key components that form the backbone of this powerful system.

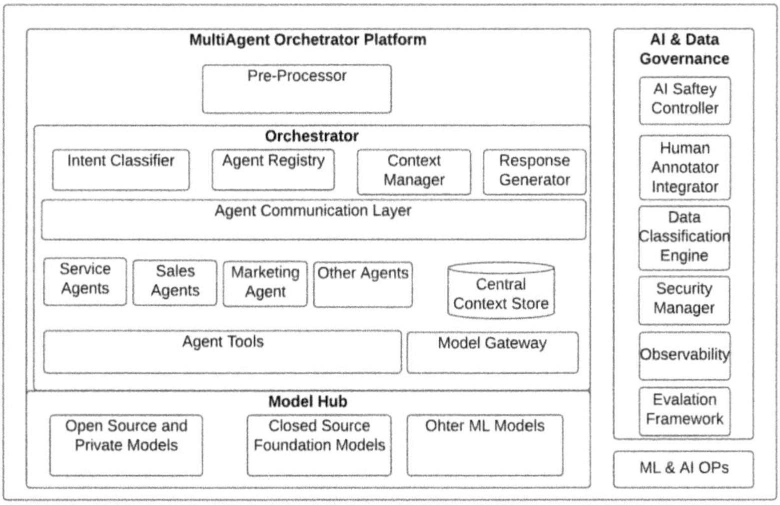

The Orchestrator: Central Coordination Engine

The Orchestrator serves as the central coordination engine within MOP, breaking down complex tasks into subtasks, assigning them to appropriate agents, and ensuring coherent, goal-oriented execution. It acts as the conductor of the cognitive enterprise, ensuring that all components work together harmoniously.

When a ComPlus customer reports internet connectivity issues, the Orchestrator breaks this down into subtasks like connection diagnostics, router configuration verification, network status checking, and relevant troubleshooting steps. Rather than following predefined pathways, it dynamically generates workflows based on the specific situation, adapting as new information becomes available. It identifies and assigns the most appropriate agents for each subtask, coordinating their activities to ensure coherent execution.

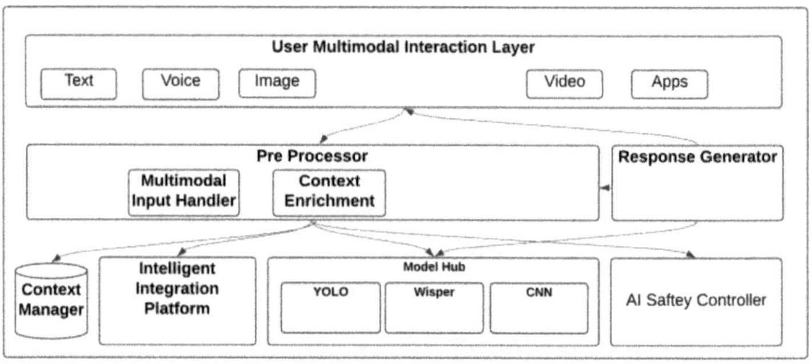

At LegalDeal, the Orchestrator manages complex legal workflows by breaking down processes such as contract analysis into components like document review, risk assessment, precedent research, and compliance verification. It considers factors like jurisdiction, client industry and regulatory landscape when designing workflows, ensuring comprehensive and compliant outcomes.

1. Pre-Processor Layer: Gateway to Intelligent Input Handling

The Pre-Processor Layer serves as the critical entry point for all inputs entering MOP, transforming raw, unstructured, or multimodal data into standardised formats that downstream components can efficiently process. It handles diverse input types – from text and audio to images, video, and sensor data – creating the essential bridge between user interactions and intelligent processing capabilities.

The Pre-Processor Layer is highly modular and adaptable, capable of performing **image processing, audio processing, sensor data analysis, gesture recognition, and multimodal fusion**. By leveraging specialised AI models (e.g., CNNs for images, RNNs for audio, or multimodal models), it extracts meaningful features, normalizes raw inputs, and enriches them with metadata for downstream processing. For example, in a broadband support context, it can transcribe customer queries, analyse speed test screenshots and detect anomalies in router sensor data. These outputs are transformed into structured formats, such as JSON or database-ready objects, enabling downstream components like the **Orchestrator** and diagnostic agents to perform their tasks with precision and agility.

Key Functionalities of the Pre-Processor Layer

1. **Image Processing**
    - **Role:** Extracts meaningful features from images for tasks like object detection, classification, or scene understanding.
    - **Techniques:**
        - Convolutional Neural Networks (CNNs) for image classification and segmentation.
        - Pre-trained models for real-time object detection or image-text understanding.
    - **Use Case:** In broadband support, analyse speed test screenshots to extract metrics like download/upload speeds and latency.

2. **Audio Processing**
    - **Role:** Processes audio inputs to extract features like pitch, tone, and sentiment for transcription, intent recognition, or emotion analysis.

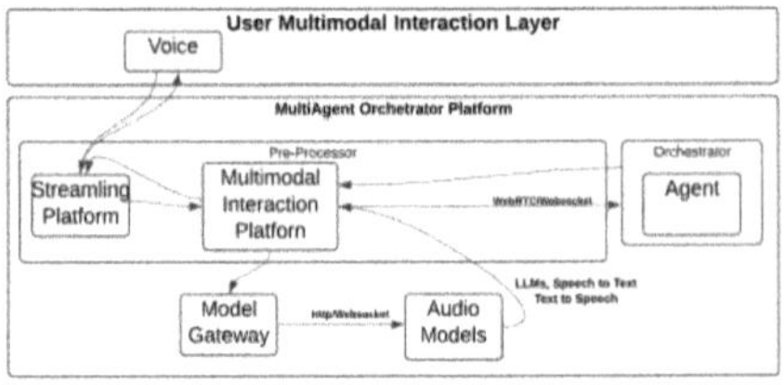

    - **Use Case:** Voice interactions between customer and voice bots.
    - Pre-Processor layer is responsible for processing the stream of audio, managing the state, integrating with LLMs or other models, pass on the output to relevant agent for further processing. It also processes the agent output, converts that back to audio, and responds back to the customer, all done in real-time.
3. **Video Processing**
    - **Role:** Processes video as a sequence of frames to analyse motion, context, and objects.
    - **Techniques:**
        - 3D Convolutional Neural Networks (3D CNNs) for spatial-temporal analysis.
    - **Use Case:** Summarize surveillance footage to detect and flag security incidents.
4. **Sensor Data Processing**
    - **Role:** Analyses multidimensional data from IoT sensors for anomaly detection, predictive maintenance, or monitoring.
    - **Techniques:**
        - Machine learning models like Decision Trees and LSTMs for pattern recognition.
    - **Use Case:** Identify anomalies in broadband router metrics (e.g., temperature, signal strength) to predict failures.
5. **Touch and Gesture Inputs**
    - **Role:** Interprets touch or gesture inputs from devices like touchscreens or motion sensors.
    - **Techniques:**
        - Gesture recognition algorithms using accelerometer data or computer vision.

   - **Use Case:** Enable gesture-based navigation in AR systems for immersive customer support applications.
6. **Multimodal Processing**
   - **Role:** Combines text, image, and audio data using multimodal AI models.
   - **Use Case:** Generate video captions by integrating audio and image cues, improving accessibility for visually impaired users.

Best Practices for the Pre-Processor Layer

1. **Multimodal Input Handling:** Design the Pre-Processor to support and integrate diverse input types (e.g., text, audio, images) to accommodate varied use cases.
2. **Dynamic Model Selection:** Leverage the **Model Gateway** to select optimal AI models for processing inputs based on task requirements.
3. **Contextual Enrichment:** Add metadata (e.g., customer IDs, timestamps) to enhance downstream processing accuracy.
4. **Compliance and Privacy:** Ensure compliance with regulatory standards (e.g., GDPR, EU AI Act) by anonymizing sensitive data during pre-processing.
5. **Scalability:** Optimize workflows for high-volume, low-latency processing to meet enterprise performance requirements.

Once the pre-processing is finished, the next step is to understand the customer/user intent.

2. Intent Classifier: Understanding User Needs

The Intent Classifier identifies the underlying intent in user inputs, determining what the user is trying to accomplish. This critical step ensures that the Orchestrator can assemble the right workflow and agents to address the specific need effectively.

The evolution of intent recognition has progressed through several stages: from simple rule-based systems that relied on manually crafted rules to modern transformer-based models with attention mechanisms that understand context and leverage transfer learning. These advanced models can accurately identify intents like "InternetRepair" from queries such as "Why is my internet so slow?" while understanding the contextual nuances that differentiate similar queries with different intents.

Key Functionalities of the Intent Classifier

1. **Intent Identification**
    - **Role:** Recognizes the primary goal or purpose behind a user query, such as diagnosing an outage or resolving a billing issue.

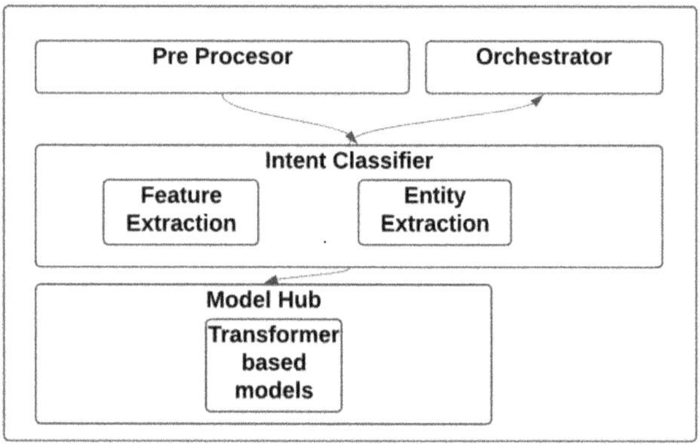

    - **Techniques:** Utilizes NLP models ranging from traditional supervised learning to advanced transformer-based models like BERT.
    - **Example Use Case:** For the query, "Why is my internet so slow?" the classifier identifies the intent as "InternetRepair."
2. **Contextual Understanding**
    - **Role:** Understand the context of user queries by analysing semantic relationships between words and phrases.
    - **Techniques:** Uses attention mechanisms in transformer models to process contextual clues.
    - **Example Use Case:** Differentiates between "I need faster internet" (intent: UpgradeRequest) and "My internet is too slow" (intent: InternetRepair).
3. **Multilingual Support**
    - **Role:** Handles diverse languages and dialects, enabling global deployment.

- **Techniques:** Incorporates pre-trained multilingual models like XLM-R or fine-tuned language-specific models.
- **Example Use Case:** Classifies intents in multiple languages, such as identifying "¿Por qué es tan lento mi internet?" as "InternetRepair" in Spanish.

4. **Ambiguity Management**
   - **Role:** Handles ambiguous queries by leveraging probabilistic scores or confidence thresholds to determine intent.
   - **Techniques:** Implements fallback mechanisms or requests clarification from the user when intent cannot be confidently identified.
   - **Example Use Case:** For a query like "I need help," the classifier might trigger a clarification workflow asking, "What do you need help with—billing or internet performance?"
5. **Entity Recognition Integration**
   - **Role:** Extract entities (e.g., "bill," "router," "New York") from user input to complement intent classification.
   - **Techniques:** Integrates entity extraction pipelines like spaCy or transformer-based models.
   - **Example Use Case:** For "Is there an outage in my area?" the classifier identifies the intent as "OutageCheck" and extracts the entity "area."

Best Practices for Intent Classification

1. **Model Selection Based on Task Complexity**
   - Use lightweight ML models for straightforward intent classification tasks and transformer-based models for nuanced, context-rich queries.
2. **Continuous Learning and Feedback Loops**
   - Implement mechanisms to retrain models using real-world customer interactions and feedback to improve accuracy over time.
3. **Confidence Thresholds for Ambiguity**
   - Set confidence thresholds to trigger fallback workflows when the model is uncertain about the intent.
4. **Support for Multimodal Inputs**

    - Design the Intent Classifier to handle text, speech, and multimodal inputs seamlessly.
5. **Explainability for Trust**
    - Leverage explainable AI techniques to provide insights into how intents are classified, building trust with end-users and stakeholders.
6. **Scalability for High Volumes**

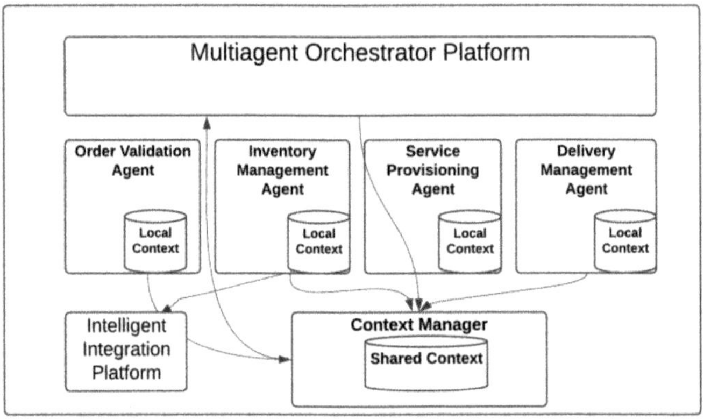

    - Optimize intent classification workflows for scalability to handle large volumes of concurrent user queries.

3. Context Manager: Enabling Coherent Interactions

The Context Manager maintains and shares context across agents and components, ensuring that all parts of the system have access to relevant information and can collaborate effectively. Context refers to all relevant data pertaining to a task, including user inputs, prior interactions, agent responses, diagnostics, and system states.

Through centralized context storage, the Context Manager maintains a unified repository of all relevant task data, capturing details about each interaction and dynamically updating context as new information becomes available. Context propagation ensures collaboration by allowing agents to share and propagate context data relevant to their specific operations. The system tracks changes to context through versioning to enable traceability, conflict resolution, and rollback mechanisms when needed.

At LegalDeal, when processing a complex regulatory compliance matter, the Context Manager ensures that all aspects of the client's situation – including previous advice, relevant jurisdictions, and specific industry regulations – are available to each specialised agent working on the case. This enables the ClauseAnalysisAgent to understand the broader implications of contract language and make appropriate recommendations within the full context of the client's situation.

4. Agent Registry: The Backbone of Agent Management

The Agent Registry serves as a centralized hub for managing and orchestrating agents within MOP. It plays a pivotal role in ensuring efficient, scalable, and modular agent interactions by maintaining metadata, enabling dynamic discovery, monitoring health, and supporting secure, real-time operations.

Agent metadata management maintains a repository of agent information, including capabilities, supported intents, API endpoints, versioning, and health status. Dynamic agent discovery enables the orchestrator to locate agents based on specific criteria, such as intent or capability. The registry continuously monitors agent health, flagging agents as "inactive" if they fail consecutive checks and automatically routing tasks away from degraded or unavailable agents.

For ComPlus's network operations centre, the Agent Registry maintains detailed profiles of specialised agents like the FaultDiagnosisAgent, NetworkOptimisationAgent, and CustomerNotificationAgent. When a service degradation occurs, the Orchestrator queries the registry to identify available agents with the appropriate capabilities, ensuring tasks are assigned efficiently even during peak incident periods.

5. AI Agents: The Building Blocks

An AI agent is an autonomous software entity designed to perform specific tasks, either independently or in collaboration with other agents and humans. Unlike traditional software components that simply execute predefined functions, agents can perceive their environment, make decisions based on reasoning, and take action to achieve their goals.

In the context of MOP, agents are specialised components that excel at particular tasks – from customer support and network diagnostics to document analysis and regulatory compliance. These agents leverage various AI technologies, including large language models, expert systems, and machine learning, to deliver capabilities that far exceed traditional automation. Agents perform several key functions within the MOP ecosystem: executing specific tasks assigned by the orchestrator, mapping incoming tasks to supported intents, retrieving and updating context via the Context Manager, communicating with other components to fulfil tasks collaboratively, reporting health status and performance metrics and supporting multiple instances to handle high workloads and ensure redundancy.

Key Functionalities of Agents

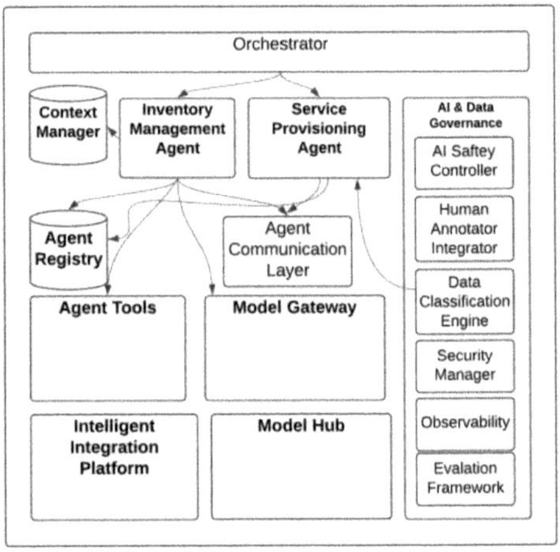

1. Task Execution

- **Role:** Perform specific tasks or subtasks assigned by the orchestrator, such as diagnosing a network issue or processing a payment.
- **Responsibilities:**
  - Execute tasks based on the assigned intent or capability.
  - Return results or statuses to the orchestrator after task completion.
- **Example Use Case:** The ***TechSupportAgent*** diagnoses a router issue and reports, "No hardware issues detected."

2. Intent Handling

- **Role:** Handle specific intents, as defined in the Agent Registry, to fulfil user requests.
- **Responsibilities:**
  - Map incoming tasks to supported intents.

    - Respond intelligently based on the identified intent.
- **Example Use Case:** For the intent "InternetRepair," the **TechSupportAgent** performs diagnostics while the ***NetworkDiagnosticsAgent*** analyses network performance.

3. Context Interaction

- **Role:** Retrieve, update, and propagate context via the Context Manager to ensure synchronized task execution.
- **Responsibilities:**
    - Retrieve relevant context data for task execution.
    - Update context with task outcomes or intermediate results.
- **Example Use Case:** The ***TechSupportAgent*** retrieves the issue context ("Internet not working") from the Context Manager and updates it after diagnosing the router.

4. Communication with Other Components

- **Role:** Interact with the orchestrator, Context Manager, and other agents to fulfil tasks collaboratively.
- **Responsibilities:**
    - Receive task assignments and instructions from the orchestrator.
    - Share results with other agents through the orchestrator or directly via the Context Manager.
- **Example Use Case:** The ***BillingAgent*** retrieves the user's payment history from the Context Manager and informs the orchestrator of any discrepancies.

5. Health and Performance Monitoring

- **Role:** Report health status and performance metrics to the Agent Registry for real-time monitoring and load balancing.
- **Responsibilities:**
    - Periodically report health status (e.g., active, inactive, overloaded).

- Provide performance metrics, such as task completion time and success rates.
- **Example Use Case:** The ***TechSupportAgent*** reports an "active" status and a 98% task success rate to the Agent Registry.

6. Scalability and Redundancy

- **Role:** Scale horizontally to handle high workloads and ensure redundancy during agent failures.
- **Responsibilities:**
    - Support multiple instances of the agent to distribute workloads.
    - Provide failover mechanisms to ensure continuity during outages.
- **Example Use Case:** Multiple instances of the ***NetworkDiagnosticsAgent*** process simultaneous diagnostic requests during peak hours.

Best Practices for Agent Implementation

1. **Single Responsibility Principle:**
    - Design agents to perform a single, well-defined function to ensure simplicity and maintainability.
2. **Modularity and Reusability:**
    - Build agents as modular components that can be reused across different workflows.
3. **Stateless Design:**
    - Design agents to be stateless, relying on the Context Manager for state management to improve scalability and fault tolerance.
4. **Dynamic Registration:**
    - Ensure agents can register and deregister themselves dynamically with the Agent Registry to support scalability and flexibility.
5. **Interoperability:**
    - Use standardised communication protocols (e.g., REST, gRPC) to ensure seamless interaction with other components.

6. Agent Communication Layer: The Nervous System

The Agent Communication Layer functions as the nervous system of MOP, enabling agents to share information and collaborate seamlessly. It supports message exchange between agents, maintains shared context across agents, orchestrates complex tasks involving multiple agents, and manages situations where multiple agents might clash over shared resources using priority systems and locking mechanisms.

As organisations rely more on AI agents, it becomes crucial for these agents to communicate in a standard, efficient way. This is where protocols like Google's A2A come in. A2A is an open protocol that lets agents from different vendors and frameworks talk to each other securely—without sharing their private memory or tools. A2A provides a common language for agents, making it easier for them to:

- Share context and data: Agents can send structured information to each other, so everyone is working with the latest facts.
- Coordinate actions: Agents can plan and adjust their roles in real-time based on what's happening in the system.
- Work across platforms: By following standard rules, agents from different systems can work together without extra effort.
- Stay secure: A2A includes strong authentication and authorization, so only trusted agents can communicate, and sensitive data stays protected.

Key Features of Agent Communication Protocols (ACPs) like A2A

- Contextual Messaging: Agents exchange detailed, structured information to make better decisions.
- Dynamic Coordination: Agents can change their behavior and responsibilities on the fly, depending on real-time needs.
- Interoperability: Standard protocols mean agents from different backgrounds can work together easily.
- Security and Governance: Built-in security features keep communication safe and compliant with company policies.

The Agent Communication Layer supports multiple communication models to meet different workflow requirements:

Model	Description	Example Use Case
Direct Communication	Agents communicate synchronously via REST, gRPC, or WebSocket APIs.	Low-latency tasks like triggering traffic rerouting in ComPlus.
Message Broker Integration	Agents exchange messages asynchronously through brokers like Kafka or RabbitMQ.	Fault notifications in ComPlus or compliance alerts in LegalDeal.
Shared Context Store	Agents share data indirectly by reading/writing to a centralized context store.	Regulatory analysis in LegalDeal or progress tracking in ComPlus workflows.
Event-Driven Triggers	Agents trigger workflows dynamically based on predefined events.	Clause analysis workflows in LegalDeal or fault recovery in ComPlus.

In summary, the Agent Communication Layer—especially when powered by protocols like A2A—ensures that agents can collaborate, coordinate, and make smart decisions together, no matter where they come from or what tools they use.

7. Agent Tools

The Agent Tools component is a foundational element of the Multi-Agent Orchestrator Platform (MOP), designed to empower agents with the operational capabilities required to perform tasks effectively. Unlike the Model Hub, which provides decision-making capabilities, Agent Tools focuses on the execution layer—bridging the gap between agents and external systems. These tools equip agents to interact with external systems, retrieve and process data, handle files, communicate with users, and ensure secure task execution.

For enterprises like ComPlus and LegalDeal, Agent Tools play a critical role in enabling agents to perform real-world operations. Whether querying APIs for network diagnostics at ComPlus or processing legal documents at LegalDeal, this component ensures seamless integration with external systems while maintaining security and compliance.

Core Functions of Agent Tools

The Agent Tools component provides a comprehensive suite of functionalities that empower agents to execute tasks efficiently. Its core functions include:

1. **External System Integration:** Enables agents to interact with third-party systems, APIs, and databases.
2. **Data Fetching Tools:** Allows agents to query internal or external data sources for specific information retrieval.
3. **File Handling Tools:** Supports file uploads, downloads, parsing, and management.
4. **Communication Tools:** Facilitates communication between agents, users, and external systems.
5. **Security and Compliance Tools:** Ensures secure task execution through authentication, authorization, logging, and monitoring.

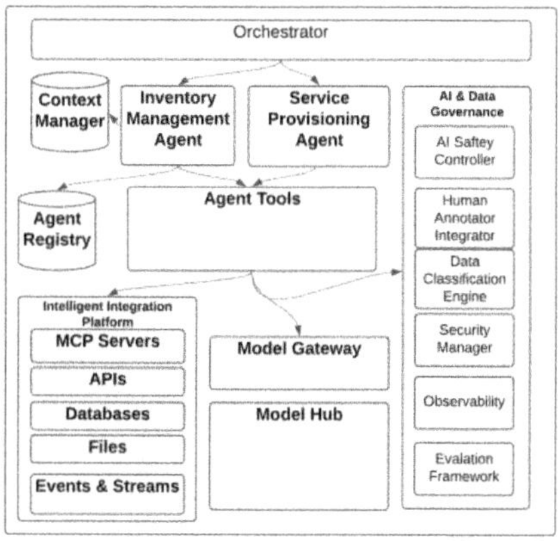

Technical Integration with MOP Components

Agent Tools integrates seamlessly with other MOP components to enable efficient workflows and secure operations. Its integration points include:

Orchestrator Integration

The Orchestrator coordinates workflows by assigning tasks to agents equipped with Agent Tools. This integration ensures that workflows are carried out effectively by leveraging the appropriate tools for each task.

- **Example:** At ComPlus, when a ServiceProvisioningAgent is tasked with rerouting network traffic during an outage, the

Orchestrator uses External System Integration tools to connect the agent to network management systems.

Model Hub Integration

Agent Tools works closely with the Model Hub by executing operational tasks based on decisions made by AI models. While the Model Hub provides insights or predictions, Agent Tools handles downstream execution.

Context Manager Integration

The Context Manager enriches Agent Tools by providing real-time contextual metadata that informs tool usage. This integration allows agents to dynamically adapt their actions based on current workflow conditions.

- **Example:** At ComPlus, when a CustomerAgent fetches account details from a CRM system, the Context Manager provides contextual information such as customer preferences or previous interactions.

AI Safety Controller Integration

The AI Safety Controller ensures that all actions performed via Agent Tools comply with ethical guidelines and organisational policies. This integration enforces dynamic policy checks during tool usage.

- **Example:** At LegalDeal, when a DocumentAutomationAgent retrieves confidential client documents using Data Fetching Tools, the AI Safety Controller validates access permissions before granting retrieval rights.

Security Manager Integration

The Security Manager safeguards interactions facilitated by Agent Tools through encryption protocols and access controls. This integration ensures secure communication between agents and external systems.

- **Example:** At ComPlus, when a TechSupportAgent downloads router logs using File Handling Tools, encryption enforced by the Security Manager protects sensitive data during transfer.

Interaction with Agents

Agent Tools are directly called by agents during task execution. This interaction ensures that agents can access tools dynamically based on their specific operational needs without requiring manual intervention or complex configurations.

- **Example:** At ComPlus, a FaultManagementAgent calls Data Fetching Tools to retrieve diagnostic logs from external systems while simultaneously using Communication Tools to notify administrators of detected issues.
- **Example:** At LegalDeal, a ClientEngagementAgent uses Communication Tools like messaging platforms to update clients on case progress while leveraging File Handling tools for document management.

Core Responsibilities of Agent Tools

- External System Integration: Agent Tools enable seamless interaction with third-party systems such as APIs or databases.
- Data Fetching Tools: Agents can query internal or external data sources for specific information retrieval.
- File Handling Tools: These tools support file uploads, downloads, parsing, and management.
- Communication Tools: Facilitates communication between agents and users or external systems via notifications or messaging platforms.
- Security and Compliance Tools: Ensures secure task execution through robust authentication mechanisms and activity logging.

Practical Implementation for Cognitive Enterprises

The Agent Tools component operates continuously within MOP to support diverse enterprise workflows requiring interaction with external systems or data sources. Its practical applications include:

- **For ComPlus:** The TechSupportAgent uses External System Integration tools to fetch router logs while leveraging File Handling tools to parse configuration data during diagnostics.
- **For LegalDeal:** The ClauseAnalyserAgent processes uploaded contracts using File Handling tools while ensuring secure access through Security Manager integration.

Governance and Compliance Benefits

By embedding robust operational capabilities into MOP's architecture, Agent Tools deliver significant governance benefits:

1. **Operational Efficiency:** Streamlines agent workflows by providing prebuilt tools for common tasks such as data retrieval or file handling.
2. **Security Assurance:** Ensures all interactions are encrypted and logged for auditability.
3. **Compliance Adherence:** Enforces organisational policies through dynamic checks during tool usage.
4. **Scalability:** Supports complex workflows requiring simultaneous interaction with multiple external systems.

For global enterprises like ComPlus operating across diverse regulatory environments, Agent Tools applies region-specific rules during system integration to ensure compliance with local laws. Similarly, LegalDeal benefits from automated safeguards that maintain client confidentiality while enabling efficient collaboration on sensitive legal matters.

8. Model Gateway: Dynamic Interface for AI Model Execution

The Model Gateway is a critical component of the Multi-Agent Orchestrator Platform (MOP), serving as the operational bridge between agents and AI models housed in the Model Hub. While the

Model Hub focuses on hosting, versioning, and managing AI models, the Model Gateway abstracts the complexities of model selection, invocation, and execution. It dynamically matches agent task requirements with the most suitable model, executes the selected model, and returns results in formats that agents can process efficiently.

For enterprises like ComPlus and LegalDeal, the Model Gateway enables intelligent decision-making by retrieving and executing best-fit models for specific workflows. Optimizing model invocation and handling complexities such as load balancing and fallback mechanisms ensures seamless integration of AI into enterprise workflows while maintaining scalability, flexibility, and performance.

Core Functions of the Model Gateway

The Model Gateway provides a robust operational layer that connects agents to AI models in real time. Its core functions include:

1. **Dynamic Model Selection:** Matches agent task requirements with the most relevant model in the Model Hub based on metadata such as task type, domain specificity, performance metrics, inference cost, scalability, and criticality.
2. **Model Invocation:** Executes selected models while managing input/output formats to meet task-specific requirements.
3. **Load Balancing:** Ensures high-volume requests are handled efficiently by managing resource allocation across concurrent workflows.
4. **Abstraction of Complexity:** Provides a simplified API interface for agents, hiding complexities like model versioning or execution pipelines.
5. **Fallback Mechanisms:** Implements robust strategies to handle model unavailability or execution failures.

Technical Integration with MOP Components

The Model Gateway integrates seamlessly with other MOP components to ensure efficient workflows, secure operations, and intelligent model utilization. Its integration points include:

Orchestrator Integration

The Orchestrator relies on the Model Gateway to dynamically request and execute AI models during task orchestration. This integration ensures that agents are equipped with the most appropriate models for their assigned tasks.

- **Example:** At ComPlus, when a FaultManagementAgent is tasked with diagnosing network issues, the Orchestrator routes this request through the Model Gateway to retrieve and execute a fault prediction model from the Model Hub.

Context Manager Integration

The Context Manager provides task-specific metadata that informs model selection within the Model Gateway. This integration ensures that selected models are contextually relevant to specific workflows.

- **Example:** At LegalDeal, when analyzing a high-risk legal contract flagged by the Context Manager, the ClauseAnalyserAgent leverages a compliance analysis model retrieved via the Model Gateway for precise evaluation.

Model Hub Integration

The Model Gateway serves as an operational extension of the Model Hub by dynamically selecting and invoking models stored within it. The integration ensures that agents access only optimized and approved models for their tasks.

AI Safety Controller Integration

The AI Safety Controller enforces governance policies during model invocation by ensuring that selected models comply with ethical guidelines and regulatory standards. This integration guarantees responsible AI usage.

Security Manager Integration

The Security Manager protects sensitive data processed during model execution by enforcing encryption protocols and access controls. This integration ensures secure communication between agents and models.

- **Example:** At ComPlus, when a bandwidth optimisation model processes customer data retrieved via the Model Gateway, encryption enforced by the Security Manager safeguards this information.

Factors Influencing Dynamic Model Selection

The Model Gateway employs sophisticated criteria to select optimal AI models for execution based on the following:

1. **Performance Metrics:** Prioritizes models with high accuracy, precision, recall, or F1 scores for specific tasks.
2. **Inference Cost:** Considers computational costs associated with executing models to optimize resource usage.
3. **Scalability:** Evaluate whether selected models can handle concurrent requests efficiently during peak usage.
4. **Task Criticality:** Ensures critical tasks (e.g., compliance checks or network fault diagnosis) are assigned to highly reliable models.
5. **Latency Requirements:** Selects low-latency models for real-time applications where rapid responses are essential.
6. **Domain Specificity:** Matches agent tasks with domain-specific models fine-tuned for particular use cases (e.g., legal document analysis or telecommunications diagnostics).

Practical Implementation for Cognitive Enterprises

The Model Gateway operates continuously within MOP to support diverse enterprise workflows with high-performing AI models. Its practical applications include:

- **For ComPlus:** The Model Gateway retrieves diagnostic models from the Model Hub to help FaultManagementAgents predict network outages in real-time while balancing resource usage across multiple requests.

- **For LegalDeal:** It dynamically invokes multilingual legal analysis models for cross-border compliance checks during contract reviews while ensuring fallback mechanisms are in place.

Governance and Compliance Benefits

By embedding robust operational mechanisms into MOP's architecture, the Model Gateway delivers significant governance benefits:

1. **Operational Efficiency:** Dynamically matches agent tasks with optimal AI models to maximize workflow efficiency.
2. **Scalability:** Handles high-volume requests from multiple agents without performance degradation.
3. **Continuity Assurance:** Implements fallback mechanisms to ensure uninterrupted workflows even during failures.
4. **Transparency:** Logs all interactions between agents and models for auditability and compliance purposes.

For global enterprises like ComPlus operating across diverse regulatory environments, the Model Gateway applies region-specific rules during model selection to ensure compliance with local laws. Similarly, LegalDeal benefits from automated safeguards that maintain client confidentiality while enabling efficient collaboration on sensitive legal matters.

9. Model Hub: Central Repository for AI Model Management

The Model Hub is a foundational component of the Multi-Agent Orchestrator Platform (MOP), serving as the backbone for managing, governing, and optimizing AI models. It hosts a diverse repository of models, including Large Language Models (LLMs), Small Language Models (SLMs), and highly specialised task-specific models. Acting as the single source of truth for all AI models within MOP, the Model Hub ensures that agents have access to the most appropriate and optimized models to perform their tasks effectively.

For enterprises like ComPlus and LegalDeal, the Model Hub is indispensable for enabling workflows that require advanced reasoning, prediction, and domain-specific expertise. While the Model Gateway dynamically selects and routes the best model for specific tasks, the Model Hub focuses on managing the entire lifecycle of models—providing a robust infrastructure for storage, fine-tuning, monitoring, and governance.

Core Functions of the Model Hub

The Model Hub provides a comprehensive framework for managing AI models throughout their lifecycle. Its core functions include:

1. **Model Lifecycle Management:** Onboarding, fine-tuning, versioning, and retiring models to ensure relevance and performance.
2. **Centralized Repository:** Acting as a single source of truth for all AI models used within MOP.
3. **Model Governance:** Enforcing ethical use, compliance with regulations, and maintaining audit trails.
4. **Performance Monitoring:** Tracking metrics like accuracy and latency to ensure optimal model performance.
5. **Scalability and Security:** Supporting seamless integration of new models while maintaining enterprise-grade security.

Technical Integration with MOP Components

The Model Hub integrates seamlessly with other MOP components to ensure efficient workflows, secure operations, and consistent model usage across the platform. Its integration points include:

Orchestrator Integration

The Orchestrator relies on the Model Hub to provide agents with access to accurate and up-to-date AI models for their tasks. This integration ensures that workflows are powered by optimized models tailored to specific requirements.

- **Example:** At ComPlus, when a FaultManagementAgent is assigned a task to diagnose network issues, the Orchestrator retrieves a fault prediction model from the Model Hub to guide decision-making.

Context Manager Integration

The Context Manager provides contextual metadata that informs model selection and usage. This integration ensures that agents leverage models tailored to specific scenarios.

- **Example:** At LegalDeal, when analyzing a contract flagged as high-risk by the Context Manager, the ClauseAnalyserAgent uses a specialised compliance model retrieved from the Model Hub.

Data Classification Engine Integration

The Data Classification Engine identifies sensitive data elements such as PII or financial records. The Model Hub uses this classification metadata to ensure that only authorized models process sensitive data.

- **Example:** At ComPlus, customer PII tagged by the Data Classification Engine is processed exclusively by privacy-compliant models retrieved from the Model Hub.

AI Safety Controller Integration

The AI Safety Controller enforces governance policies on model usage based on ethical guidelines and regulatory requirements. The integration ensures that only compliant models are deployed in workflows.

- **Example:** At LegalDeal, before deploying a new regulatory analysis model from the Model Hub, the AI Safety Controller validates it against ethical guidelines to ensure fairness in decision-making.

Security Manager Integration

The Security Manager protects sensitive data handled by models in the Model Hub through encryption and access controls. This integration ensures enterprise-grade security during model usage.

- **Example:** At ComPlus, when a bandwidth optimisation model processes sensitive network data, encryption protocols enforced by the Security Manager safeguard this information.

Model Gateway Integration

The Model Gateway dynamically selects and routes inference requests to appropriate models hosted in the Model Hub based on task requirements. This integration ensures seamless execution of AI-driven workflows.

- **Example:** At LegalDeal, when a ContractReviewAgent requests an analysis of multilingual contracts for cross-border cases, the Model Gateway retrieves an appropriate language processing model from the Model Hub for inference.

Practical Implementation for Cognitive Enterprises

The Model Hub operates continuously within MOP to support diverse enterprise workflows with high-performing AI models. Its practical applications include:

- **For ComPlus:** The Model Hub hosts specialised fault prediction and bandwidth optimisation models fine-tuned with telecommunications-specific data.
- **For LegalDeal:** It provides legal language processing models customized for compliance checks and contract analysis in cross-border legal cases.

Governance and Compliance Benefits

By embedding robust governance mechanisms into MOP's operations, the Model Hub delivers significant benefits:

1. **Regulatory Compliance:** Tracks all model-related activities to ensure adherence to standards like GDPR.
2. **Operational Resilience:** Maintains version control to prevent disruptions caused by outdated or underperforming models.
3. **Ethical Assurance:** Evaluate models for bias and fairness before deployment.
4. **Transparency:** Logs all updates and usage activities for auditability.

For global enterprises like ComPlus operating across diverse regulatory environments, the Model Hub applies region-specific rules during model fine-tuning to ensure compliance with local laws. Similarly, LegalDeal benefits from automated safeguards that maintain client confidentiality while enabling efficient collaboration on sensitive legal matters.

10. AI Safety Controller: Ensuring Ethical and Secure AI Operations

As AI systems become more integral to enterprise workflows, ensuring their safety, ethical compliance, and adherence to organisational policies is paramount. The AI Safety Controller is a cornerstone of the Multi-Agent Orchestrator Platform (MOP), designed to embed safety mechanisms, mitigate risks, and enforce transparency across all agent operations. By integrating real-time monitoring, policy enforcement, bias detection, explainability, and detailed audit logging, the AI Safety Controller ensures that AI agents remain responsible, trustworthy, and aligned with enterprise objectives.

The introduction of the EU AI Act marks a watershed moment in AI regulation, setting comprehensive standards for risk management, transparency, and accountability. Organisations must now classify their AI systems according to risk, implement robust governance frameworks, and ensure ongoing compliance with evolving legal requirements. For high-risk AI, this means establishing risk management systems, maintaining detailed technical documentation, ensuring data quality, and embedding human oversight into automated decision-making. These requirements are not limited to the EU; they are likely to influence global best practices and regulatory trends, making proactive compliance a strategic imperative for all cognitive enterprises.

The AI Safety Controller is purpose-built to operationalise the EU AI Act's requirements for trustworthy, transparent, and compliant AI. Acting as a central governance and oversight layer, it continuously monitors agent workflows for alignment with organisational policies, ethical guidelines, and regulatory obligations-including those defined by the EU AI Act. It enforces risk management protocols by dynamically evaluating agent actions and outputs for potential bias, discrimination, or drift, leveraging both automated detection and human-in-the-loop review for high-risk cases. It ensures transparency and explainability by logging all agent decisions, providing human-readable rationales, and maintaining comprehensive audit trailskey for regulatory reporting and stakeholder trust. By orchestrating these controls in real-time, the AI Safety Controller enables enterprises to meet the EU AI Act's demands for risk classification, technical documentation, ongoing monitoring, and human oversight-transforming regulatory compliance from a static requirement into an active, adaptive capability within the cognitive enterprise.

For enterprises like ComPlus and LegalDeal, where workflows involve sensitive data and high-stakes decisions, the AI Safety Controller plays a critical role in safeguarding operations against risks while maintaining compliance with ethical guidelines and regulatory standards.

Core Functions of the AI Safety Controller

The AI Safety Controller employs a range of sophisticated mechanisms to ensure safe and ethical agent operations. Its core functions include:

1. **Policy Compliance Enforcement:** Dynamically enforces predefined policies to ensure workflows adhere to organisational rules, ethical standards, and regulations.
2. **Bias Detection and Mitigation:** Identifies and mitigates discriminatory patterns in agent outputs to ensure fairness.
3. **Risk Assessment:** Evaluates tasks to identify potential risks and escalates high-stakes actions for human oversight.

4. **Explainability and Transparency:** Ensures all agent actions are interpretable and provide clear rationales.
5. **Audit Logging:** Tracks agent interactions for compliance reporting and forensic analysis.
6. **Real-Time Monitoring:** Detects anomalies in agent behaviour and initiates corrective actions.

Technical Integration with MOP Components

The AI Safety Controller integrates seamlessly with other MOP components to provide comprehensive governance across workflows. Its integration points include:

Orchestrator Integration

The AI Safety Controller works closely with the Orchestrator to enforce safety policies during task assignment and execution. It evaluates agent actions dynamically against predefined rules stored in the Policy Engine.

- **Example:** When a FaultManagementAgent at ComPlus attempts to reroute network traffic during an outage, the AI Safety Controller ensures that critical services like healthcare networks are prioritized.

Context Manager Integration

The Context Manager provides essential metadata that informs the AI Safety Controller about workflow context. This integration enables adaptive policy enforcement based on real-time conditions.

- **Example:** At LegalDeal, when a RegulatoryAgent analyses client data for compliance checks, the Context Manager supplies contextual information about data sensitivity levels. This ensures anonymization policies are applied appropriately.

Data Classification Engine Integration

The Data Classification Engine identifies sensitive data elements such as PII or financial records. The AI Safety Controller uses this classification metadata to enforce privacy safeguards dynamically.

- **Example:** When customer billing information is tagged as PII at ComPlus, the AI Safety Controller ensures that only authorized agents can access or process this data.

Security Manager Integration

The Security Manager provides encryption services and access controls that complement the AI Safety Controller's safety mechanisms. Together, they protect sensitive data from unauthorized access or breaches.

- **Example:** At LegalDeal, when a ClauseAnalyserAgent accesses legal contracts containing privileged information, the Security Manager encrypts sensitive sections while the AI Safety Controller monitors adherence to ethical guidelines.

Behaviour Analytics Engine Integration

The Behaviour Analytics Engine continuously monitors agent activities for anomalies or policy violations. The AI Safety Controller leverages these insights to detect risks proactively.

- **Example:** If a BillingAgent at ComPlus exhibits unusual behaviour by attempting unauthorized access to payment records, the Behaviour Analytics Engine flags this activity for immediate intervention by the AI Safety Controller.

Practical Implementation for Cognitive Enterprises

The AI Safety Controller operates continuously within the MOP ecosystem to ensure safe operations across diverse workflows. Its practical applications include:

- **For ComPlus:** The AI Safety Controller monitors bandwidth allocation models for fairness while ensuring compliance with regional privacy regulations.
- **For LegalDeal:** It tracks ClauseAnalyserAgent decisions during contract reviews to ensure they align with legal standards and ethical practices.

Governance and Compliance Benefits

By embedding robust safety mechanisms into every aspect of MOP's operations, the AI Safety Controller delivers significant governance benefits:

1. **Regulatory Compliance:** Maintains audit trails of all agent actions for adherence to standards like GDPR.
2. **Operational Resilience:** Flags high-risk actions for human review to prevent costly failures.
3. **Ethical Assurance:** Ensures agents operate within defined ethical boundaries.
4. **Transparency:** Provides explainable decision-making processes that build trust in AI systems.

For global enterprises like ComPlus operating across diverse regulatory environments, the AI Safety Controller applies region-specific rules based on workflow context to ensure compliance with local laws. Similarly, LegalDeal benefits from automated safeguards that protect client confidentiality while enabling efficient collaboration on sensitive legal matters.

11. Security Manager: Ensuring Robust Security and Compliance

In an era of increasing cybersecurity threats and stringent regulatory requirements, the Security Manager serves as a critical component of the Multi-Agent Orchestrator Platform (MOP). It ensures that all AI-driven operations are secure, compliant, and resilient against evolving threats. Acting as the central governance layer for security, the Security Manager enforces Zero Trust Security (ZTS) principles, implements role-based access controls, monitors agent behaviour in real-time, and mitigates risks associated with data breaches, unauthorized access, and malicious actions.

For enterprises like ComPlus and LegalDeal, where workflows involve sensitive customer data, proprietary models, or regulatory compliance requirements, the Security Manager is indispensable. It prevents breaches, detects anomalies, and secures communications across the platform while ensuring adherence to industry standards and organisational policies.

Key Capabilities of the Security Manager

The Security Manager employs advanced mechanisms to safeguard sensitive data and ensure operational trustworthiness. Its key capabilities include:

1. **Zero Trust Security (ZTS):** Verifies every interaction to secure operations regardless of origin.
2. **Role-Based Access Control (RBAC):** Minimizes privileges by restricting access based on roles and context.
3. **Real-Time Behaviour Monitoring:** Detects anomalies or unauthorized actions using AI-driven analytics.
4. **Secure Communication:** Protects data exchanges through encryption protocols like TLS/SSL.
5. **Incident Response Automation:** Mitigates threats by isolating compromised agents or escalating incidents.
6. **Compliance Assurance:** Tracks adherence to regulatory standards like GDPR through detailed audit logs.

Technical Integration with MOP Components

The Security Manager integrates seamlessly with other MOP components to provide a unified security framework across workflows. Its integration points include:

Orchestrator Integration

The Security Manager collaborates with the Orchestrator to enforce security policies at every stage of agent workflows. It evaluates access requests dynamically based on agent roles, task types, and data sensitivity levels before allowing task execution.

- **Example:** When a ServiceProvisioningAgent requests access to configuration data at ComPlus, the Security Manager ensures that only agents with appropriate clearances can access sensitive information by ensuring role-based access control.

Context Manager Integration

The integration with the Context Manager ensures that security policies are context-aware and adaptive. Classification metadata from the Context Manager is used to dynamically adjust access controls and enforce security measures.

- **Example:** If a legal document at LegalDeal is flagged as containing sensitive client information, this classification metadata informs the Security Manager to apply stricter access controls throughout the workflow.

AI Safety and Control Integration

The Security Manager works closely with the AI Safety and Control component to enforce privacy policies dynamically based on security events or detected anomalies. This integration ensures that agents handle information in compliance with organisational policies.

- **Example:** When unusual behaviour is detected in a BillingAgent at ComPlus (e.g., accessing restricted customer data), the AI Safety component triggers immediate policy enforcement actions such as revoking access or isolating the agent.

Data Classification Engine Integration

The Data Classification Engine provides critical metadata that informs the Security Manager about data sensitivity levels. This collaboration enables automated encryption, anonymization, or tokenization of sensitive data fields.

- **Example:** If customer financial information is detected in a LegalDeal contract, the Data Classification Engine triggers encryption services from the Security Manager before storing or processing the data further.

Security Monitoring System

The Security Manager integrates with MOP's logging and auditing systems to maintain comprehensive records of all interactions. These logs are essential for compliance reporting and forensic analysis in case of incidents.

- **Example:** Logs generated during a RegulatoryAgent's compliance analysis are stored securely for future audits or investigations.

Practical Implementation for Cognitive Enterprises

The Security Manager operates continuously within the MOP ecosystem to protect workflows involving sensitive data. Its real-world applications include:

- **For ComPlus:** The Security Manager encrypts customer billing information during transmission and monitors agent activities for unauthorized access attempts.
- **For LegalDeal:** It ensures secure communication between ClauseAnalyserAgent and legal databases while maintaining detailed audit trails for compliance purposes.

Governance and Compliance Benefits

By embedding robust security mechanisms into every aspect of MOP's operations, the Security Manager delivers significant governance benefits:

1. **Regulatory Compliance:** Ensures adherence to standards like GDPR by maintaining comprehensive audit logs.
2. **Operational Resilience:** Automates threat responses to minimize downtime during security incidents.

3. **Data Protection:** Safeguards sensitive information through encryption and anonymization techniques.
4. **Trustworthiness:** Builds confidence in AI-driven operations by ensuring secure interactions across agents, tools, and external systems.

For global enterprises like ComPlus operating across diverse regulatory environments, the Security Manager applies region-specific rules based on data origin to ensure compliance with local laws. Similarly, LegalDeal benefits from automated safeguards that protect client confidentiality while enabling efficient collaboration.

12. Data Classification Engine: Privacy and Compliance

In today's data-driven world, organisations handle vast amounts of information ranging from harmless public data to highly sensitive personal and financial details. As cognitive enterprises evolve, the ability to properly classify this data becomes not just a compliance requirement but a fundamental business necessity. The Data Classification Engine serves as the guardian of information within the Multi-Agent Orchestrator Platform (MOP), ensuring that every piece of data is properly identified, categorized, and handled according to its sensitivity level.

At its core, data classification is about understanding what information you have and how it should be protected. For telecommunications giant ComPlus, this might involve categorizing customer billing information, network usage patterns, and personal details. Similarly, legal services firm LegalDeal must carefully classify client information, case details, and sensitive contractual terms. Without proper classification, these organisations risk not only compliance violations but also potentially damaging data breaches.

The Data Classification Engine handles this critical task automatically, examining incoming data streams in real-time and applying appropriate classification tags based on content, context, and regulatory requirements. This process ensures that every agent in the MOP ecosystem interacts with data in a manner appropriate to its sensitivity level, maintaining security and compliance throughout all workflows.

Key Capabilities of the Data Classification Engine

The Data Classification Engine employs several sophisticated mechanisms to identify and categorize data effectively. At its foundation is content-based analysis, which examines the actual information within documents, messages, and data fields to identify sensitive elements such as credit card numbers, social security numbers, and health information. This analysis occurs in real-time as data flows through the system, ensuring that classification happens before any agent processing begins.

Pattern recognition algorithms within the engine can identify common formats of sensitive information even when they appear within unstructured text. For example, the engine can recognize the distinctive pattern of a credit card number embedded in a customer service transcript at ComPlus or identify personal health information in case notes at LegalDeal. Once identified, this information is tagged with appropriate classification labels such as "PII" (Personally Identifiable Information), "Financial," or "Health Data," creating a metadata layer that travels with the information throughout its lifecycle in the system.

Context-aware classification extends beyond simple pattern matching to understand the broader context in which data appears. This capability allows the engine to make more nuanced classification decisions based on where the data originated, who created it, and how it's being used. For instance, a customer's address in a public directory might be classified differently than the same address in a financial document, reflecting the different privacy implications of each context.

Technical Integration with MOP Components

The Data Classification Engine integrates seamlessly with other MOP components through a series of carefully designed interfaces that ensure efficient data flow while maintaining security boundaries. This integration enables the entire platform to respect data sensitivity throughout complex workflows. The Data Classification Engine connects directly with the Orchestrator through a pre-processing pipeline that examines all incoming data before task assignment. This integration ensures that the Orchestrator can make informed decisions about which agents should handle specific data based on classification levels and security requirements. The technical implementation uses a stream processing model where data flows through classification before entering the main orchestration workflow.

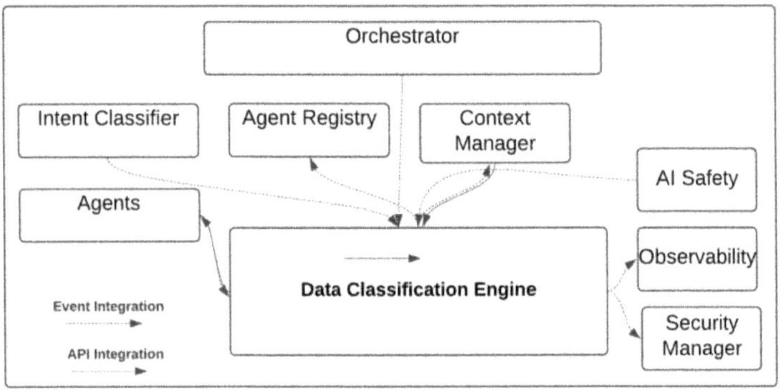

When a customer contacts ComPlus with a billing inquiry, the Orchestrator routes the incoming data through the Classification Engine first. The engine identifies and tags sensitive elements like account numbers and payment details before the Orchestrator assigns the task to appropriate agents with the necessary security clearances.

Context Manager Integration

The Connection with the Context Manager ensures that classification metadata becomes part of the shared context available to all agents in a workflow. This bidirectional integration allows classification decisions to be influenced by existing context while simultaneously enriching that context with new classification information. The implementation uses a metadata enhancement pattern where classification tags are stored alongside other contextual information in the central context store.

For LegalDeal, this means that when a legal document is analysed, its classification becomes part of the context available to all agents in the workflow. If the document contains sensitive client information, this classification travels with the document through every step of the analysis process, ensuring appropriate handling throughout.

AI Safety and Control Integration

Perhaps the most crucial integration is with the AI Safety and Control Component, which relies on classification metadata to enforce privacy and compliance policies. This connection enables dynamic policy enforcement based on data sensitivity levels, ensuring that agents handle information in accordance with organisational and regulatory requirements. The implementation uses an event-driven architecture where classification changes trigger immediate policy evaluations.

When the Classification Engine identifies PII in a customer support request at ComPlus, it immediately triggers appropriate controls in the AI Safety component. These controls might include data masking for certain agents, restrictions on how the information can be stored, or requirements for explicit consent before processing.

Security Manager Integration

The Data Classification Engine works closely with the Security Manager to implement technical protection measures based on classification levels. This integration enables automated encryption, anonymization, or tokenization of sensitive data fields based on their classification tags. The implementation uses a service-oriented architecture where the Classification Engine can request security services for specific data elements.

For example, when customer financial information is detected in a LegalDeal contract, the Classification Engine can automatically request encryption services from the Security Manager before this information is stored or processed further in the workflow.

Practical Implementation for Cognitive Enterprises

In practice, the Data Classification Engine operates continuously as data flows through the MOP ecosystem, providing real-time classification that adapts to changing data patterns and regulatory requirements. For ComPlus, this means customer service interactions are automatically scanned for sensitive information, with appropriate protections applied before any processing occurs.

When a customer discusses account details with a ComPlus representative, the Data Classification Engine analyses the conversation in real-time, identifying and tagging elements like phone numbers, addresses, and account details. These classifications trigger appropriate security controls, such as masking sensitive fields when displaying information to certain agents or encrypting specific data before storage.

For LegalDeal, the engine might classify different sections of legal contracts based on their sensitivity, ensuring that personally identifiable information receives higher protection than general terms and conditions. This granular approach allows the system to apply appropriate controls to specific data elements rather than treating entire documents with the same security level.

The implementation uses a tiered classification approach that typically includes categories such as:

1. Public Information - Data that can be freely shared without restrictions
2. Internal Use Only - Information restricted to within the organisation
3. Confidential - Sensitive business information requiring careful handling
4. Highly Confidential - Critical data requiring the strictest protection measures
5. Regulated Data - Information subject to specific regulatory requirements (PII, health data, financial records)

Each category triggers specific handling requirements, access controls, and security measures that are automatically enforced throughout the MOP ecosystem.

Governance and Compliance Benefits

The Data Classification Engine provides significant governance and compliance benefits by creating a consistent, automated approach to data handling. By maintaining detailed audit logs of all classification decisions, the engine supports compliance with regulations like GDPR and industry-specific requirements.

For ComPlus, operating across multiple countries with varying privacy regulations, the Classification Engine can apply region-specific rules based on data origin and applicable laws. This capability ensures that customer data is handled according to the appropriate regulatory framework regardless of where it's processed within the global organisation.

Similarly, LegalDeal benefits from automated compliance checks that ensure client confidentiality is maintained throughout all workflows. The engine's ability to identify privileged communications and apply appropriate protections helps the firm meet its ethical and legal obligations while still enabling efficient collaboration.

13. Evaluation Framework: Performance Assessment

The Evaluation Framework assesses the performance, reliability, and compliance of AI agents, models, and workflows to ensure they operate optimally while meeting enterprise standards. It tracks key performance indicators such as task completion time and success rates, continuously evaluates AI models for accuracy and bias, assesses agent actions to ensure they align with predefined policies, analyses end-to-end workflows to identify bottlenecks, ensures operations adhere to regulatory requirements, collects feedback from agents and users and identifies unusual patterns in agent behaviour or workflow execution.

The effectiveness of AI agents directly impacts business outcomes in cognitive enterprises. This section explores how to measure agent performance and integrate evaluation systems with Multi-Agent Orchestrator Platforms (MOPs). Using examples from ComPlus and LegalDeal, we'll examine practical approaches to agent evaluation that drive continuous improvement.

Creating an Effective Evaluation Framework

Agent performance goes beyond simple technical metrics. For the telecommunications company ComPlus, agents handling internet connectivity issues must be evaluated based on technical accuracy and customer satisfaction. Similarly, at LegalDeal, legal research agents need to assess legal accuracy and regulatory compliance. A comprehensive framework includes task completion rates, response accuracy, and interaction efficiency alongside business-specific metrics.

Context retention represents how well agents maintain awareness of important background information. At ComPlus, this means tracking if the Network Diagnostics Agent remembers customer equipment details and service history when troubleshooting. Collaboration effectiveness measures how well agents work together in multi-step processes—critical when several specialised agents must coordinate to resolve complex network problems at ComPlus or analyse intricate legal documents at LegalDeal.

Technical Integration with the Multi-Agent Orchestrator

The evaluation system must connect seamlessly with the Multi-Agent Orchestrator Platform through a dedicated Evaluation Layer. This integration requires careful technical design to enable real-time monitoring without disrupting existing workflows. The Evaluation Layer interfaces with several key MOP components through standardised APIs and event-based integration.

Context Manager Integration

Modern evaluation systems connect to the Context Manager (via Evaluation Framework) using standardised observability patterns and lightweight protocols. This integration should:

1. Use OpenTelemetry standards for tracing and context propagation
2. Implement WebSocket connections for real-time updates rather than polling
3. Support structured query capabilities for retrieving specific contextual elements
4. Provide abstractions that simplify access to context data

At ComPlus, this modernised approach reduced integration complexity while providing richer contextual data for evaluation metrics, particularly for assessing how effectively agents leverage historical interaction data.

Agent Registry Integration

Contemporary evaluation systems maintain detailed performance profiles for agents by connecting to the Agent Registry through flexible, standardised interfaces. Modern implementation patterns include:

1. GraphQL API support for schema-aware querying of agent capabilities
2. Integration with popular agent frameworks like AutoGen and LangChain
3. Version-aware performance tracking that monitors changes across agent updates
4. Benchmark comparisons against similar agents and industry standards

At LegalDeal, this approach allows performance metrics to be queried across multiple dimensions, providing insights into how different legal domains affect agent performance, with results displayed through an interactive dashboard.

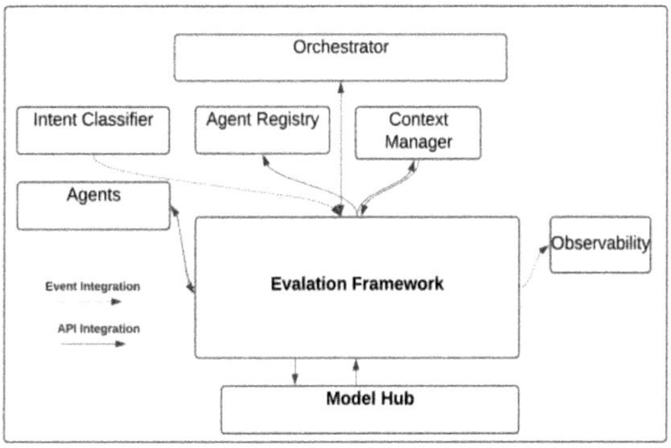

Task Orchestrator Integration

For comprehensive workflow assessment, modern evaluation systems integrate with the Task Orchestrator using current best practices:

1. Distributed tracing to follow entire workflow execution paths
2. Performance metrics at both the individual step and end-to-end process levels
3. Support for A/B testing of alternative workflow paths
4. Integration with CI/CD pipelines for automated testing as part of deployment workflows

This approach provides visibility into multi-step agent processes, helping ComPlus identify bottlenecks in customer service resolution pathways.

Model Gateway Integration

For evaluation of AI model performance, the Evaluation Layer connects to the Model Gateway to monitor:

1. Model confidence scores and uncertainty estimates
2. Inference latency and resource utilization
3. Prediction accuracy against ground truth when available

This integration uses a combination of synchronous API calls for real-time metrics and asynchronous processing for deeper analysis. At LegalDeal, this tracks how accurately the Legal Research Agent's underlying models interpret case law and statutes, flagging instances where confidence is low for human review.

Implementing Real-Time Evaluation at ComPlus and LegalDeal

A practical evaluation system for ComPlus focuses on customer experience metrics collected as interactions unfold. When a customer reports slow internet, the system tracks each agent's performance from initial classification to final resolution. The technical implementation uses a stream processing architecture that:

1. Captures interaction events through instrumentation code in agent interfaces
2. Processes these events through an analysis pipeline using Kafka Streams or similar technology
3. Computes real-time metrics using sliding window algorithms
4. Triggers alerts when performance falls below thresholds

The evaluation component maintains a database of performance metrics, integrating with visualisation tools through a GraphQL API that allows flexible querying of performance data. This enables ComPlus managers to identify improvement opportunities across their agent ecosystem.

At LegalDeal, the evaluation system focuses on legal accuracy and processing efficiency. The implementation includes specialised components for comparing agent outputs against legal standards, using a combination of rule-based verification and expert review. A document processing pipeline tracks how efficiently agents handle different document types, storing performance data in a time-series database that enables trend analysis across different legal domains and document complexities.

Governance and Automated Improvement

The evaluation system not only measures performance but also drives improvement through automated feedback loops. The technical implementation includes:

1. An anomaly detection system that identifies performance patterns requiring attention
2. Automated retraining triggers that initiate model updates when performance degrades
3. A/B testing infrastructure to evaluate potential improvements before full deployment

At both ComPlus and LegalDeal, these systems connect to continuous integration pipelines, automatically generating test cases from identified weaknesses. This creates a virtuous cycle where evaluation directly drives improvement without constant human intervention.

Implementation Recommendations

To implement these modern integration patterns, consider:

1. Adopting a modular architecture that separates core evaluation capabilities from integration adapters
2. Providing SDKs and libraries in multiple languages with simple, well-documented interfaces
3. Supporting both real-time evaluation and batch processing for different use cases
4. Implementing standardised metrics aligned with industry frameworks while allowing custom extensions

By aligning with modern evaluation frameworks while preserving domain-specific evaluation needs, the updated evaluation framework will offer a more developer-friendly, flexible approach to AI system assessment, ultimately driving continuous improvement and quality assurance. This approach transforms evaluation from a periodic assessment into an integral part of the agent lifecycle, enabling data-driven optimisation and ensuring alignment with enterprise objectives.

14. Observability Framework: System Transparency and Insights

When Maria Chen logged into ComPlus's operations dashboard at the beginning of her shift, she immediately understood the state of their Multi-Agent Orchestrator Platform across 25 countries. Not through a dozen separate monitoring screens as in the past but through a unified observability interface that presented a clear picture of how every agent in the system was performing. She noticed an emerging pattern in response latency when the Customer Service Agent interacted with the Knowledge Retrieval Agent—something that would have gone undetected until customers started calling with complaints in the past. The system had not only identified the anomaly but traced its origin through the entire agent workflow, identifying that the Context Manager was receiving unusually large payload sizes that affected downstream processing. Within minutes, she implemented the system's suggested resolution, preventing what once would have triggered a major service degradation affecting thousands of customers.

Understanding the Observability Framework

The Observability Framework provides comprehensive visibility into the operation, behaviour, and performance of the Multi-Agent Orchestrator Platform (MOP). Unlike traditional monitoring that tracks predefined metrics, observability enables teams to understand the internal state of complex, distributed agent systems through their external outputs. This capability becomes critical as cognitive enterprises deploy sophisticated multi-agent systems where interactions between components create emergent behaviours that simple monitoring cannot capture.

For the MOP—which functions as the "central nervous system" of the cognitive enterprise—observability creates transparency across the entire orchestration layer, providing insights into how agents interact, how workflows execute, and how the system responds to different inputs and conditions. This visibility is essential not just for technical operations but for building trust in AI systems by making their behaviour transparent, explainable, and accountable.

Observability Pillars for Multi-Agent Systems

Effective observability for the MOP encompasses three fundamental pillars:

Metrics that provide quantitative measurements of system performance and behaviour. For multi-agent systems, these include agent response times, task completion rates, model inference latency, and orchestration efficiency. Rather than viewing these metrics in isolation, the Observability Framework correlates them across components to identify patterns and relationships.

Logs that capture detailed records of system events and agent actions. In the MOP context, these include agent reasoning steps, decision points in workflows, context updates, and error conditions. Advanced log analysis techniques help extract meaningful insights from these high-volume data streams.

Traces that track the execution path of requests across the distributed components of the MOP. When a user query enters the system, tracing follows its journey from the Pre-Processor through the Orchestrator to specialised agents and back, creating a complete picture of the interaction. This end-to-end visibility is crucial for understanding complex multi-agent workflows.

Beyond these traditional pillars, the Observability Framework for MOPs adds specialised capabilities for AI systems:

Model Observability provides visibility into AI model behaviour, including input distributions, confidence scores, token usage, and attention patterns. This capability helps teams understand not just that a model produced a particular output but how and why it reached that conclusion.

Agent Interaction Analysis visualises the communication patterns between agents, identifying collaboration patterns, information flows, and potential bottlenecks. This visibility is particularly valuable for understanding how multiple specialised agents coordinate to solve complex problems.

Technical Integration with the Multi-Agent Orchestrator

The Observability Framework is tightly integrated with the MOP through instrumentation points across all key components. This integration enables comprehensive visibility without disrupting operational workflows or adding significant performance overhead. The framework connects with core MOP components through standardised telemetry collection, context enrichment, and visualisation capabilities.

Pre-Processor Integration

The Observability Layer connects to the Pre-Processor through lightweight instrumentation that captures input characteristics and transformation metrics. This connection enables:

1. Visibility into input distributions across different channels and modalities
2. Performance metrics for input normalization and enrichment processes
3. Early detection of anomalous or potentially problematic inputs

The technical implementation uses non-blocking telemetry collection to avoid adding latency to critical processing paths. At ComPlus, this integration allows operations teams to understand how different input types affect downstream processing, identifying when certain input patterns (like complex customer queries about network outages) might require additional resources or alternative routing.

Orchestrator Integration

For the central Orchestrator component, the Observability Framework provides comprehensive visibility into the intelligence that routes requests and coordinates workflows. This integration enables:

1. Monitoring of intent classification accuracy and confidence levels
2. Visualisation of task planning processes and decision trees
3. Performance metrics for context management operations
4. End-to-end tracing of workflow execution

The implementation uses OpenTelemetry-based distributed tracing that follows requests through the entire orchestration process. At LegalDeal, this integration creates visual maps of how contract analysis requests flow through multiple specialised agents, helping identify which branches of their agent workflow contribute most to processing latency.

Agent Integration

The Observability Framework connects to individual agents through standardised instrumentation APIs that capture performance metrics, reasoning steps, and resource utilization. This connection provides:

1. Visibility into agent-specific performance characteristics and behaviour patterns
2. Metrics for agent execution time, memory usage, and API call patterns
3. Detailed logs of agent reasoning steps and decision processes

The technical implementation uses a lightweight SDK that agents incorporate during development, ensuring consistent observability across both custom and third-party agents. At ComPlus, this allows operations teams to understand how their Network Diagnostics Agent interacts with external systems, tracking API dependencies that might affect reliability.

Model Gateway Integration

For the Model Gateway and Hub, the Observability Framework captures detailed metrics on model performance, usage patterns, and infrastructure utilization. This integration enables:

1. Real-time monitoring of model inference latency and throughput
2. Visibility into model selection decisions made by the gateway
3. Resource utilization metrics across the model serving infrastructure
4. Early detection of model drift or performance degradation

The implementation uses a combination of infrastructure-level metrics and model-specific telemetry. At LegalDeal, this integration provides visibility into how their language models perform across different document types, identifying which models struggle with certain legal domains and might require additional training or fine-tuning.

Context Manager Integration

The Observability Framework connects to the Context Manager to provide visibility into how context flows throughout the system. This integration enables:

1. Monitoring of context size, complexity, and update frequency
2. Tracing of how context information influences agent decisions
3. Performance metrics for context storage and retrieval operations

The technical implementation captures key metrics without storing sensitive context contents, ensuring privacy while maintaining operational visibility. At ComPlus, this integration allows operations teams to identify when context overload affects system performance, particularly during complex customer support scenarios where context accumulates across multiple interaction turns.

Implementing Real-Time Observability at ComPlus and LegalDeal

A practical observability implementation at ComPlus focuses on unifying visibility across their complex MOP deployment. When customers interact with any service, the system tracks the complete journey across the orchestration layer, specialised agents, and supporting systems. The technical implementation uses a centralized observability platform that:

1. Collects telemetry from all MOP components through standardised instrumentation
2. Correlates events across components using distributed tracing and context propagation
3. Applies AI-assisted anomaly detection to identify emerging issues
4. Visualises system behaviour through intuitive, role-specific dashboards

The observability platform maintains a time-series database of performance metrics, a distributed tracing system for request flows, and centralized logging with advanced search capabilities. This comprehensive approach ensures that when issues arise, teams have complete context rather than fragmented views across disconnected tools.

"*Before implementing our observability framework, troubleshooting MOP issues was like solving a mystery with half the clues missing,*" explains Maria Chen, Senior Network Engineer at ComPlus. "*We might see symptoms in the customer experience but couldn't trace them back through the agent workflow to identify root causes. Now, we have end-to-end visibility that shows exactly how requests flow through our system, where delays occur, and why certain interactions perform differently than others. Problems that once took days to diagnose are now understood in minutes.*"

At LegalDeal, the observability implementation focuses on their document processing workflows and the MOP components that drive them. The approach includes specialised observability components for legal-domain systems:

1. Document workflow tracing that follows materials from intake through analysis to review
2. Agent interaction visualisation that shows how specialised legal agents collaborate
3. Model performance monitoring that tracks accuracy across different legal domains
4. Integration of health dashboards that show connectivity with external legal resources

This implementation provides attorneys and managers with real-time visibility into matter status, potential bottlenecks, and quality metrics through intuitive dashboards tailored to legal operations.

For David Torres, a contract attorney at LegalDeal, the impact on daily work has been profound: "*Before our observability framework, I had no visibility into what happened after I submitted a document for processing. Now, I can see exactly where a contract is in our workflow—which agents have processed it, what they've found, and whether any components are taking longer than expected. This transparency has transformed how we work and communicate with clients.*"

Governance and Continuous Improvement

The observability framework drives continuous improvement through automated feedback loops and governance processes. The technical implementation includes:

1. An anomaly detection system that identifies performance patterns requiring attention
2. Automated alerting and incident management workflows
3. A continuous improvement process that translates observability insights into actionable improvements
4. Architecture compliance monitoring that ensures systems adhere to design standards

At both ComPlus and LegalDeal, these systems connect to continuous integration and deployment pipelines, automatically generating test cases from identified weaknesses. This creates a virtuous cycle where observability directly drives improvement without constant human intervention.

Effective observability requires thoughtful integration with the Multi-Agent Orchestrator Platform through well-designed instrumentation of key components. By implementing a comprehensive Observability Framework that connects with the Pre-Processor, Orchestrator, specialised agents, Model Gateway, and Context Manager, cognitive enterprises gain unprecedented visibility into their operations. Companies like ComPlus and LegalDeal demonstrate how this visibility transforms troubleshooting from a reactive, time-consuming process into a proactive practice that enhances system reliability, performance, and trust. As multi-agent systems become increasingly central to business operations, observability transitions from a technical capability to a strategic asset that ensures cognitive systems deliver consistent, explainable value.

15. Response Generator : Ensuring Unified & Context-Aware Communication

The Response Generator is a vital component of the Multi-Agent Orchestrator Platform (MOP), designed to create consistent, coherent outputs from agent activities. Acting as the communication hub for agents, it ensures that responses are accurate, context-aware, and tailored to user needs and workflow requirements. By supporting multimodal outputs such as text, audio, video, PDFs, and structured JSON, the Response Generator bridges the gap between complex agent orchestration and user-facing communication.

For enterprises like ComPlus and LegalDeal, the Response Generator plays a critical role in translating complex operations into user-friendly formats. Whether generating personalised summaries for legal clients at LegalDeal or crafting notifications for customers during network outages at ComPlus, this component ensures seamless communication tailored to individual preferences and contexts.

Core Functions of the Response Generator

The Response Generator provides a robust framework for generating outputs that align with user expectations and workflow requirements. Its core functions include:

1. **Multimodal Output Generation:** Produces responses in various formats such as text, audio, video, PDFs, and structured JSON.
2. **Context-Aware Customization:** Tailors responses based on user preferences and historical interactions stored in the Context Manager.
3. **Integration of Multiple Modalities:** Combines outputs from different sources into cohesive and consistent responses.
4. **Dynamic Adaptation:** Adjusts tone, format, and content dynamically based on task requirements and recipient profiles.

Technical Integration with MOP Components

The Response Generator integrates seamlessly with other MOP components to ensure efficient workflows and context-rich communication. Its integration points include:

Orchestrator Integration

The Orchestrator coordinates workflows by routing agent outputs through the Response Generator for formatting and delivery. This integration ensures that responses are aligned with task requirements and user expectations.

- **Example:** At ComPlus, when a FaultManagementAgent diagnoses network issues, the Orchestrator routes the diagnostic results through the Response Generator to create a customer-facing notification explaining the outage.

Context Manager Integration

The Context Manager enriches response generation by providing historical interaction data and user preferences. This integration ensures that responses are personalised and contextually relevant.

- **Example:** At ComPlus, when sending service updates to customers, the Response Generator uses Context Manager data to tailor notifications based on customer preferences (e.g., SMS vs. email).

AI Safety Controller Integration

The AI Safety Controller ensures ethical compliance during response generation by validating content against organisational policies. This integration prevents inappropriate or biased outputs.

- **Example:** At LegalDeal, before generating legal summaries for clients, the AI Safety Controller verifies that sensitive information is excluded from unauthorized recipients.

Security Manager Integration

The Security Manager safeguards sensitive data embedded in generated responses through encryption protocols and access controls. This integration ensures the secure delivery of outputs.

- **Example:** At ComPlus, when generating billing updates containing customer account details, encryption enforced by the Security Manager protects these communications during transmission.

Core Responsibilities of the Response Generator

1. Multimodal Output Generation

The Response Generator supports diverse output formats to cater to varied communication needs.

- **Example (ComPlus):** Generates audio notifications for customers about service disruptions.
- **Example (LegalDeal):** Creates PDFs summarizing compliance risks for legal clients.

2. Context-Aware Customization

Tailored responses are based on user preferences stored in the Context Manager.

- **Example (ComPlus):** Sends personalised outage notifications via SMS or email depending on customer preferences.
- **Example (LegalDeal):** Formats legal analyses into executive summaries for senior management or detailed reports for technical teams.

3. Integration of Multiple Modalities

Combines outputs from different sources into cohesive communications.

- **Example (ComPlus):** Merges network diagnostic results with customer account details into unified service updates.
- **Example (LegalDeal):** Integrates compliance analysis with visual risk assessments for client presentations.

4. Dynamic Adaptation

Adjusts tone, format, and content dynamically based on recipient profiles.

- **Example (ComPlus):** Crafts empathetic messages during major service outages to maintain customer trust.
- **Example (LegalDeal):** Generates formal legal summaries for corporate clients while using casual language for individual clients.

Practical Implementation for Cognitive Enterprises

The Response Generator operates continuously within MOP to support diverse enterprise workflows requiring tailored communication outputs. Its practical applications include:

- **For ComPlus:** The Response Generator creates real-time service notifications, combining network diagnostics with personalised customer details.
- **For LegalDeal:** It translates complex legal analyses into client-friendly formats such as executive summaries or detailed technical reports depending on recipient needs.

Governance and Compliance Benefits

By embedding robust communication capabilities into MOP's architecture, the Response Generator delivers significant governance benefits:

1. **Operational Efficiency:** Streamlines communication workflows by automating response generation across multiple modalities.
2. **Personalisation Assurance:** Ensures responses are tailored to individual preferences for enhanced engagement.
3. **Compliance Adherence:** Validates generated content against organisational policies through AI Safety Controller integration.

4. **Security Assurance:** Protects sensitive data embedded in responses through encryption protocols enforced by the Security Manager.

For global enterprises like ComPlus operating across diverse regulatory environments, the Response Generator applies region-specific rules during content creation to ensure compliance with local laws. Similarly, LegalDeal benefits from automated safeguards that maintain client confidentiality while enabling efficient collaboration on sensitive legal matters.

16. Human Annotator Component: Expert Oversight

The Human Annotator component bridges the gap between human expertise and AI capabilities, ensuring high-quality data annotation, validation, and refinement to support AI models and workflows. It enables human annotators to label, validate, or refine raw data to train AI models with higher accuracy, review and correct AI-generated outputs to ensure quality and reduce errors, identify and address biases in training datasets or model predictions, provide nuanced judgment for tasks where AI struggles with ambiguity or contextual subtleties, offer feedback to improve AI models iteratively through active learning mechanisms and ensure compliance with regulatory requirements and ethical guidelines during data processing.

In cognitive enterprises, human expertise remains vital even with advanced AI systems. This section explains how human annotators can be integrated with Multi-Agent Orchestrator Platforms (MOPs) to improve performance, provide oversight, and facilitate continuous learning.

The Role of Human Annotators

Human annotators provide crucial input that AI systems cannot generate themselves. They validate outputs, correct errors, provide domain expertise, and help train agents with real-world knowledge. When ComPlus addresses complex network issues or LegalDeal analyses intricate contracts, human annotation ensures the accuracy of agent outputs and helps systems learn from these interactions.

Human annotation takes various forms—from simple approval/rejection decisions to detailed feedback on agent responses or even step-by-step demonstrations of how to complete complex tasks. These contributions help agents improve over time and handle increasingly difficult situations.

Technical Integration with MOP Components

The integration of human annotators with the Multi-Agent Orchestrator Platform requires dedicated technical connections to key components:

The system requires a specialised Human Annotation component that connects with core MOP components. This layer manages how human input flows into the system and how feedback is processed. The implementation includes:

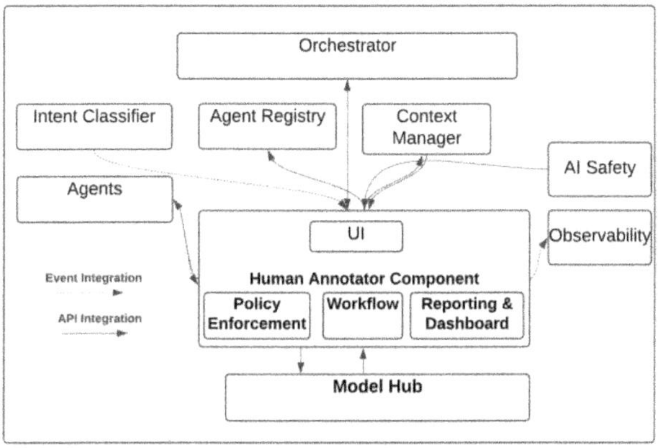

1. User interfaces that allow annotators to view, modify, and create annotations
2. Feedback collection systems that standardize human input
3. Priority queuing that identifies which tasks most need human review

Context Manager Integration

For effective annotation, humans need access to relevant context. This integration:

1. Provides annotators with background information about the task
2. Shows the history of agent actions and decisions

3. Highlights areas of uncertainty where human input is most valuable

The technical implementation uses a bidirectional data flow where annotators receive context information and return enriched annotations that become part of the system's knowledge base. At ComPlus, this allows technical experts to review automated network diagnostics with all relevant customer history displayed alongside.

Agent Registry Integration

The Human Annotation Layer connects to the Agent Registry to:

1. Identify which agents handle which tasks
2. Track which agents most frequently require human intervention
3. Update agent capability profiles based on human feedback

This integration uses a database of agent performance metrics that is continually updated based on annotation quality scores. At LegalDeal, this helps identify which legal domain agents most benefit from attorney review.

Feedback Integration System

A critical component is the system that processes human feedback and turns it into improvements:

1. Annotation classification that categorizes different types of feedback
2. Learning mechanisms that incorporate annotations into agent training
3. Quality monitoring that measures annotation consistency

The implementation uses structured JSON formats to standardize feedback across different annotation types, from simple corrections to complex explanations. These structured formats allow the system to automatically incorporate certain types of feedback while flagging others for deeper review.

Integration with AI Safety

The AI Safety Controller flags tasks that violate policies or ethical guidelines, routing them to the Human Annotator Integration Component for review. e.g., a biased or unfair decision by an AI model is flagged and corrected by a human annotator before being finalized.

Practical Implementation for Cognitive Enterprises

In practice, human annotation fits into MOP workflows through carefully designed touchpoints. At ComPlus, when the Network Diagnostics Agent encounters an unusual connection issue, the system can:

1. Route the case to an appropriate technical expert
2. Present them with the agent's analysis alongside relevant customer data
3. Allow them to correct misdiagnosis or confirm the agent's solution
4. Feed this annotation back into the system to improve future performance

The human annotation process uses a web-based interface that presents information in an intuitive format, requiring minimal training for annotators. The system employs priority algorithms to ensure human attention focuses on cases where it adds the most value—typically those with high uncertainty, potential high impact, or novel characteristics.

Step-by-Step Workflow

1. **Task Identification:**
    - An AI agent encounters a task requiring manual intervention (e.g., ambiguous classification or high-risk decision-making).
2. **Task Routing:**
    - The Orchestrator routes the task to the Human Annotator Integration Component.
3. **Context Sharing:**

    - The Context Manager provides relevant data, logs, and instructions to annotators.
4. **Annotation Process:**
    - Annotators complete the task using an integrated interface or external platform.
5. **Feedback Integration:**
    - Annotated data is returned to the Orchestrator and stored in the Model Hub for future model improvement.
6. **Model Update:**
    - Feedback is used to fine-tune AI models, ensuring continuous learning and improvement.

Benefits of Integrated Human Annotation

This integrated approach offers several advantages:

1. Continuous improvement through ongoing human feedback
2. Balanced workloads where routine tasks are handled automatically while complex cases receive human attention
3. Knowledge capture that preserves human expertise in the system
4. Quality assurance for critical decisions

As cognitive enterprises evolve, the role of human annotators shifts from routine checking to handling edge cases and novel situations. The MOP's integration with human annotators creates a symbiotic relationship—humans help agents improve, while agents handle increasing workloads so humans can focus on high-value contributions. This approach ensures cognitive enterprises maintain high quality while scaling their capabilities.

17. AI/ML Operations for Cognitive Enterprises

In today's competitive landscape, businesses are increasingly relying on artificial intelligence and machine learning to gain a competitive edge. However, as search results indicate, nearly 80% of AI/ML projects fail before deployment due to challenges like data discrepancies, lack of model versioning, and implementation difficulties. AI/ML Operations

(MLOps) solves these problems by bringing structure and reliability to the development and management of AI systems.

For cognitive enterprises – organisations that leverage AI at scale to transform their operations – MLOps is not just helpful but essential. It creates the foundation that allows AI agents to remain effective as business conditions change. Without proper MLOps practices, even the most sophisticated multi-agent systems will deliver diminishing value over time as models drift, data changes, and business requirements evolve.

Core Elements of MLOps in Multi-Agent Systems

MLOps extends DevOps principles to AI systems, creating automated pipelines for model development, deployment, monitoring, and maintenance. For multi-agent systems, this means establishing consistent processes for managing the lifecycle of multiple specialised agents that work together. This includes continuous integration for code changes, continuous delivery for deploying updates safely, and continuous training to help agents adapt to new data patterns.

Unlike traditional software systems, AI agents learn and evolve over time, requiring specialised operational approaches. MLOps provides the framework to manage this complexity through version control for both models and data, automated testing to verify performance, and monitoring systems that detect when models begin to drift from expected behaviour.

Technical Integration with the Multi-Agent Orchestrator Platform

The Multi-Agent Orchestrator Platform requires specific integration points with MLOps systems to maintain high-performance agent operations. These connections enable seamless model updates, performance monitoring, and continuous improvement.

Orchestrator Integration

The MLOps pipeline connects directly with the Orchestrator component through standardised APIs. When the MLOps system detects that an agent model needs updating, it coordinates with the Orchestrator to manage the transition with minimal disruption. This integration uses event-driven architecture patterns where model update events trigger appropriate handling by the Orchestrator.

The technical implementation requires:

1. Event notification systems for model updates
2. Version coordination between MLOps and the Orchestrator
3. Fallback mechanisms when model updates encounter issues

Model Gateway Integration

The Model Gateway serves as the primary interface between MLOps and the Model Hub. This component manages model versioning, deployment, and runtime access. The MLOps pipeline publishes updated models to the Model Gateway's registry, which maintains records of all available model versions and their performance characteristics.

This integration enables:

1. Seamless model updating without disrupting ongoing operations
2. A/B testing of new models against existing ones
3. Rollback capabilities when updates don't perform as expected

The technical implementation typically uses REST APIs for model registration and GraphQL for flexible querying of model metadata and performance metrics.

Context Manager Integration

The MLOps system connects to the Context Manager to access interaction data essential for model retraining. This bidirectional connection allows MLOps to:

1. Extract real-world interaction patterns for model improvement
2. Inform the Context Manager about model updates and capability changes
3. Analyse how different contexts affect model performance

This integration uses data streaming technologies like Apache Kafka for high-volume data transfer between systems, ensuring that training data accurately reflects real-world usage patterns.

Agent Registry Integration

The MLOps pipeline maintains agent specifications through integration with the Agent Registry. This connection ensures that technical capabilities, performance requirements, and version histories remain synchronized. The implementation uses versioned JSON schema definitions to maintain consistent agent specifications across systems.

Practical Benefits in Cognitive Enterprises

For cognitive enterprises, the integration between MLOps and the Multi-Agent Orchestrator Platform delivers several practical benefits:

1. Reliability improvements through automated monitoring and intervention when agent performance degrades
2. Adaptation to changing conditions through continuous learning and model updates

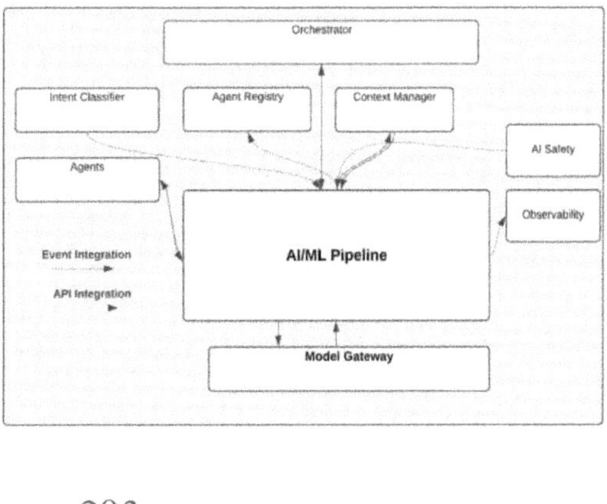

3. Governance and compliance through comprehensive tracking of model lineage and decision factors
4. Cost optimisation by identifying and addressing inefficient agent behaviours

This integrated approach ensures that AI agents continue to deliver value even as business conditions evolve. For example, when customer service patterns change at telecommunications company ComPlus, the MLOps system can detect these shifts and initiate retraining for relevant agents. Similarly, legal service provider LegalDeal can rapidly adapt to regulatory changes by updating models through the integrated pipeline.

Effective AI/ML Operations form the foundation for sustainable cognitive enterprises by ensuring that agent-based systems deliver consistent value over time. By integrating MLOps practices with the Multi-Agent Orchestrator Platform through well-defined technical interfaces, organisations can achieve greater reliability, adaptability, and performance from their AI systems.

This integration transforms AI management from a series of one-off projects into a continuous improvement cycle that keeps agent capabilities aligned with business objectives. As AI becomes increasingly central to business operations, this operational excellence becomes not just beneficial but essential for maintaining competitive advantage in the rapidly evolving cognitive enterprise landscape.

Summary:

Chapter 11 provides a comprehensive exploration of the Multi-Agent Orchestrator Platform (MOP), a critical component of the Cognitive Enterprise Architecture Framework (CeAF). The MOP serves as the "central nervous system" of a cognitive enterprise, orchestrating intelligent workflows across AI agents, enterprise systems, and data platforms. Each component of the MOP plays a vital role in enabling seamless collaboration between specialised agents, ensuring real-time decision-making, and maintaining governance and security.

The chapter emphasizes that while some frameworks and tools may offer partial capabilities of MOP, enterprises must carefully evaluate their unique needs and design a detailed implementation strategy to achieve desired outcomes. The MOP is not just a technical solution but an enabler of business transformation, bridging operational silos and embedding intelligence into every layer of the organisation.

Key Components of the MOP

The chapter outlines several interconnected components that collectively enable the MOP to function effectively:

1. **Pre-Processor Layer**: Converts diverse inputs (text, audio, images) into standardised formats for downstream processing.
2. **Orchestrator**: Coordinates workflows by interpreting user intent, managing interaction context, and planning tasks across multiple agents.
3. **Specialised Agents**: Execute domain-specific tasks such as knowledge retrieval, reasoning, or action execution.
4. **Model Gateway and Hub**: Manages AI model access, ensuring optimal performance and resource allocation.
5. **AI Safety and Control**: Embeds governance mechanisms to monitor compliance, mitigate risks, and enforce ethical boundaries.
6. **Human Annotator Component**: Facilitates human-in-the-loop validation for data labeling and output refinement.
7. **Observability Framework**: Provides visibility into system operations, enabling real-time monitoring and troubleshooting.
8. **Evaluation Framework**: Measures AI model performance against business objectives to ensure continuous improvement.
9. **Security Manager**: Safeguards data access and system integrity with robust controls.

Each component is interdependent, contributing to the overall effectiveness of the platform while addressing specific challenges such as data silos, governance complexities, or operational inefficiencies.

Critical Insights for Enterprises

The chapter highlights several key takeaways for organisations planning to implement MOP:

- **Holistic Design is Essential**: While some frameworks offer partial capabilities (e.g., orchestration or model management), enterprises must ensure all components are integrated to achieve cohesive functionality.
- **Customization is Key**: Off-the-shelf solutions may not align perfectly with unique business needs. Enterprises must plan for customization to address domain-specific requirements.
- **Governance Cannot Be Overlooked**: The AI Safety and Control layer ensures ethical compliance and builds trust—critical for scaling AI capabilities responsibly.
- **Continuous Improvement Matters**: The Evaluation Framework ensures that AI systems evolve based on real-world performance data.

Step-by-Step Implementation Plan for ComPlus and LegalDeal

Step 1: Assess Current State

- *ComPlus*: Conduct an audit of existing customer service workflows, network operations systems, and agent capabilities to identify integration points.
- *LegalDeal*: Map current contract review processes and knowledge management systems to pinpoint inefficiencies.

Step 2: Define Business Objectives

- *ComPlus*: Focus on reducing customer complaint resolution times by 50% through intelligent orchestration.
- *LegalDeal*: Aim to cut contract review time by 75% while improving accuracy with AI-assisted workflows.

Step 3: Build the Foundation

- Establish a unified Customer Context Hub or Legal Knowledge Graph as the central repository for enriched data.

Step 4: Implement Core Orchestration

- Develop an Intent Classifier to route requests dynamically based on context (e.g., customer inquiries at ComPlus or legal clauses at LegalDeal).
- Integrate Task Planners for breaking down complex workflows into manageable steps.

Step 5: Enable Specialised Agents

- *ComPlus*: Deploy NetworkDiagnosticsAgent for outage detection and CustomerServiceAgent for personalised recommendations.
- *LegalDeal*: Introduce ClauseAnalysisAgent for identifying key provisions and ComplianceAgent for regulatory checks.

Step 6: Integrate Governance Mechanisms

- Embed AI Safety and Control components to monitor compliance with GDPR (for ComPlus) or client confidentiality standards (for LegalDeal).
- Implement Observability Frameworks for real-time monitoring of agent performance.

Step 7: Optimize Through Feedback Loops

- Use the Evaluation Framework to measure outcomes such as customer satisfaction scores (ComPlus) or contract review accuracy (LegalDeal).
- Continuously retrain models using updated interaction data from Analytical Learning Systems.

Step 8: Scale Gradually

- Expand MOP capabilities incrementally—starting with high-impact use cases before rolling out across other domains.

Conclusion

The Multi-Agent Orchestrator Platform is more than a technical solution; it is a strategic enabler of cognitive transformation. By integrating these components thoughtfully and aligning them with business goals, enterprises like ComPlus and LegalDeal can unlock unprecedented levels of efficiency, intelligence, and customer-centricity. However, success requires more than adopting frameworks—it demands a deep understanding of each component's role and meticulous planning to ensure cohesive implementation. Only then can organisations fully realise the transformative potential of cognitive enterprise architecture.

Looking Ahead

As we move into the next chapter, we'll explore how AI systems have evolved with advancements in agentic architectures, prompting techniques, function calling, and advanced reasoning. These innovations enable AI agents to collaborate, reason, and act autonomously in complex environments. Organisations now face a key decision: whether to build these Multiagent Orchestrator Platform (MOP) capabilities in-house for greater control or buy ready-made solutions for faster deployment. The chapter will unpack these choices and show how MOP integrates these cutting-edge technologies to drive smarter, more adaptive enterprises.

Chapter 12: Intelligent Agents Evolution: From Automation to Autonomous Reasoning

The evolution of intelligent agents represents one of the most significant transformative journeys in modern computing. Today's sophisticated agent systems, capable of reasoning across complex scenarios, retrieving relevant knowledge, and taking autonomous actions, have emerged through distinct developmental stages. This chapter explores the maturity progression of agent systems, the core technologies enabling their capabilities, and the critical implementation considerations organisations must navigate when adopting these powerful technologies.

The Agent Maturity Model: A Progressive Journey

Intelligent agents have evolved through clearly defined maturity levels, each representing significant advancements in capabilities, autonomy, and intelligence. Understanding this evolutionary progression provides essential context for organisations seeking to implement or enhance agent-based systems.

Level 0: Fixed Automation

At this foundational level, agents operate through pre-defined rule-based workflows with deterministic logic and no contextual understanding. These basic agents rely on IF-THEN rules, hardcoded scripts, and basic workflow engines to perform simple, repetitive tasks.

While effective for highly structured scenarios, Level 0 agents struggle with ambiguity and require frequent human intervention. Their brittle design makes them vulnerable when facing novel scenarios outside their programmed parameters. A typical example is a router status checker that follows fixed logic to check if a device is online/offline.

Level 1: AI-Augmented Automation

Level 1 represents the first meaningful integration of artificial intelligence into agent systems. These agents feature basic AI for specific tasks, improved categorization and better routing of interactions. They leverage simple ML models, basic NLP, and classification algorithms to enhance their capabilities.

Though more advanced than Level 0, these agents still struggle with complex processing and cross-context interactions. Their awareness remains limited to narrow domains. A common implementation is a customer query classifier that routes support tickets to appropriate departments based on content analysis.

Level 2: Agentic Assistance

At this level, agents become context-aware, providing responses based on knowledge retrieval and personalisation. Their capabilities expand to include multi-step planning with minimal reasoning capabilities. They utilize prompting techniques, retrieval-augmented generation, and knowledge graph capabilities to deliver more sophisticated assistance.

Level 2 agents face challenges with complex multi-step planning and reasoning, with limited generative capabilities that may produce inconsistent outputs. Broadband support agents exemplify this level, diagnosing issues by following contextual troubleshooting paths and accessing relevant documentation.

Level 3: Reasoning Agents

These advanced agents demonstrate sophisticated reasoning across contexts, can generate creative solutions to complex problems, and understand nuanced human instructions. They employ large language models with chain-of-thought reasoning, recursive refinement, and symbolic reasoning techniques to achieve these capabilities.

While powerful, Level 3 agents still face limitations in handling complex ethical trade-offs, may struggle with transparency in decision processes, and require careful monitoring. Financial advisors utilizing these agents can analyse client portfolios, consider market trends and generate personalised investment strategies with supporting rationales.

Level 4: Autonomous Agents

At the highest maturity level, agents operate with minimal supervision, continuously learn from interactions, and can execute complex workflows while adapting to changing conditions. They incorporate feedback mechanisms, self-improvement capabilities, and autonomous decision-making within defined boundaries.

Level 4 agents represent both the greatest potential and highest risk, requiring robust ethical guardrails and human oversight. Complete autonomy remains inappropriate for many scenarios despite their advanced capabilities. These agents can be found in automated trading systems that continuously adapt strategies based on market conditions while operating within risk parameters.

Implementing Agents in Enterprise Architecture

The journey from basic automation to autonomous agents represents not merely a technical evolution but a fundamental shift in how organisations approach intelligent systems. Organisations must consider several factors when implementing agent-based architectures:

Architectural Considerations

Successful agent implementations require thoughtful integration with enterprise systems. Key considerations include:

- **Agent Coordination Patterns**: How multiple agents communicate and collaborate to achieve complex goals
- **Interface Standardisation**: Ensuring consistent communication protocols between agents and other enterprise systems
- **Monitoring Frameworks**: Implementing real-time performance tracking and anomaly detection

- **Security Controls**: Establishing appropriate boundaries for agent actions and data access

Ethical Implementation Framework

As agent capabilities advance, ethical considerations become increasingly critical. Organisations must establish:

- **Transparency Mechanisms**: Ensuring agent reasoning and decisions can be explained to stakeholders
- **Human Oversight Protocols**: Determining when and how humans should review agent recommendations
- **Boundary Setting**: Clearly defining the limits of agent autonomy based on risk assessment
- **Continuous Evaluation**: Regularly assessing agent performance against ethical standards and business objectives

Navigating the Agent Maturity Journey

Organisations seeking to implement intelligent agents should take a measured approach, advancing through maturity levels as their capabilities and governance frameworks mature. A strategic implementation typically follows these phases:

1. **Assess Current Capabilities**: Evaluate existing automation and identify opportunities for intelligent agent enhancement
2. **Start with Focused Use Cases**: Begin with well-defined scenarios where agent assistance provides clear value
3. **Establish Governance Early**: Implement oversight mechanisms before deploying advanced reasoning capabilities
4. **Incrementally Expand Autonomy**: Gradually increase agent independence as confidence and capabilities grow
5. **Maintain Human-Centric Design**: Ensure agents support and enhance human work rather than replacing human judgment

The Future of Intelligent Agents

The evolution of agent systems continues to accelerate, with several emerging developments shaping their future trajectory:

- **Multi-Modal Reasoning**: Agents that seamlessly integrate understanding across text, images, audio, and other data types
- **Collaborative Agent Networks**: Ecosystems of specialised agents working together to solve complex problems
- **Explainable Agency**: Advanced techniques for making agent reasoning transparent and understandable
- **Adaptive Learning**: Systems that continuously refine their capabilities based on ongoing interactions and feedback

As organisations implement these increasingly sophisticated systems, maintaining a human-centered approach becomes even more essential. The most successful implementations will view agents not as replacements for human judgment but as powerful tools that amplify human capabilities, allowing people to focus on the complex, creative, and empathetic aspects of work that remain uniquely human.

The journey from fixed automation to autonomous reasoning represents one of the most profound technological transitions in enterprise architecture. Organisations that thoughtfully navigate this evolution—balancing technological capability with ethical considerations and human needs—will unlock unprecedented value while avoiding the pitfalls that accompany increasingly autonomous systems.

The Foundation of Agent Intelligence: Prompting

The interface between human intent and intelligent systems lies at the heart of cognitive transformation. Prompting has emerged as the fundamental mechanism through which users and systems interact with large language models, serving as the critical translation layer that converts human requests into structured directives that models can interpret and act upon. As organisations like ComPlus and LegalDeal integrate sophisticated AI agents into their workflows, understanding the evolution of prompting techniques becomes essential for maximizing agent effectiveness.

The Evolution of Prompting Approaches

Prompting methodologies have undergone a remarkable transformation, with each evolutionary stage enabling more sophisticated capabilities and interactions. This progression reflects a journey from simple query-response patterns to complex reasoning frameworks that enable agents to tackle increasingly nuanced tasks.

Static Instructions: The Foundation

The journey begins with static instructions—simple, direct prompts that provide basic task definitions with minimal guidance. These straightforward directives excel in simplicity and ease of implementation, requiring minimal computational overhead. A network technician at ComPlus might use this approach with a prompt like "List steps to restart a router," receiving a standardised response suitable for uncomplicated scenarios.

However, static prompting quickly reveals its limitations when faced with ambiguity or complexity. Without contextual awareness, these prompts generate generic responses that often miss critical nuances of specific situations. In enterprise environments where context determines appropriate actions, this approach proves insufficient for sophisticated workflows.

Context-Aware Prompting: Adding Situational Intelligence

The next significant advancement incorporates relevant context, user-specific details, and current state information into prompts. This approach generates more personalised and relevant responses by providing agents with the specific circumstances surrounding a request.

At ComPlus, support agents might use context-aware prompts such as "Customer with 100Mbps plan reporting speeds of 25Mbps. Suggest diagnostic steps." This additional context enables the agent to provide targeted troubleshooting guidance specific to the customer's service tier and reported issue, significantly improving response relevance.

While context-aware prompting marked a substantial improvement, it still lacks sophisticated reasoning capabilities and struggles to adapt to rapidly changing scenarios. The responses, though more relevant, often fail to demonstrate the depth of analysis required for complex problem-solving that cognitive enterprises demand.

Few-Shot Learning: Teaching Through Examples

Few-shot learning represents a pedagogical approach to prompting, where the system receives examples of desired outputs before being asked to generate new responses. By demonstrating both format and reasoning patterns, this technique creates a template for agents to follow when addressing similar requests.

At LegalDeal, attorneys might use few-shot prompting when generating initial contract drafts, providing examples of properly formatted clauses that reflect the firm's preferred language and structure. This approach ensures consistency across documents while significantly improving accuracy and alignment with expectations.

The primary drawbacks include increased token usage—which affects both processing speed and operational costs—and the potential for pattern overfitting, where agents reproduce example characteristics too rigidly rather than adapting to the unique aspects of new situations.

Chain-of-Thought Prompting: Structured Reasoning

Chain-of-thought prompting represents a significant leap forward in agent intelligence, guiding models through step-by-step reasoning processes that break complex problems into logical stages. This approach mirrors how human experts tackle multifaceted challenges, leading to substantially enhanced accuracy and logical consistency.

Network operations teams at ComPlus implement this approach with prompts that structure the troubleshooting process: "First check for regional outages, then analyse router logs for error patterns, then examine recent configuration changes, and finally recommend appropriate remediation steps." By explicitly outlining the reasoning sequence, the agent maintains logical coherence throughout complex diagnostics.

While chain-of-thought prompting delivers superior results for complex tasks, it comes with higher computational requirements and increased response times. For time-sensitive operations, organisations must carefully balance the improved quality against performance considerations.

Tool-Augmented Prompting: Bridging Thought and Action

The most advanced prompting approach currently deployed incorporates instructions for utilizing external tools and systems, enabling agents to bridge the gap between reasoning and execution. Tool-augmented prompting combines cognitive processing with real-world interactions, supporting end-to-end workflows that previously required constant human intervention.

ComPlus has implemented this approach in their customer support operations, with prompts that not only analyse connectivity issues but also include instructions for generating API calls to network management systems: "Analyse customer connection status, identify potential issues, and if appropriate, generate the API call to reset their router remotely." This capability transforms agents from advisory systems to operational partners that can directly resolve customer issues.

While offering unprecedented capabilities, tool-augmented prompting requires robust function-calling infrastructure and careful handling of execution permissions to prevent errors. Organisations implementing this approach must develop comprehensive safety protocols and oversight mechanisms to manage these enhanced capabilities responsibly.

Strategic Implementation in Cognitive Enterprises

The progression from static to tool-augmented prompting offers a clear development path for organisations building intelligent agent capabilities. Rather than viewing these approaches as mutually exclusive, cognitive enterprises typically deploy a spectrum of prompting techniques based on task complexity, risk profile, and performance requirements.

At ComPlus, routine customer inquiries might utilize context-aware prompting for efficiency, while complex network diagnostics employ chain-of-thought techniques to ensure thorough analysis. Similarly, LegalDeal applies different prompting strategies across their practice areas—using few-shot approaches for standardised document generation while implementing chain-of-thought prompting for complex compliance assessments that require careful reasoning.

As organisations advance their cognitive capabilities, the sophistication of their prompting strategies typically evolves in parallel with their broader transformation journey. The mastery of advanced prompting techniques represents a critical competency for cognitive enterprises, enabling them to fully realise the potential of intelligent agents across their operations.

Enabling Action Through Function Calling

The cognitive capabilities of AI agents reach their full potential when they can not only reason about the world but also take action within it. Function calling serves as the critical bridge between intelligence and execution, enabling AI systems to transform insights into tangible outcomes. As organisations like ComPlus and LegalDeal advance in their cognitive transformation journeys, the ability of their systems to interact with operational environments becomes increasingly essential.

The Evolution of Function Calling Capabilities

Function calling capabilities have evolved dramatically, moving from rigid, programmer-defined integrations to flexible, context-aware implementations that can adapt to novel situations. This evolution mirrors the broader maturity progression of intelligent agents, with each stage delivering greater autonomy and effectiveness.

Manual Integration: The Foundation

At its most basic level, function calling begins with manual integration—hardcoded scripts that execute predefined sequences with minimal variation. These implementations feature straightforward, predictable behavior that engineers can easily troubleshoot and maintain. At ComPlus, early network management systems utilized this approach with scripts that would check router status and execute reboot commands when devices appeared offline.

While simple to implement, these manual integrations suffer from significant limitations. Their rigid logic cannot adapt to unexpected scenarios, modifications require developer intervention, and they operate based on narrow assumptions about operational conditions. When ComPlus network engineers encountered unique failure patterns or needed to adjust diagnostic sequences, they faced time-consuming recoding efforts rather than simple configuration changes.

Rule-Based Execution: Adding Flexibility

As cognitive systems mature, rule-based execution introduces conditional logic and dynamic selection capabilities that significantly enhance adaptability. These systems evaluate runtime conditions, select appropriate functions from a wider repertoire, and navigate branching workflows based on predefined criteria. LegalDeal implemented this approach in their initial contract review systems, where different analysis functions would trigger based on contract type, jurisdiction, and identified clauses.

Rule-based systems handle common variations effectively and support basic decision trees that can navigate predictable scenarios. However, they still face considerable constraints. As rule complexity increases, maintenance becomes challenging, with interdependencies creating unexpected behaviors when modified. More fundamentally, these systems cannot reason about novel situations that fall outside their predefined rule sets—they can only execute logic explicitly programmed by their developers.

LLM-Driven Execution: Reasoning in Action

The most sophisticated function-calling approach leverages large language models to provide genuinely intelligent execution control. These systems dynamically select, sequence, and parameterize functions based on contextual understanding and real-time conditions. Rather than following predetermined scripts or rules, they reason about the most appropriate actions to take given the specific situation at hand.

At ComPlus, customer support systems now employ this approach to troubleshoot connection issues. When a customer describes a problem, the LLM analyses the complaint, determines relevant diagnostic steps, and orchestrates a sequence of API calls to appropriate network systems—checking outages, testing line quality, reviewing recent changes, and initiating appropriate remediation. The system adapts its approach based on customer responses and diagnostic findings, creating truly conversational troubleshooting experiences.

The advantages of LLM-driven execution are substantial. These systems handle complex, ambiguous scenarios by reasoning about appropriate actions rather than following fixed patterns. They adapt to unique situations by considering specific context and constraints. Perhaps most importantly, they support natural language control that allows non-technical users to guide sophisticated technical operations through conversation.

Despite these strengths, LLM-driven function calling presents significant implementation challenges. It requires robust infrastructure to manage security, error handling, and access control across potentially hundreds of function definitions. Organisations must carefully address the risk of hallucination, where models might attempt to call non-existent functions or provide invalid parameters. Finally, these systems demand greater computational resources than their simpler predecessors, requiring careful optimisation for performance-sensitive applications.

Practical Implementation Considerations

When implementing function-calling capabilities, cognitive enterprises must balance several critical factors. First, they must carefully define the scope and permissions of available functions, ensuring systems can take meaningful actions while maintaining appropriate security boundaries. Second, they must implement robust validation and error handling to manage unexpected inputs or failure conditions. Finally, they must design observability systems that maintain transparency in function execution, ensuring that both users and operators understand what actions the system is taking and why.

ComPlus has addressed these considerations through a graduated implementation approach. They began with basic functions in lower-risk domains, carefully monitoring performance and gathering feedback before expanding to more critical operational areas. This cautious expansion has allowed them to build organisational confidence in autonomous functions while refining their governance approach based on real-world experience.

As function calling capabilities continue to evolve, we can expect even deeper integration between reasoning and action, with systems that can compose complex workflows from primitive functions, learn from execution outcomes, and continuously improve their operational effectiveness. For cognitive enterprises, mastering this capability represents a crucial step toward systems that don't just provide insights but actively help implement solutions.

Advanced Reasoning Patterns in Agent Systems

The evolution of intelligent systems has introduced increasingly sophisticated reasoning patterns that enable agents to navigate complex challenges with greater effectiveness. As cognitive enterprises like ComPlus and LegalDeal integrate multi-agent platforms into their operations, these advanced reasoning approaches become critical for orchestrating workflows across specialised agents and diverse knowledge sources. Understanding these patterns and their appropriate applications helps organisations select the right cognitive approaches for specific business needs.

The Evolution of Reasoning Capabilities

Reasoning represents the cognitive heart of intelligent agent systems—their ability to process information, draw inferences, and solve problems in increasingly human-like ways. As agent systems mature from simple rule-based automation to sophisticated autonomous reasoning, their underlying reasoning patterns grow correspondingly more powerful. These patterns determine not just what agents can accomplish but how they approach problems and the quality of insights they generate.

Traditional RAG: The Foundation of Knowledge-Grounded Responses

Retrieval Augmented Generation (RAG) serves as the foundation for knowledge-informed agent systems. This approach retrieves relevant information from knowledge bases before generating responses, grounding AI outputs in factual information rather than relying solely on parametric knowledge encoded in language models.

The core mechanism of Traditional RAG follows a streamlined process: when a query arrives, the system searches appropriate knowledge sources, retrieves relevant information, and incorporates this material when generating its response. This relatively straightforward approach requires moderate implementation complexity while delivering significant benefits in accuracy and reliability.

For organisations beginning their cognitive transformation journey, Traditional RAG provides an accessible entry point with tangible benefits. ComPlus initially implemented this pattern in their customer support operations, enabling agents to answer questions about service offerings, billing policies, and basic troubleshooting by drawing on up-to-date knowledge bases. The approach dramatically reduced hallucinations and factual errors while ensuring customers received current information despite frequent service changes.

This reasoning pattern excels in straightforward information retrieval scenarios such as question answering, documentation searches, and basic support interactions. However, it shows limitations when confronting multi-step problems that require iterative reasoning or adaptation based on progressive findings.

ReAct: Combining Reasoning and Action

ReAct (Reasoning, Action, Observation) represents a significant advancement in agent cognitive capabilities by alternating between thinking, doing, and observing in an iterative cycle. Unlike Traditional RAG's linear approach, ReAct enables agents to adjust their problem-solving strategy based on intermediate findings.

The pattern follows a cyclical process: the agent first reasons about the current situation, then takes a specific action based on that reasoning, observes the results, and incorporates these observations into its next reasoning step. This iterative approach mirrors how humans tackle complex problems, adjusting course as new information emerges.

LegalDeal leveraged ReAct patterns when developing contract analysis workflows. Their system first examines a contract section, identifies key provisions, takes actions to retrieve relevant precedents or regulations, observes how these compare to the contract language, and then reasons about potential risks or improvements. This cyclical process continues until the entire agreement has been thoroughly analysed, with each step building upon previous findings.

With moderate implementation complexity, ReAct proves particularly valuable for troubleshooting workflows, diagnostic processes, and multi-step investigations where initial assumptions may need revision based on discovered information. The pattern enables adaptive problem-solving that more closely resembles human expert approaches while maintaining the efficiency of automated systems.

GraphRAG: Leveraging Relationship Intelligence

GraphRAG enhances retrieval capabilities by leveraging knowledge graphs to understand contextual relationships between entities. Rather than treating information as isolated documents, GraphRAG maps complex interconnections that enable more sophisticated reasoning about systems and organisations.

This approach captures entity relationships explicitly, allowing agents to identify both direct and indirect connections that might not be apparent through traditional retrieval methods. By modelling complex systems with their dependencies and relationships, GraphRAG enables a more nuanced understanding of interconnected problems.

ComPlus implemented GraphRAG to manage their network infrastructure knowledge, mapping relationships between services, hardware components, software dependencies and customer impacts. When service issues arise, agents can traverse these relationship graphs to understand potential root causes and downstream effects that might not be obviously connected in linear documentation.

While requiring moderate to high implementation complexity, GraphRAG delivers exceptional value for applications involving network topology analysis, service dependency mapping, and complex system diagnostics. The pattern particularly excels when problems require understanding how changes in one system component might affect seemingly unrelated areas through indirect relationships.

Retrieval-Augmented Reasoning (RAR): Precision Throughout Complex Workflows

Retrieval Augmented Reasoning (RAR) represents an advanced evolution that integrates information retrieval throughout multi-step reasoning processes. Unlike Traditional RAG, which retrieves information primarily at the beginning, RAR performs targeted retrieval at each reasoning step to maintain precision throughout complex workflows.

This sophisticated approach ensures that each step of a multi-stage reasoning process has access to the most relevant information for that specific sub-problem. As the agent's understanding evolves during the reasoning process, its retrieval requirements change correspondingly, with RAR adapting dynamically to these shifting needs.

LegalDeal implemented RAR for complex regulatory compliance analysis, where different stages of reasoning require distinct types of information. The system progressively retrieves relevant regulatory texts, precedent cases, client documentation, and industry standards as it works through multi-stage analyses that might span dozens of reasoning steps, each grounded in appropriate knowledge sources.

While RAR involves high implementation complexity, it delivers exceptional value for sophisticated applications like complex diagnostics, multi-stage legal analysis, and advanced technical support scenarios. The pattern's ability to maintain precision across extended reasoning chains makes it particularly valuable for high-stakes decision contexts where accuracy throughout the entire process is critical.

Task Decomposition: Divide and Conquer Approach

Task Decomposition addresses complexity by systematically breaking problems into manageable subtasks that can be solved independently before recombining results. This pattern enables cognitive systems to tackle problems that would be overwhelming if approached holistically.

The core mechanism involves analyzing a complex request, identifying logical components, creating a structured plan of subtasks, distributing these to appropriate specialised agents or capabilities, and finally synthesizing the individual results into a coherent solution. This approach enables parallel processing and leverages specialised capabilities for different aspects of complex problems.

ComPlus deployed Task Decomposition when handling multi-faceted customer issues that span different service areas. When a business customer reports connectivity issues affecting multiple locations with different service configurations, the system breaks this into location-specific diagnostics, service-type analyses, and historical pattern reviews before synthesizing recommendations that address the overarching problem.

With moderate implementation complexity, Task Decomposition excels in scenarios involving cross-domain problems, multi-part customer issues, and complex project planning. It proves particularly valuable when different aspects of a problem require distinct expertise or approaches that can be executed independently before integration.

Dynamic Graph Augmentation: Reasoning in Changing Environments

Dynamic Graph Augmentation represents the frontier of reasoning capabilities by continuously updating knowledge graphs with real-time information. This advanced pattern enables cognitive systems to maintain accuracy in rapidly changing environments by capturing temporal changes and evolving conditions.

Unlike static knowledge approaches, Dynamic Graph Augmentation continuously refreshes its understanding as systems change, configurations are updated, or new information becomes available. This temporal awareness ensures that reasoning remains grounded in current reality rather than potentially outdated knowledge.

For network operations at ComPlus, this pattern proved transformative. Their system continuously updates infrastructure knowledge graphs based on deployment changes, configuration updates, and performance metrics. When troubleshooting occurs, the system reasons using the current state rather than potentially outdated documentation, dramatically improving diagnostic accuracy during and after maintenance periods.

While implementing Dynamic Graph Augmentation involves very high complexity, its benefits for systems with frequent changes justify the investment for specific use cases. The pattern delivers exceptional value for network operations, infrastructure monitoring, and any system where configurations change frequently, and reasoning based on outdated information could lead to costly errors.

Strategic Implementation in Cognitive Enterprises

Organisations implementing cognitive capabilities should view these reasoning patterns as complementary approaches rather than mutually exclusive options. Mature cognitive enterprises typically deploy multiple patterns based on use case requirements, complexity, and business value.

For routine interactions, Traditional RAG may provide sufficient capabilities with optimal efficiency, while complex diagnostics might warrant Retrieval-Augmented Reasoning despite its higher implementation complexity.

The progression toward more sophisticated reasoning patterns often mirrors the overall maturity of an organisation's cognitive capabilities. As ComPlus and LegalDeal demonstrate, organisations typically begin with foundational patterns before gradually implementing more advanced approaches as their expertise, data infrastructure, and governance capabilities mature. This evolutionary approach ensures that reasoning capabilities align with business needs while developing the organisational readiness required for more sophisticated implementations.

Implementation Considerations: Build vs. Buy

The journey toward implementing a multi-agent orchestration platform presents organisations with a fundamental strategic decision that will shape their cognitive capabilities for years to come. Should they build a custom platform tailored to their specific requirements, purchase a commercial solution, or leverage open-source frameworks? This critical choice requires careful evaluation of organisational capabilities, strategic priorities, and resource constraints.

Strategic Approaches to Platform Implementation

The Custom Development Path

Organisations that choose to build custom multi-agent platforms gain unparalleled flexibility and control over their cognitive capabilities. This approach allows for precise alignment with unique business processes and integration with existing systems. ComPlus initially considered this route for their network operations platform, recognising that their complex infrastructure monitoring requirements might benefit from a tailored solution.

Custom development, however, comes with significant considerations. The initial investment is substantial, requiring specialised AI talent, experienced developers, and dedicated project management. Organisations typically face development timelines measured in months or even years before realizing value, creating a prolonged gap between investment and return. Once deployed, custom platforms demand ongoing maintenance commitments, with internal teams assuming full responsibility for updates, enhancements, and troubleshooting.

The control afforded by custom development proves particularly valuable for organisations where agent capabilities represent core competitive differentiators or where highly specialised workflows cannot be adequately addressed by commercial offerings. However, this control comes with increased risk exposure—development challenges, evolving requirements, and potential skills gaps can all threaten successful implementation.

Commercial Solutions: Accelerating Time to Value

For organisations prioritising rapid deployment and proven functionality, commercial platforms offer compelling advantages. These solutions typically provide comprehensive capabilities out-of-the-box, reducing implementation timelines from months to weeks. LegalDeal adopted this approach for its document analysis system, leveraging a specialised legal AI platform that offered pre-trained models for contract review and due diligence.

Commercial solutions require moderate initial investment for licensing and implementation services, though ongoing subscription costs can be significant, especially as usage scales. While customization options exist, they remain constrained by vendor-provided configuration capabilities, potentially limiting adaptation to unique organisational requirements. Organisations become dependent on vendor roadmaps for new features, though they benefit from regular updates and professional support services.

This approach significantly reduces technical risk, as vendors have typically addressed common implementation challenges and continuously refine their platforms based on broad customer feedback. For standard workflows with moderate customization needs, commercial solutions offer an optimal balance of speed, reliability, and fit, particularly for organisations with limited internal AI expertise.

Open-Source Frameworks: The Middle Path

Between fully custom development and commercial platforms lies a third option: leveraging open-source frameworks like LangChain and LangGraph. This approach offers substantial flexibility while reducing the development burden associated with building from scratch. ComPlus adopted this strategy for certain agent capabilities, using open-source components as building blocks while adding custom elements for telecommunications-specific functions.

These frameworks present an attractive financial profile, with minimal licensing costs and moderate ongoing maintenance requirements. Implementation timelines typically fall between custom and commercial approaches, depending on the complexity of the desired capabilities. Organisations retain significant control over architecture and functionality while benefiting from community contributions and established patterns.

The open-source approach requires substantial technical expertise—teams must understand framework capabilities, integration approaches, and implementation patterns. Scaling these solutions to enterprise levels often requires additional engineering effort beyond the core framework capabilities. Organisations must carefully evaluate framework maturity and community support to ensure long-term viability for production deployments.

Open-Source Framework Dynamics

The open-source landscape offers several frameworks that support multi-agent orchestration, each with distinct characteristics aligned to different use cases and requirements.

LangChain has emerged as a popular framework offering modular components for building LLM-powered applications. Its strength lies in straightforward task-chaining capabilities and a rich ecosystem of integrations that accelerate development. Organisations have successfully deployed LangChain for chatbots, document question-answering systems, and basic agent implementations that follow primarily linear workflows. However, complex non-linear workflows present challenges, as the framework offers only basic state management and relatively simple agent coordination mechanisms.

For more sophisticated orchestration requirements, LangGraph provides graph-based workflow capabilities that support complex decision trees and state management across execution cycles. This framework excels in scenarios requiring multi-agent coordination, stateful applications and workflows with cyclical or branching logic. These advanced capabilities come with tradeoffs—LangGraph presents a steeper learning curve, documentation continues to evolve, and enterprise support options remain limited. Organisations adopting LangGraph should be prepared for substantial integration work to create production-ready systems.

The framework selection process should align closely with specific use case requirements and organisational capabilities. LegalDeal, for example, initially prototyped their legal knowledge system using LangChain, which adequately supported their document Q&A needs. As they expanded to more complex workflows involving multiple specialised legal agents, they transitioned certain components to LangGraph to support the required coordination complexity.

Aligning Requirements with Implementation Strategies

Organisations can navigate implementation decisions more effectively by mapping their specific requirements to the most appropriate approach:

When agent capabilities directly differentiate the business—such as ComPlus's network diagnostic system that fundamentally transformed their service quality—custom development ensures unique capabilities and complete control. This approach proves essential when competitive advantage derives directly from agent intelligence.

For scenarios demanding rapid deployment, commercial platforms offer the fastest path to production. LegalDeal leveraged this advantage when implementing their contract analysis system, reducing time-to-value from potentially years to mere months—a critical consideration in their competitive legal technology landscape.

Organisations facing moderate customization needs with budget constraints often find open-source frameworks provide an ideal balance. These frameworks offer flexibility without high licensing costs, though they require technical expertise and integration effort. This approach works particularly well for experimental initiatives or when exploring capabilities before committing to larger investments.

Industry-specific workflows with complex requirements typically benefit from custom development that ensures precise alignment with specialised processes. ComPlus took this approach with its network operations platform, where telecommunications-specific protocols and integration requirements could not be adequately addressed by commercial offerings.

Standard workflows requiring some tailoring are often best served by commercial platforms with configuration options. This approach balances implementation speed with adequate customization flexibility. LegalDeal selected this path for their client portal, leveraging a configurable platform that supported their specific client interaction patterns without requiring extensive custom development.

Organisations in highly regulated environments must prioritize compliance, often leading them toward either custom development with full control or commercial solutions from trusted vendors with proven compliance capabilities. Both approaches enable rigorous validation and documentation of system behavior—which is essential for maintaining regulatory standing.

Implementation Guidance

Successful organisations typically adopt hybrid approaches tailored to their specific context. ComPlus implemented a strategy combining commercial platforms for standard functions like customer support, open-source frameworks for moderately specialised capabilities, and custom development for their core network intelligence systems where competitive differentiation was crucial.

Similarly, LegalDeal leveraged commercial legal AI for document analysis while building custom components for attorney-client collaboration where their unique practice methodology created specific requirements. This balanced approach optimized their investment while ensuring capabilities aligned precisely with strategic priorities.

The build-vs-buy decision ultimately requires careful evaluation of strategic objectives, available resources, timing considerations, and risk tolerance. By aligning these factors with the appropriate implementation strategy, organisations can create multi-agent orchestration platforms that deliver maximum value while minimising implementation challenges.

The Future of Intelligent Agents

The evolution of intelligent agents from basic automation to autonomous reasoning systems represents one of the most significant technological transformations in modern computing. As we've explored through ComPlus and LegalDeal's journeys, these capabilities have already begun reshaping organisations across industries. Looking ahead, several important trends are emerging that will further transform the landscape of agent-based systems.

Agent Autonomy and Self-Improvement

The next 2-3 years will see significant advances in agents' ability to optimize their own performance without explicit programming. These self-learning capabilities will enable systems to adapt their approaches based on outcomes, continuously refining their effectiveness. ComPlus has already begun implementing early versions of these capabilities, with their network diagnostic agents automatically adjusting detection parameters based on false positive/negative rates.

The impact of this trend will be multifaceted: reduced requirements for human oversight of routine operations, enhanced problem-solving capabilities for complex scenarios, and greater adaptability to novel situations that weren't explicitly anticipated in the original design. Organisations implementing these self-improving systems will need robust governance frameworks to ensure that optimisation occurs within appropriate boundaries, particularly for critical functions.

Cross-Enterprise Collaboration

Within 3-5 years, we'll see the emergence of secure agent collaboration across organisational boundaries, enabling new forms of partnership and coordination. This evolution will require standardised protocols for agent interaction, clear permission models, and shared knowledge ecosystems that respect proprietary information while enabling collective intelligence.

The potential impact is particularly significant for complex multi-party workflows like supply chains, where coordinated optimisation across partners could dramatically improve efficiency. ComPlus is exploring early applications in their wholesale telecom business, where their network provisioning agents could eventually coordinate directly with enterprise customers' systems to optimize service delivery and capacity planning.

LegalDeal envisions similar cross-firm collaboration for complex transactions, where intelligent agents from multiple legal practices, financial institutions, and corporate clients could securely coordinate due diligence processes while maintaining appropriate confidentiality and oversight.

Advanced Human-AI Teaming

Perhaps the most transformative trend emerging over the next 2-4 years involves increasingly sophisticated models for human-AI collaboration. Future systems will recognize user intent with minimal explicit instruction, adapt their support based on individual work patterns, and provide contextually relevant assistance that feels like working with a skilled colleague rather than operating a tool.

These advanced teaming capabilities will enable truly synergistic problem-solving, where the combined human-AI system achieves outcomes neither could reach independently. We already see early examples in LegalDeal's litigation practice, where case analysis systems work alongside attorneys to develop novel legal arguments by connecting precedents in ways human researchers might not have considered.

Ethical and Responsible AI Evolution

Running parallel to these technical advancements, ongoing evolution in ethical reasoning and governance will be essential for the widespread adoption of advanced agent systems. Organisations like ComPlus and LegalDeal recognize that trust is the foundation of successful AI implementation, making investments in explainability, bias mitigation, and governance frameworks as critical as technical capabilities themselves.

Future agent systems will incorporate increasingly sophisticated ethical reasoning that can navigate complex trade-offs while maintaining alignment with human values. This evolution isn't a separate trend but a necessary companion to technical advancement—the development of capabilities that ensure intelligent agents remain beneficial partners in human endeavors rather than sources of new risks.

Conclusion

The evolution of intelligent agents represents more than just technological progress—it's a reimagining of how organisations operate, make decisions, and create value. Moving from fixed automation to autonomous reasoning mirrors the shift to cognitive enterprises, where success depends on blending human creativity with AI's capabilities. The experiences of ComPlus and LegalDeal show that true transformation isn't just about adopting technology but about fostering a meaningful partnership between humans and machines.

At the core of this shift is the Multiagent Orchestration Platform, which unifies data, applications, and expertise into intelligent workflows. By automating routine tasks and enabling seamless collaboration, it empowers employees to focus on high-value activities while driving efficiency, personalisation, and innovation. As these capabilities advance, they will accelerate the move toward cognitive enterprises—organisations that are adaptive, innovative, and capable of delivering exceptional value through the combined power of human and artificial intelligence.

Looking Ahead

In the next chapter, we'll explore how the Cognitive Enterprise Architecture Framework (CeAF) and concepts like Data Mesh, the Multiagent Orchestrator Platform (MOP), and intelligent integration platforms can transform operations for a telecommunications giant like ComPlus. By adopting decentralised models like Data Mesh, telcos can gain real-time insights from their vast, scattered data. MOP further enhances operations by orchestrating AI agents to drive automation and adaptive workflows in areas like network optimisation and customer experience. Together, these frameworks enable telcos to boost efficiency, deliver personalised services and innovate at scale—redefining their role in the digital era.

Chapter 13: AI Compute – Strategic Choices for Enterprises

Introduction: Navigating the AI Compute Landscape

As enterprises embrace artificial intelligence (AI) to drive innovation and efficiency, they face critical decisions about how to build and deploy AI systems. These decisions often revolve around whether to **buy or build models**, adopt **open-source or closed-source solutions,** and choose between **fine-tuning foundational models or developing custom solutions**. Each choice has significant implications for cost, scalability, security, and alignment with business objectives.

This chapter provides a structured approach to navigating these strategic choices, helping enterprises evaluate their options and align their AI computing strategies with their goals. By examining the benefits, trade-offs, and practical considerations for each decision, organisations can make informed choices that maximize value while minimising risks.

1. Buy vs. Build Models

One of the most fundamental decisions enterprises face is whether to buy pre-built AI models or build custom models tailored to their specific needs. This decision depends on factors such as the complexity of the use case, time-to-market requirements, and available resources.

Buy: Leveraging Pre-Built Models

Pre-built AI solutions are ideal for common, well-defined tasks like sentiment analysis, image recognition, or document classification. Vendors typically offer these models as ready-to-use services or APIs.

Pros:

- Faster time-to-market: Pre-built models can be deployed quickly without extensive development effort.
- Reduced development effort: Enterprises can leverage vendor expertise without needing in-house AI teams.
- Access to vendor expertise: Vendors often provide support, updates, and performance optimisations.

Cons:

- Limited customization: Pre-built models may not fully address domain-specific needs.
- Potential vendor lock-in: Dependence on a single vendor can limit flexibility and increase long-term costs.

Build: Developing Custom Models

Developing custom AI models is suited for tasks requiring domain-specific expertise or differentiation. This approach allows enterprises to tailor solutions to unique business needs.

Pros:

- Full control: Custom models can be optimized for specific use cases and integrated seamlessly with existing systems.
- Differentiation: Tailored solutions provide a competitive edge by addressing unique challenges.
- No vendor lock-in: Enterprises maintain ownership of their models and data.

Cons:

- Higher development costs: Building custom models requires skilled teams and significant investment.
- Longer timelines: Development cycles can be lengthy, delaying deployment.

When to Choose:

- **Buy** when tasks are generic (e.g., sentiment analysis) or time-sensitive (e.g., launching a new feature quickly).
- **Build** when differentiation or domain specificity is critical (e.g., legal contract analysis at LegalDeal or network optimisation at ComPlus).

2. Open vs. Closed Source Solutions

Another key decision revolves around adopting open-source frameworks versus closed-source platforms for AI development and deployment. Each option offers distinct advantages depending on enterprise priorities, such as flexibility, cost, and security.

Open-source frameworks like TensorFlow, PyTorch, and Hugging Face provide flexibility, cost-efficiency, and community support. These tools are widely used for experimentation and custom development.

Pros:

- Customization: Open-source tools allow enterprises to modify code to meet specific needs.
- Transparency: Code is publicly available, enabling greater trust and auditability.
- No vendor lock-in: Enterprises retain full control over their AI stack.
- Cost-efficiency: Open-source software is free to use, reducing licensing costs.

Cons:

- Technical expertise required: Deployment and maintenance require skilled teams with deep technical knowledge.
- Limited enterprise-grade support: Community-based support may not meet the needs of mission-critical systems.

Closed-Source Platforms

Proprietary platforms like AWS SageMaker, Azure AI, and Google Vertex AI offer managed services with enterprise-grade features such as scalability, security, and integration with cloud ecosystems.

Pros:

- Simplified operations: Managed services handle infrastructure, scaling, and updates.
- SLA guarantees: Vendors provide service-level agreements for reliability and uptime.
- Ease of integration: Closed-source platforms integrate seamlessly with other enterprise tools.

Cons:

- Higher costs: Licensing fees can add up over time.
- Vendor dependency: Enterprises may face challenges if they need to switch providers.

When to Choose:

- Use **open-source** for experimentation, cost savings, or custom workflows requiring flexibility.
- Use **closed-source** for critical systems requiring reliability, security, managed support, and seamless integration with cloud ecosystems.

3. Fine-Tuning vs. Foundational Models

As large language models (LLMs) like GPT evolve into foundational technologies across industries, enterprises must decide whether to fine-tune these models or develop entirely new ones. This decision depends on the complexity of the task and the availability of domain-specific data.

Fine-Tuning Foundational Models

Fine-tuning involves adapting pre-trained foundational models like GPT or BERT to specific use cases by training them on domain-specific datasets. This approach leverages the general knowledge embedded in foundational models while tailoring them to enterprise needs.

Pros:

- Cost-efficiency: Fine-tuning requires fewer resources than training a model from scratch.
- Faster deployment: Enterprises can build on existing capabilities rather than starting from zero.
- High accuracy: Foundational models provide strong baselines that improve with fine-tuning.

Cons:

- Data dependency: Fine-tuning requires high-quality domain-specific data.
- Limited control over architecture: Foundational models may not fully align with enterprise goals.

Building New Models from Scratch

Building new models involves training neural networks from raw data using custom architectures designed for specific tasks. This approach offers maximum flexibility but requires significant resources.

Pros:

- Full customization: New models can be designed specifically for unique requirements.
- Ownership of IP: Enterprises retain complete control over model architecture and data usage.

Cons:

- High development costs: Training from scratch demands extensive computational resources and expertise.

- Long timelines: Model development cycles can delay deployment significantly.

When to Choose:

- **Fine-tune foundational models** when tasks align with existing capabilities (e.g., customer sentiment analysis at ComPlus).
- **Build new models from scratch** when use cases require novel architectures or proprietary solutions (e.g., legal compliance analysis at LegalDeal).

4. Infrastructure Considerations for AI Compute

Beyond model decisions, enterprises must also evaluate their infrastructure strategies for deploying AI workloads effectively. Key considerations include scalability, security, cost-efficiency, and alignment with operational goals.

Cloud vs. On-Premises Deployment

Enterprises must decide whether to deploy AI workloads in the cloud or on-premises based on factors such as scalability requirements and regulatory constraints:

1. **Cloud Deployment**
   - Ideal for dynamic workloads requiring scalability (e.g., seasonal demand spikes).
   - Offers managed services that reduce operational overhead.
   - Challenges include data sovereignty concerns in regulated industries like finance or healthcare.
2. **On-Premises Deployment**
   - Suitable for industries requiring strict control over sensitive data (e.g., legal contracts at LegalDeal).
   - Provides greater customization but requires significant capital investment in hardware and maintenance teams.

Edge Computing vs. Centralized Processing

For real-time applications like network diagnostics at ComPlus or IoT device management in smart cities:

1. **Edge Computing**
   - Processes data locally at the source (e.g., routers or IoT devices).
   - Reduces latency by eliminating round-trip delays to centralized servers.
   - Challenges include limited computing power at edge devices compared to centralized systems.
2. **Centralized Processing**
   - Aggregates data in a central location for large-scale analysis using powerful compute clusters.
   - Suitable for batch processing tasks requiring high computational power but less time sensitivity.

Conclusion: Strategic Alignment in AI Compute Decisions

The decisions enterprises make about buying versus building models, adopting open versus closed solutions, fine-tuning versus building new architectures, and selecting deployment infrastructure will shape their ability to harness AI effectively. Each choice must align with broader business objectives while balancing cost-efficiency, scalability, security, and innovation potential. For organisations like ComPlus and LegalDeal navigating these choices:

- ComPlus leverages pre-built foundational models fine-tuned for telecommunications workflows while adopting edge computing for real-time network diagnostics.
- LegalDeal builds custom compliance analysis models using open-source frameworks deployed on-premises for secure handling of sensitive legal documents.

By following structured decision-making frameworks outlined in this chapter—grounded in practical examples—enterprises can craft AI compute strategies that deliver transformative value while mitigating risks associated with scalability limitations or vendor dependencies.

Chapter 14: Building Cognitive Networks – The AI-Driven Telecommunications Revolution

---

Maria Rodriguez, VP of Network Operations at ComPlus, stands in front of a holographic dashboard displaying real-time network health metrics. "*Five years ago, we spent 70% of our budget fixing outages,*" *she explains.* "*Today, our network anticipates problems before they occur—like predicting a router failure in Chicago three hours before it happened last week. Our AI rerouted traffic seamlessly, and customers never noticed. This isn't just efficiency—it's a fundamental shift in how we operate.*"

This chapter provides a blueprint for transforming traditional telecommunications networks into cognitive ecosystems that think, learn, and act autonomously. For organisations like ComPlus, this means modernising legacy systems, organizing data intelligently, and deploying AI agents that collaborate to deliver unprecedented reliability and innovation. We'll explore how these changes align with the Cognitive Enterprise Architecture Framework (CeAF) and leverage the Multi-Agent Orchestrator Platform (MOP) introduced earlier.

Four Steps to Build a Cognitive Network

Building on the architecture foundation principles we explored in the previous chapters, cognitive networks represent the next frontier for telecommunications providers like ComPlus. While a solid data architecture creates the underlying capability to manage information effectively, transforming the network itself into a cognitive system requires specific architectural and operational changes. This chapter explores four essential steps organisations can take to build truly cognitive networks that not only transmit data but actively leverage it to enhance operations, customer experiences, and business models.

Modernising Operational Support Systems with AI and APIs

Traditional Operational Support Systems (OSS) were designed for stability rather than agility, making them ill-suited for cognitive operations that require flexibility and intelligence. The first step toward a cognitive network involves transforming these legacy systems through three key approaches.

Microservices architecture breaks monolithic OSS applications into smaller, independent components that can evolve separately. For ComPlus, this meant dividing their unified operations platform into discrete services for service assurance, fault management, performance monitoring, and service provisioning. Each service can now be updated independently, allowing ComPlus to introduce new capabilities without disrupting the entire system. When they recently enhanced their network troubleshooting capabilities, they only needed to update the fault management microservice rather than the entire OSS platform.

APIs-as-Products transform network capabilities into programmable services that both internal teams and external partners can consume. Rather than treating APIs as mere technical interfaces, ComPlus now manages them as valuable products with clear documentation, service levels, and governance. Their Network Performance API, for example, exposes real-time latency metrics that application developers use to optimize customer experiences. Similarly, their Location Services API provides secure access to anonymized customer location data that enhances emergency services and enables location-based applications.

Hyper-automation leverages AI to handle routine operational tasks without human intervention. ComPlus implemented an intelligent FaultResolutionAgent that automatically diagnoses and resolves common network issues based on historical patterns and current conditions. This AI system now handles approximately 80% of routine network faults, dramatically reducing resolution times while freeing engineers to focus on complex problems and strategic initiatives. When a fibre optic cable experiences signal degradation, the FaultResolutionAgent can identify the issue, reroute traffic, and dispatch maintenance crews without human intervention.

Organizing Data for Collective Network Intelligence

As we explored in the previous chapter, effective data organisation is essential for cognitive capabilities. For networks specifically, three approaches help create the collective intelligence needed for truly cognitive operations.

Data Mesh principles, when applied to network operations, empower individual network domains to manage their own data as products while adhering to global standards. ComPlus reorganized its data governance model to give its wireless, fibre and core network teams direct ownership of their respective data domains. The wireless team now independently manages their coverage maps, tower performance metrics, and customer connection data as standardised data products that other teams can easily consume. This domain-oriented ownership ensures that the teams with the deepest technical understanding maintain their specific network data while enabling enterprise-wide access through consistent interfaces.

Knowledge graphs map complex relationships between network components, services, and customers, enabling AI systems to understand dependencies and impacts. When a server failure occurred at ComPlus's Frankfurt data centre, their knowledge graph immediately identified all affected services, applications, and customer segments by traversing the connections between infrastructure components and business services. This comprehensive view enabled the operations team to prioritize repairs based on customer impact rather than technical severity, resolving critical services within minutes instead of hours.

Network ontologies provide the semantic foundation for cognitive networks by establishing a common vocabulary and relationship model across all network domains. ComPlus developed a comprehensive telecommunications ontology that defines concepts like "Network Element," "Service," "Latency," and "Quality of Experience" along with their relationships and business rules. This shared understanding enables AI systems to correctly interpret that a "latency spike" means different things in different contexts—for video streaming services, latency over 50 milliseconds creates visible disruption, while email services can tolerate delays up to 100 milliseconds without user impact. By implementing this ontology, ComPlus reduced AI model training time by 40% while improving prediction accuracy for service impacts.

Deploying Open RAN and AI-Enhanced Radio Networks

Traditional radio access networks relied on proprietary, integrated equipment from single vendors, limiting flexibility and innovation. Cognitive networks require more open, intelligent approaches to radio infrastructure.

Open Radio Access Network (Open RAN) architectures disaggregate hardware and software components, allowing telecommunications providers to select best-of-breed solutions from multiple vendors. ComPlus implemented Open RAN for their 5G network deployment, combining AI capabilities from a vendor with standardised computing hardware from another vendor. This modular approach reduced their 5G infrastructure costs compared to traditional proprietary systems while providing greater flexibility to upgrade specific components as technology evolves.

AI-enhanced Radio Access Networks (AI-RAN) embed intelligence directly into network infrastructure rather than treating it as an external overlay. ComPlus implemented AI-RAN capabilities that continuously analyse network conditions and user behaviour to optimize performance in real-time. These systems predict traffic surges by correlating historical usage patterns with external data sources like weather forecasts, event calendars, and social media activity. When a major sporting event is scheduled, the system automatically increases capacity in the surrounding area hours before the event begins. Similarly, their AI-RAN dynamically allocates bandwidth based on service priority, ensuring critical applications receive necessary resources during peak demand periods. During a recent natural disaster, the system automatically prioritized connections to hospitals and emergency services while maintaining basic connectivity for affected residents.

Launching a Network API Economy

The ultimate expression of a cognitive network is its ability to transform from a cost centre into a revenue-generating platform through programmable capabilities offered to the broader ecosystem.

Developer ecosystems enable external partners to build applications and services that leverage network capabilities through well-defined, secure APIs. ComPlus created an API marketplace that offers specialised network services to developers and enterprise customers. Their Location Precision API enables retailers to anonymously analyse customer movements within stores for improved layout optimisation and personalised offers. Their Quality of Service Guarantee API allows gaming companies and streaming services to purchase prioritized bandwidth that ensures consistent low-latency experiences during peak usage periods. By exposing these network capabilities as services, ComPlus transformed network functions from internal resources into revenue-generating products.

Network-as-a-service models take this concept further by allowing enterprise customers to create customized virtual networks with specific characteristics. ComPlus now offers specialised virtual networks for industries with unique requirements. An automotive manufacturer uses this capability to maintain secure, reliable connections with 500,000 vehicles, enabling real-time software updates and performance monitoring. The healthcare system in one of ComPlus's operating countries leverages a dedicated virtual network for telemedicine services with guaranteed privacy, compliance features, and quality of service. These specialised networks generate premium subscription revenue while creating significant switching costs for enterprise customers who build their operations around these capabilities.

Conclusion

Building a cognitive network requires more than simply adding AI capabilities to existing telecommunications infrastructure. It demands fundamental changes to how networks are designed, deployed, and monetized. By modernising operational systems, organizing data for collective intelligence, implementing open and intelligent radio networks, and creating new business models through network APIs, telecommunications providers like ComPlus are transforming passive infrastructure into active, intelligent systems that create new value for customers, partners, and shareholders.

As we'll explore in the next chapter, these cognitive network capabilities create the foundation for entirely new digital experiences and business models that would be impossible with traditional telecommunications approaches. For ComPlus, the cognitive network represents not just an evolution of their technical infrastructure but a transformation of their entire business model from connectivity provider to digital platform and ecosystem enabler.

Edge AI: Bringing Intelligence to the Network Periphery

As telecommunications providers like ComPlus build cognitive networks, Edge AI emerges as a critical capability for processing data close to where it's generated—delivering speed, efficiency, and new monetization opportunities.

Why Edge AI Matters for ComPlus

Global data traffic is growing at 24% annually. This explosive growth creates challenges that cloud-only AI solutions can't address:

- **Latency Requirements:** Applications like autonomous vehicles need sub-millisecond responses, which is impossible with cloud roundtrips.
- **Bandwidth Constraints:** Sending all data to centralized data centres is increasingly impractical and expensive.
- **Privacy Concerns:** Customers expect their sensitive data to remain localized.

Edge AI addresses these challenges by processing data on-device or at nearby edge nodes, reducing cloud dependence while maintaining intelligence in the network.

Edge AI within the CeAF Framework

ComPlus is leveraging the Cognitive Enterprise Architecture Framework (CeAF) to implement Edge AI systematically across its network. Key integrations include:

1. **Multi-Agent Orchestrator Platform (MOP):**
   ComPlus's *NetworkEdgeAgent* works alongside cloud-based agents, with the MOP deciding which tasks run at the edge versus in the cloud. When a cell tower in Manchester detected unusual vibrations, the edge agent identified a loose connection and dispatched maintenance within minutes.
2. **Active and Intelligent Network Systems:**
   Edge AI models embedded in network equipment enable "agentic AI networks"—interconnected LLMs and SLMs that share insights while maintaining local decision-making. ComPlus has deployed lightweight SLMs at some of its cell sites for real-time traffic optimisation, reducing congestion significantly.
3. **Data Products and Platform:**
   Using a data mesh architecture, ComPlus's edge nodes expose network telemetry as data products to edge applications. Retail partners now access anonymized foot traffic patterns via local edge servers rather than centralized databases.
4. **Model Hub:**
   ComPlus maintains a centralized Model Hub for training but deploys optimized edge variants that consume minimum power while maintaining accuracy in network diagnostics.

Before diving into the case study, let's take a moment to reflect on how the concepts discussed so far—such as Data Mesh, the Multiagent Orchestrator Platform (MOP), and Intelligent Integration Platforms—can be applied in practice. These frameworks, when combined under the Cognitive Enterprise Architecture Framework (CeAF), provide a powerful toolkit for addressing real-world challenges. From decentralizing data ownership and enabling real-time insights with Data Mesh to orchestrating intelligent workflows and AI agents with MOP, these approaches create a cohesive ecosystem for innovation. The upcoming case study will demonstrate how these ideas come together to transform operations, showcasing their potential to drive efficiency, personalization, and adaptability in complex environments like telecommunications.

Case Study

Use Case: AI-Driven Broadband Fault Diagnosis

Problem Statement:
ComPlus faced escalating operational costs and customer dissatisfaction due to inefficient fault diagnosis processes. The legacy system required technicians to manually investigate over 2,000 monthly broadband fault reports, with 35% resulting in unnecessary truck rolls (field visits). The average diagnostic time was **47 minutes,** and customer satisfaction scores lagged at 62/100.

Solution Overview

ComPlus deployed a cognitive fault diagnosis system powered by the Multi-Agent Orchestrator Platform (MOP) and CeAF principles. The solution reduces human intervention through AI-driven automation while improving diagnostic accuracy. Here's how it works:

Step 1: Customer-Initiated Fault Reporting

Agent: *BroadbandDiagnosticAgent*
MOP Components: *Agent Tools, Context Manager*

Automated Interaction:
When a customer reports an issue via ComPlus's app or IVR system, the *BroadbandDiagnosticAgent* initiates a conversational interface.

Example: "Hello, I'm ComPlus AI. Let's start with basic checks. Is your router's power light green?"

Contextual Awareness:
The *Context Manager* pulls the customer's service history, equipment details, and past issues to tailor the diagnostic flow.

Example: If the customer's router was replaced recently, the agent skips basic hardware checks.

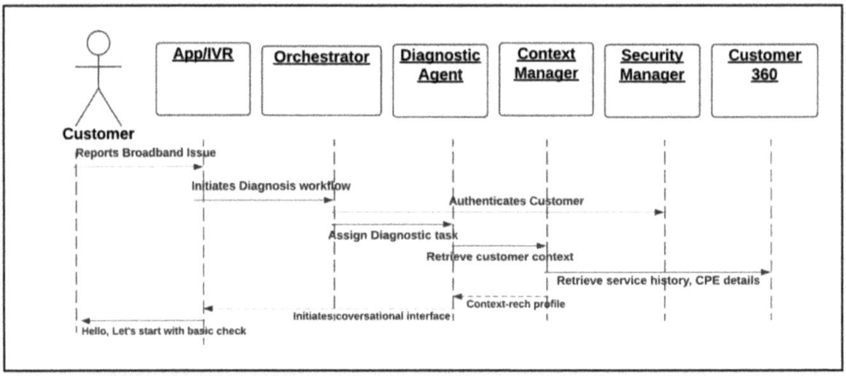

Step 2: Progressive Diagnostic Testing

Agents: *BroadbandDiagnosticAgent, Model Gateway*
MOP Components: *Knowledge Graph, Model Hub*

Tier 1 Tests:
The agent guides the customer through simple checks using predefined scripts:

Router reboot

Microfilter inspection

Ethernet cable connections

Tier 2 Tests:
If issues persist, the agent runs automated line tests:

Speed Test: Measures upload/download speeds.

Line Attenuation: Checks signal degradation over copper lines.

Packet Loss Analysis: Identifies network congestion.

AI-Powered Analysis:
Test results are sent to the *Model Gateway*, which selects the best fault-classification AI model from the *Model Hub*.

Example: A "Noise Margin" drop below 6dB triggers a "Line Interference" classification.

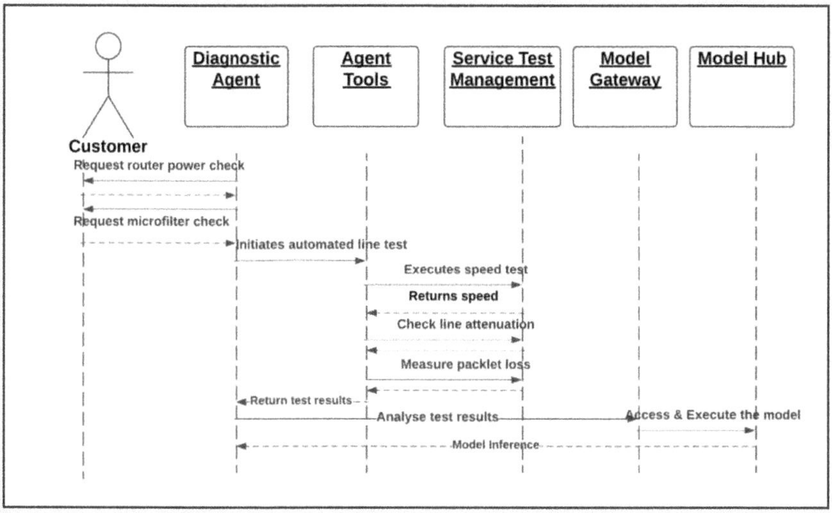

Step 3: Root Cause Identification

Agents: *PredictiveResolutionAgent*
MOP Components: *Knowledge Graph, Data Classification Engine*

Pattern Matching:
The *PredictiveResolutionAgent* cross-references the fault type with ComPlus's *Knowledge Graph*, which maps:

Historical fault patterns (e.g., "rainfall → line corrosion").

Geographic data (e.g., flood-prone areas).

Equipment lifespans (e.g., routers nearing EOL).

Confidence Scoring:
The system ranks potential causes by likelihood:

High Confidence (80%+): "Microfilter fault" → remote fix.

Medium Confidence (50-80%): "Line interference" → technician dispatch with specific tools.

Low Confidence (<50%): Escalate to human engineers.

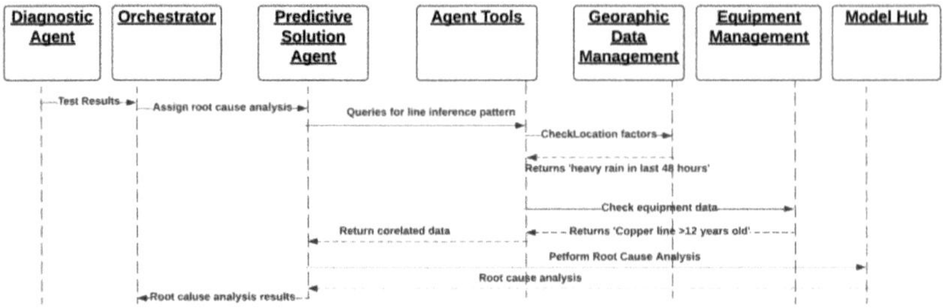

Step 4: Automated Remediation

Agents: *RemoteRepairAgent*
MOP Components: *Security Manager, AI Safety Controller*

Remote Fixes:
For high-confidence issues, the *RemoteRepairAgent* executes repairs:

Router configuration resets.

Firmware updates.

Bandwidth reallocation.

Safety Checks:
The *AI Safety Controller* validates actions against compliance policies, while the *Security Manager* authenticates access to customer equipment.

Example: After resetting a router, the agent monitors line stability for 5 minutes before closing the case.

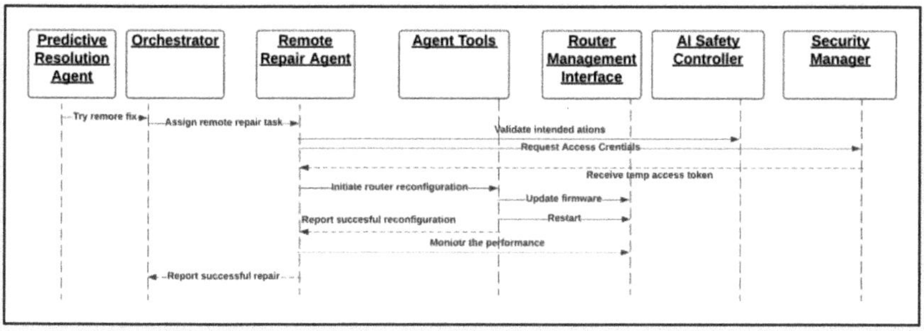

Step 5: Technician Dispatch (If Needed)

Agents: *PredictiveResolutionAgent*
MOP Components: *Response Generator, Agent Tools*

Smart Work Orders:
If onsite repairs are required, the system generates a work order with:

Predicted fault cause.

Required tools/parts (e.g., "Bring DSLAM test equipment").

Priority level based on customer SLA.

Real-Time Updates:
The *Response Generator* sends automated SMS/email updates to the customer:

"Technician Emma will arrive between 2-3 PM with a replacement router."

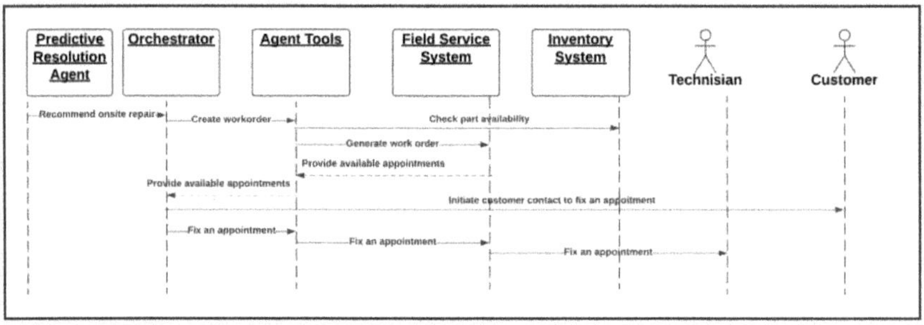

Step 6: Continuous Learning

Agents: *LearningAgent*
MOP Components: *Model Hub, Knowledge Graph*

Feedback Loop:
Post-resolution, the *LearningAgent* updates:

AI Models: Retrains fault-classification models with new data.

Knowledge Graph: Adds new fault patterns (e.g., "Heatwave → increased DSLAM failures").

Performance Monitoring:
Tracks key metrics like:

False positive/negative rates.

Average resolution time.

Customer satisfaction scores.

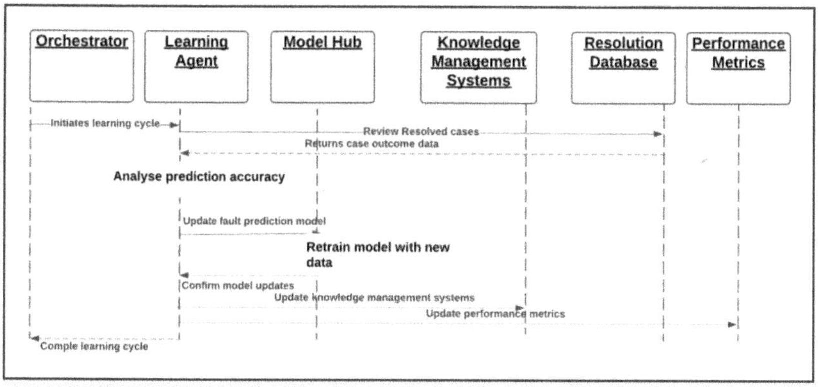

Why It Works

1. **MOP Orchestration:** Seamlessly coordinates agents, models and tools.
2. **CeAF Alignment:** Embeds intelligence across data (knowledge graphs), processes (automated workflows), and infrastructure (edge AI).
3. **Scalability:** Handles 5,000+ concurrent diagnostics without performance loss.

By combining MOP's agentic workflows with CeAF's architectural rigour, ComPlus transformed fault diagnosis from a cost centre into a competitive advantage—proving that cognitive networks aren't just faster but fundamentally *smarter.*

Conclusion: The Cognitive Advantage

Cognitive networks aren't a distant future—they're the present for leaders like ComPlus. By modernising OSS, organizing data intelligently, deploying collaborative AI agents, and implementing Edge AI throughout their infrastructure, telecommunications providers can:

- **Reduce Costs**: Automate 80% of routine tasks.
- **Boost Revenue**: Monetize network APIs and services.
- **Future-Proof Infrastructure**: Adapt seamlessly to 6G, quantum networking, and beyond.

Chapter 15: AI's Transformative Impact on Software Engineering

Artificial Intelligence (AI) is redefining the landscape of software engineering, introducing intelligent automation, predictive analytics, and enhanced collaboration across the Software Development Life Cycle (SDLC). By embedding AI into SDLC practices, organisations can achieve faster development cycles, more accurate decision-making, and higher software quality. Beyond the SDLC, AI is also revolutionizing operational methodologies such as DevOps, DevSecOps, and MLOps while introducing innovative paradigms like "Architecture as Code" (AaC).

This chapter explores AI's transformative impact on software engineering, detailing its role in each SDLC phase, its integration into operational methodologies, and its potential to reshape architectural practices. We will also examine how organisations like ComPlus and LegalDeal can strategically adopt these advancements to accelerate their transformation journeys.

AI Across the Software Development Life Cycle (SDLC)

The SDLC consists of multiple phases that span from requirements gathering to maintenance. Each phase benefits significantly from AI-driven advancements. By automating repetitive tasks, providing predictive insights, and enhancing collaboration, AI enables teams to focus on strategic activities while improving software reliability and delivery speed.

1. Requirement Gathering and Planning

The requirement gathering and planning phase is foundational to the success of any software project. AI-powered tools streamline this phase by automating the identification, analysis, and validation of requirements.

Capabilities of AI in Requirement Gathering:

- **Automated Requirement Elicitation**: AI leverages Natural Language Processing (NLP) to extract requirements from emails, meeting transcripts, and documentation. This reduces manual effort and ensures comprehensive coverage of stakeholder needs.
- **Impact Analysis**: AI assesses how changes in requirements affect timelines, resource allocation, or design components, enabling data-driven decision-making.
- **Predictive Analytics**: By analysing historical project data, AI forecasts potential risks, resource needs, and project timelines, allowing teams to proactively address challenges.
- **Real-Time Collaboration**: AI-powered collaboration tools provide intelligent suggestions during stakeholder discussions, improving communication and decision-making.

ComPlus Example: ComPlus uses an NLP-powered tool to analyse customer service feedback and identify new feature requirements for their telecommunications platform. This ensures that customer needs are prioritized in the planning phase.

LegalDeal Example: LegalDeal leverages AI to extract regulatory requirements from legal documents and map them to system features for compliance tracking.

2. Design Phase

In the design phase, AI enhances the creation of architectural blueprints and system designs by automating complex processes and providing actionable recommendations.

Capabilities of AI in Design:

- **Automated Prototyping**: AI generates rapid prototypes for user interfaces and system components based on high-level requirements, enabling faster feedback cycles.

- **Architecture Assistance**: AI tools create architectural diagrams, sequence flows, and component specifications while ensuring adherence to industry standards.
- **Design Recommendations**: AI suggests optimal design patterns, such as microservices or event-driven architectures, based on project requirements and historical data.
- **Dependency Mapping and Bottleneck Detection**: AI identifies interdependencies between components and highlights potential risks or performance bottlenecks.

ComPlus Example: ComPlus uses an AI-driven architecture tool to generate microservices-based designs for its network operations platform. The tool identifies potential bottlenecks in traffic routing workflows during peak usage periods.

LegalDeal Example: LegalDeal employs an architecture assistant that recommends optimal database structures for managing client-sensitive legal documents while ensuring compliance with data protection regulations.

3. Development Phase

The development phase is often the most resource-intensive part of the SDLC. Here, AI introduces automation for code generation, quality assurance, and intelligent collaboration.

Capabilities of AI in Development:

- **Code Generation**: AI-powered tools automatically generate boilerplate code, API specifications, and reusable components based on user input or high-level descriptions.
- **Automated Code Reviews**: Machine learning models analyse code for adherence to standards, security vulnerabilities, and inefficiencies and provide actionable feedback to developers.
- **Mock Server Creation**: AI generates mock servers for APIs to enable front-end and back-end teams to work in parallel without dependencies.

- **Programming Language Translation**: Tools facilitate seamless translation of code across programming languages while preserving functionality.

ComPlus Example: ComPlus integrates an AI-based code review tool into its development pipelines to identify security vulnerabilities during sprint cycles. This reduces post-deployment issues by 40%.

LegalDeal Example: LegalDeal uses an automated code generation tool that creates API endpoints for integrating legal research databases with internal systems.

4. Testing Phase

Testing is a critical phase of the SDLC where quality assurance ensures that the software meets functional and non-functional requirements. AI introduces intelligent automation to enhance test coverage and defect detection.

Capabilities of AI in Testing:

- **Synthetic Data Generation**: Machine learning models create realistic test data that simulate real-world scenarios while ensuring compliance with privacy regulations.
- **Automated Test Case Creation**: Models analyse code changes or requirements to dynamically generate comprehensive test cases.
- **Continuous Testing in CI/CD Pipelines**: Automated tests run after every code change to ensure only high-quality code progresses through pipelines.
- **Defect Prediction**: Predictive analytics identify areas of the codebase most likely to introduce defects based on historical patterns.

5. Deployment Phase

Deployment is one of the most critical phases of the SDLC, during which software is released into production environments. Here, too, AI ensures smooth deployments by automating workflows and providing real-time insights.

Capabilities of AI in Deployment:

- **CI/CD Pipeline Automation**: Intelligent systems automate deployment schedules, rollback strategies during failures, and environment configurations across staging/testing/production environments.
- **Predictive Monitoring During Rollouts**: Machine learning models monitor system performance during deployments for anomalies or bottlenecks before they impact end users.
- **Intelligent Orchestration Across Multi-Environments:** Ensures consistency across environments using automated orchestration tools.

ComPlus Example: During Black Friday sales events, ComPlus uses predictive monitoring powered by machine learning algorithms to ensure zero downtime despite peak loads.

LegalDeal Example: LegalDeal automates multi-environment deployments for its compliance tracking platform using CI/CD pipelines integrated with anomaly detection systems.

6. Maintenance Phase

The maintenance phase focuses on ensuring long-term reliability and performance post-deployment. Here, too, AI enhances this phase with predictive analytics and automated updates.

Capabilities of AI in Maintenance:

- **Predictive Maintenance**: Machine learning models analyse logs and usage patterns to forecast potential failures, enabling proactive issue resolution.
- **Automated Updates**: Synchronizes technical documentation with system changes and automates patch implementation upgrades

- **Root Cause Analysis:** Pinpoint underlying causes of performance issues failures, reducing resolution times, optimizing resources

ComPlus Example: Proactively resolves network outages by analysing telemetry logs, reducing downtime, improving customer satisfaction

Beyond SDLC Integration DevOps DevSecOps MLOps

DevOps emphasizes collaboration between development operations, delivering faster, reliable software. Enhanced automation monitoring predictive insights enable continuous improvement.

DevSecOps integrates security workflows, strengthening threat detection compliance enforcement incident response.

MLOps operationalizes machine learning model production, managing lifecycle retraining and scaling governance.

Revolutionizing Architecture Code AaC

Architecture Code treats architectural artefacts as executable, enabling automation validation iterative refinement.

Benefits include Impact Assessment Automation analysing changes, predicting impacts, performance scalability, Continuous Validation, and aligning evolving goals.

AI-Based Legacy Application Migration

In many organisations, legacy applications and codebases represent rich operational knowledge acquired over decades. However, they often hinder the seamless integration of modern cognitive technologies. Rather than undertaking a full-scale rearchitecting—which can entail significant disruption and risk—many enterprises are turning to AI-driven legacy migration tools that focus purely on transforming and modernising existing code. These tools leverage advanced machine learning algorithms to analyse, refactor, and migrate legacy applications incrementally, preserving core functionality while enabling integration with contemporary systems.

Key capabilities of AI-based legacy migration include:

Automated Code Analysis and Refactoring: Tools scan legacy code to identify dependencies, redundant logic, and inefficiencies. By automating the process of refactoring, organisations can modernise applications without disrupting established workflows.

Incremental Migration via API Wrapping: Instead of overhauling the entire system, AI migration solutions can create standardised API layers around legacy applications. This approach exposes existing functionalities to new digital services, ensuring continuity while opening pathways for future integration.

Preservation of Core Business Logic: AI-driven tools focus on migrating and optimizing code without altering its inherent business rules. As a result, organisations retain the essential behaviors that have proven reliable over time while still benefiting from improved maintainability and scalability.

Reduction of Technical Debt: By streamlining and cleaning up outdated code segments, these migration tools lower the cumulative technical debt, making the system more agile and easier to manage in the long term.

For enterprises like ComPlus, this targeted migration strategy ensures that their legacy systems remain operational and valuable during the transition to cognitive architectures. It enables them to integrate modern AI-driven capabilities—such as real-time analytics and enhanced customer interaction models—without the substantial risk and cost associated with complete system rearchitecture. In essence, AI-based legacy migration offers a pragmatic path forward, allowing organisations to evolve gradually while safeguarding the integrity of their core operations.

Conclusion Intelligent Era Engineering

AI fundamentally transforms engineering, automating and enhancing collaboration, enabling predictive insights, ensuring scalability, adaptability, and dynamic needs, unlocking unprecedented efficiencies, and fostering innovation.

Chapter 16: Realizing Business Vision Through Cognitive Enterprise

Introduction: From Architecture to Business Value

Throughout this book, we have explored the components and capabilities of the Cognitive Enterprise Architecture Framework (CeAF) and its implementation at ComPlus and LegalDeal. In this chapter, we will examine how these architectural components are expected to translate into tangible business outcomes by 2027. While we are writing in 2025, we will project how the technical foundations laid today will enable these organisations to achieve their strategic ambitions over the next two years. This forward-looking perspective helps connect current architectural decisions to future business value.

Both ComPlus and LegalDeal began their transformation journeys with clear business visions for 2027. Their success depends not just on implementing advanced technologies but on how effectively these technologies address specific business challenges and opportunities. The CeAF, with its integrated approach to data, applications, AI and human experience, provides the blueprint for delivering on these strategic ambitions. This chapter demonstrates how the architectural components we've explored will come together to realise business value for both organisations by 2027.

ComPlus: Transforming Telecommunications Through Cognitive Architecture

Revisiting ComPlus's 2027 Strategic Vision

In Chapter 1, we introduced ComPlus, a telecommunications giant operating across 25 countries with over 100 million customers. Their transformation vision for 2027 centres around three strategic pillars: Customer Experience Excellence, Operational Efficiency, and New

Digital Services. Each pillar represents specific business outcomes that will differentiate ComPlus in its market and drive sustainable growth.

For Customer Experience Excellence, ComPlus aims to achieve hyper-personalised, seamless interactions across channels, reducing customer effort and enhancing satisfaction. Their Operational Efficiency goals focus on building self-healing networks that predict and prevent service disruptions. Through New Digital Services, they seek to generate 25% of revenue from offerings beyond traditional telecommunications by 2027.

Now, in 2025, ComPlus has made significant progress in implementing the architectural foundations needed to achieve these 2027 ambitions. Let's examine how key components of the CeAF are expected to deliver on these strategic priorities over the next two years.

Customer Experience Excellence Through Cognitive Architecture

ComPlus's 2027 vision for customer experience excellence focuses on creating hyper-personalised, proactive, and frictionless interactions across all touchpoints. Several CeAF components are instrumental in building toward this vision:

The Customer 360 Data Product, implemented in 2024, integrates data from diverse sources to create a unified view of each customer. By combining interaction history, service usage, billing information, and demographic data, this foundation enables the personalised experiences that ComPlus's strategy demands. Maria Rodriguez, VP of Customer Experience, explains how this capability has transformed their approach: "*Before implementing our Customer 360 Data Product, our representatives had to navigate five different systems to understand a customer's situation. Now, they have a complete view instantly, reducing call handling time by 40% while significantly improving resolution rates.*"

By 2027, ComPlus plans to extend this foundation with predictive customer intent modelling, which will anticipate customer needs before they're expressed. The architecture includes expansion points for these capabilities, with the current data product designed to incorporate behavioural analytics and predictive models as they mature over the next two years.

The Multi-Agent Orchestrator Platform (MOP), partially implemented in 2025, coordinates specialised AI agents that support customer interactions. The CustomerSupportAgent handles routine inquiries autonomously, while the ServiceDiagnosticsAgent identifies and resolves technical issues proactively. By 2027, ComPlus plans to have a complete ecosystem of specialised agents working together to deliver seamless customer experiences across channels and use cases.

Digital Enablers provide the omnichannel capabilities essential for consistent customer experiences. The Intelligent Engagement Hub, currently being deployed in 2025, will enable seamless transitions between channels, preserving context as customers move from web to mobile to call centre. By 2027, ComPlus expects this system to reduce customer effort scores by 60% compared to 2023 baselines, contributing significantly to their customer experience goals.

The roadmap for achieving the 2027 customer experience vision includes several key milestones: completing the agent ecosystem by Q1 2026, implementing predictive intent modelling by Q3 2026, and achieving fully contextual cross-channel experiences by Q1 2027. With these capabilities in place, ComPlus expects to reduce churn by 35% and increase customer lifetime value by 25% by the end of 2027.

Operational Efficiency Through Network Intelligence

ComPlus's 2027 operational efficiency goals centre on creating intelligent, self-healing networks that minimize downtime, reduce costs, and improve service quality. Several CeAF components are critical to this transformation:

Active Networks and OSS, currently being implemented in 2025, provide the foundation for autonomous network operations. By implementing self-organizing network capabilities, ComPlus has already achieved dynamic optimisation of cell coverage, capacity, and handover parameters without manual intervention. Network Operations Director Thomas Chen notes that these capabilities have reduced optimisation-related site visits by 78% while improving average network capacity by 24% without additional hardware investments.

By 2027, ComPlus plans to extend these capabilities to create truly autonomous networks that can predict potential failures days in advance, automatically reroute traffic during peak periods, and optimize energy consumption based on usage patterns. The current architecture includes the necessary hooks for these advanced capabilities, with plans to implement predictive maintenance across all network elements by Q2 2026.

The Intelligent Integration Platform ensures seamless data flows between network systems, operational tools, and customer-facing applications in real-time. When fully implemented by 2027, this platform will enable real-time response to network events, reducing mean time to resolution by 85% compared to 2023 baselines. The integration architecture is being deployed in phases, with core capabilities already in place and advanced event processing scheduled for completion by Q4 2026.

The roadmap for achieving ComPlus's 2027 network vision includes implementing network digital twins by Q2 2026, deploying advanced predictive maintenance across all network elements by Q4 2026, and achieving autonomous optimisation capabilities by Q2 2027. With these capabilities in place, ComPlus expects network reliability to improve by 40%, operational costs to decrease by 45%, and customer satisfaction with service quality to increase by 60% by the end of 2027.

New Digital Services Through Innovation Enablement

ComPlus's ambition to generate 25% of revenue from new digital services by 2027 requires architectural capabilities that support rapid innovation and market entry. Several CeAF components are critical to this transformation:

The Application Architecture, with its microservices foundation and API ecosystem, enables rapid service development and deployment. In 2025, ComPlus has already implemented core microservices capabilities, reducing time-to-market for new services by 65%. By 2027, they plan to have a complete API ecosystem that enables partners to easily build on ComPlus's platform, creating a thriving digital marketplace.

The Data Foundation enables data monetization through secure sharing mechanisms and advanced analytics capabilities. These foundations have supported the launch of ComPlus's Smart City platform in 2025, which combines telecommunications data with IoT sensors to provide urban planning insights to municipal governments. By 2027, ComPlus expects to have at least five major data monetization streams generating significant revenue.

LegalDeal: Redefining Legal Practice Through Cognitive Architecture

Revisiting LegalDeal's 2027 Strategic Vision

In Chapter 1, we introduced LegalDeal, a forward-thinking legal firm facing challenges from changing client expectations, increased competition from legal tech startups, and pressure to improve efficiency while maintaining quality. Their transformation vision for 2027 centres around three strategic pillars: Client-Centric Service Delivery, Knowledge Democratization, and Operational Excellence.

For Client-Centric Service Delivery, LegalDeal aims to provide transparent, responsive, and value-based services that align with client business objectives. Their Knowledge Democratization goals focus on creating AI-enhanced legal research and drafting tools that make expertise accessible throughout the organisation. Through Operational Excellence, they seek to automate 70% of routine legal tasks by 2027.

Now, in 2025, LegalDeal has implemented key architectural foundations needed to achieve these 2027 ambitions. Let's examine how components of the CeAF are expected to deliver on these strategic priorities over the next two years.

Client-Centric Service Delivery Through Digital Engagement

LegalDeal's 2027 vision for client-centric service delivery focuses on creating transparent, responsive, and value-based legal services. Several CeAF components are instrumental in building toward this vision:

The Client Matter Data Product, implemented in 2024, integrates all information related to a client's legal matters, including documents, communications, billing, and status updates. This comprehensive view enables attorneys to understand the full context of client relationships and provide more relevant advice. Practice Group Leader Sarah Williams describes the impact: "*Previously, attorneys spent hours gathering information about a client's matters before meetings. Now, they have instant access to everything they need, allowing them to focus on strategic advice rather than information gathering.*"

By 2027, LegalDeal plans to extend this foundation with predictive insights that anticipate client legal needs based on business events, industry trends, and regulatory changes. The current architecture includes expansion points for these capabilities, with plans to implement predictive analytics by Q3 2026.

Digital Enablers provide the client portal and collaboration tools essential for transparent service delivery. By 2027, LegalDeal expects to offer a comprehensive digital experience where clients can access real-time updates, collaborate on documents, communicate with their legal team, and monitor budget status through a secure, intuitive interface. The client portal is being deployed in phases, with core capabilities already in place and advanced features scheduled for completion by Q2 2026.

The roadmap for achieving the 2027 client-centric vision includes implementing predictive client needs analysis by Q3 2026, completing the advanced client portal by Q2 2026, and deploying real-time collaboration tools by Q4 2026. With these capabilities in place, LegalDeal expects to increase client satisfaction by 40% and improve client retention by 25% by the end of 2027.

Knowledge Democratization Through Cognitive Systems

LegalDeal's 2027 knowledge democratization goals centre on making legal expertise accessible throughout the organisation, reducing dependence on individual experts. Several CeAF components are critical to this transformation:

The Legal Knowledge Graph captures relationships between legal concepts, precedents, regulations, and practice-specific knowledge. In 2025, this graph already connects over 2 million legal concepts across 14 practice areas. By 2027, LegalDeal plans to extend this to cover all jurisdictions where they operate and include predictive capabilities that identify emerging legal trends and their potential impact on clients.

The Multi-Agent Orchestrator Platform (MOP) supports knowledge work through specialised agents. The LegalResearchAgent and PrecedentAnalysisAgent, already in pilot deployment in 2025, have reduced research time by 45% while improving the comprehensiveness of legal analysis. By 2027, LegalDeal plans to deploy a complete ecosystem of specialised legal agents, including DraftingAssistants, that can generate initial drafts of common legal documents based on precedents and client requirements.

The roadmap for achieving the 2027 knowledge democratization vision includes extending the knowledge graph to all jurisdictions by Q2 2026, completing the legal agent ecosystem by Q3 2026, and implementing advanced drafting assistants by Q1 2027. With these capabilities in place, LegalDeal expects new attorneys to reach proficiency 60% faster and reduce dependency on senior partners by 50% by the end of 2027.

Operational Excellence Through Intelligent Automation

LegalDeal's 2027 operational excellence goals focus on automating 70% of routine legal tasks, reducing costs, and improving the accuracy and consistency of legal work. Several CeAF components are critical to this transformation:

The Intelligent Integration Platform connects LegalDeal's practice management, document management, billing, and client relationship systems. In 2025, this integration has already reduced administrative time by 28% while improving data accuracy. By 2027, LegalDeal plans to implement end-to-end workflow automation that handles routine tasks across systems without human intervention.

The Multi-Agent Orchestrator Platform (MOP) orchestrates complex legal workflows. The DocumentReviewAgent, ComplianceCheckAgent, and QualityAssuranceAgent, currently being deployed in 2025, are expected to reduce document review time by 35% while improving issue identification accuracy. By 2027, these agents will work together to handle entire legal processes autonomously, from initial document review to final quality checks.

The roadmap for achieving the 2027 operational excellence vision includes implementing end-to-end workflow automation by Q4 2026, completing the document processing agent ecosystem by Q2 2026, and deploying advanced analytics for continuous process improvement by Q1 2027. With these capabilities in place, LegalDeal expects to automate 70% of routine legal tasks, reduce operational costs by 35%, and improve matter profitability by 30% by the end of 2027.

The Path Forward: Bridging from 2025 to 2027

As ComPlus and LegalDeal continue their cognitive transformation journeys from 2025 to 2027, they face several key challenges and opportunities that will shape their architectural evolution:

Ecosystem Expansion

Both organisations are expanding beyond their traditional boundaries to participate in broader ecosystems. ComPlus is building partnerships with IoT providers, smart home manufacturers and content creators to expand their service offerings. LegalDeal is participating in legal innovation networks, collaborating with legal tech startups and integrating with client systems to provide more embedded legal services.

These ecosystem strategies require architectural components that support secure, scalable integration with external partners. The API

Management capabilities of the Intelligent Integration Platform will play a crucial role, as will the standardised data products that enable seamless information exchange. Both organisations have roadmaps to enhance these capabilities by 2026, positioning them for ecosystem success by 2027.

Advanced Intelligence and Autonomy

Both ComPlus and LegalDeal are pursuing higher levels of intelligence and autonomy in their operations. ComPlus is advancing toward fully autonomous networks that can predict, prevent, and resolve issues without human intervention. LegalDeal is developing more sophisticated AI legal assistants that can draft documents, conduct research, and provide preliminary advice with minimal human oversight.

These ambitions rely heavily on the Multi-Agent Orchestrator Platform, with increasingly sophisticated agents that can reason across complex domains. Both organisations plan to significantly enhance their agent capabilities between 2025 and 2027, with major milestones for autonomous operations scheduled throughout 2026.

Human-AI Collaboration Models

As AI capabilities advance from 2025 to 2027, both organisations are focusing on optimizing the collaboration between humans and intelligent systems. ComPlus is developing new interfaces that allow engineers to work more effectively with network optimisation algorithms. LegalDeal is creating tools that help attorneys and AI systems collaborate on complex legal analysis.

These collaboration models build on the Human-centric AI principles established in Chapter 2, ensuring that technology enhances rather than replaces human capabilities. Both organisations have roadmaps for enhancing these collaboration models throughout 2026, positioning them to achieve their 2027 visions of effective human-AI partnerships.

Conclusion: Architecture as the Bridge to Future Business Value

As we've seen throughout this chapter, cognitive enterprise architecture serves as the bridge between current capabilities and future business ambitions. By aligning architectural components with clear 2027 business goals, both ComPlus and LegalDeal have created roadmaps that translate technical capabilities into tangible business outcomes.

For ComPlus, the CeAF will enable the delivery of hyper-personalised customer experiences, self-healing network operations, and innovative digital services that generate 25% of revenue by 2027.

For LegalDeal, it will transform client service delivery, democratize legal knowledge through AI assistants, and automate 70% of routine legal tasks by 2027.

As organisations embark on their own cognitive transformation journeys, they should take several key lessons from these experiences:

Start with a business vision: Begin by clearly articulating the strategic outcomes you seek to achieve by a specific future date, then work backwards to identify the architectural capabilities required.

Create implementation roadmaps: Develop clear milestones and timelines that connect current architectural foundations to future business capabilities.

Integrate across domains: The most valuable capabilities emerge at the intersection of data, applications, AI, and human experience—requiring an integrated architectural approach.

Build with future expansion in mind: Design current systems with the flexibility to incorporate emerging technologies and capabilities as they mature.

Maintain human centricity: Design systems that enhance human capabilities and align with organisational values and ethical principles.

By following these principles and leveraging the Cognitive Enterprise Architecture Framework, organisations can create a clear path from current architectural foundations to future business ambitions, ensuring that technology investments deliver meaningful value in an increasingly digital world.

Chapter 17: The Future of Cognitive Enterprises

Introduction: Envisioning the Next Era of Cognitive AI

As we conclude this exploration of cognitive enterprise transformation, it is essential to look ahead at the future of cognitive AI and its profound implications for enterprises like ComPlus and LegalDeal. The evolution of AI technologies—particularly in multi-agent systems, synthetic data, human-centric design, and autonomous decision-making—is set to redefine how organisations operate, innovate and compete. This chapter envisions how cognitive AI will shape the next generation of enterprises, transitioning from tools that automate tasks to ecosystems of intelligent agents capable of collaboration, contextual awareness, and self-evolution.

For ComPlus, this journey means becoming a leader in telecommunications through intelligent networks that deliver seamless connectivity. For LegalDeal, it means redefining legal services with scalable automation while maintaining the highest standards of practice. As these organisations advance through the Agent Maturity Model—from autonomous collaboration to fully self-evolving ecosystems—they are poised to unlock unprecedented efficiencies, scalability, and innovation.

The Evolution of Cognitive AI: From Tools to Ecosystems

Cognitive AI is evolving from a set of tools designed to automate discrete tasks into an ecosystem of intelligent agents capable of collaboration, self-learning, and contextual awareness. This transformation is captured in the **Agent Maturity Model**, which progresses through five levels—from basic task automation to fully autonomous, self-regulating ecosystems.

Level 4: Autonomous and Collaborative Agents

At this stage, agents achieve a high degree of autonomy and collaboration. They dynamically interact with other agents, systems, and human stakeholders to achieve complex goals.

- **ComPlus Example**: Agents like the Fault Management Agent autonomously detect network issues, collaborate with Bandwidth Optimisation Agents to allocate resources during peak demand, and resolve problems without human intervention. During a national emergency or network outage, these agents prioritize bandwidth for critical services such as hospitals while ensuring minimal disruption for other customers.
- **LegalDeal Example**: Agents like the Clause Analysis Agent assess legal risks across contracts while collaborating with ComplianceAgents to ensure regulatory adherence. For instance, when new regulations are introduced in a specific jurisdiction, these agents autonomously identify affected contracts and recommend revisions.

Level 5: Fully Autonomous and Self-Evolving Ecosystems

The pinnacle of cognitive AI maturity is characterized by agents that self-orchestrate, self-learn, and self-regulate. These agents form intelligent ecosystems capable of adapting to dynamic environments with minimal human oversight.

- **ComPlus Example**: During a national crisis such as a natural disaster or cyberattack, fully autonomous agents reroute network traffic dynamically, prioritize bandwidth for critical infrastructure like hospitals or emergency responders, and adjust billing policies for affected customers—all without human intervention.
- **LegalDeal Example**: LegalDeal's ComplianceAgents autonomously update workflows in response to regulatory changes while redistributing workloads across teams. Risk models are refined based on real-world outcomes without requiring manual input from attorneys.

The transition from Level 4 to Level 5 represents a transformative leap where enterprises no longer simply react to challenges but proactively anticipate opportunities through intelligent ecosystems.

Key Trends Shaping the Future of Cognitive AI

Several trends are driving the evolution of cognitive AI into its next phase. These trends will redefine how enterprises like ComPlus and LegalDeal operate, innovate, and deliver value.

1. Human-Centric AI

The future of cognitive AI emphasizes human-centric design principles where technology augments rather than replaces human expertise. This ensures that AI systems remain ethical, transparent, and aligned with organisational values.

- **ComPlus Example**: Field technicians use augmented reality (AR) tools powered by AI for real-time guidance during repairs while maintaining human oversight for critical decisions. For instance, AR overlays provide step-by-step instructions for resolving complex equipment failures.
- **LegalDeal Example**: Lawyers adopt human-in-the-loop approaches where AI handles routine tasks like document drafting or clause extraction but leaves complex legal judgments under human control. This balance ensures both efficiency and accountability in legal practice.

2. Multi-Agent Orchestration at Scale

The Multi-Agent Orchestrator Platform (MOP), introduced in Chapter 12, will evolve into a decentralized framework where thousands of agents autonomously manage workflows across domains.

- **ComPlus Example**: MOP enables seamless collaboration among thousands of agents managing network infrastructure during global events such as large-scale sporting tournaments or international crises.

- **LegalDeal Example**: MOP coordinates legal research agents, compliance agents, and client interaction agents to deliver integrated solutions for complex cases involving cross-border regulations or multi-jurisdictional disputes.

3. Synthetic Data as a Catalyst for Innovation

Synthetic data will play a pivotal role in addressing challenges related to scalability, privacy, and fairness in AI training.

- **ComPlus Example**: Synthetic data simulates network scenarios such as peak traffic loads or equipment failures for training predictive maintenance models while protecting customer privacy.
- **LegalDeal Example**: Synthetic datasets enable the development of multilingual natural language processing (NLP) models for contract analysis without compromising sensitive client information.

By using synthetic data effectively, enterprises can accelerate model development while ensuring compliance with privacy regulations like GDPR.

4. Proactive Enterprise Evolution

Cognitive AI will empower enterprises not only to solve current problems but also to anticipate future opportunities through predictive analytics and proactive decision-making.

- **ComPlus Example**: MarketAnalysisAgents predict emerging customer demands such as 6G adoption trends or smart city applications. These insights enable ComPlus to recommend infrastructure upgrades before competitors.
- **LegalDeal Example**: KnowledgeManagementAgents identify gaps in legal expertise across teams and suggest targeted training programs or partnerships with external specialists to address emerging client needs.

Proactive capabilities allow organisations to stay ahead of market trends while optimizing resource allocation.

5. Ethical Governance in Autonomous Systems

As cognitive systems become more autonomous, ensuring ethical governance will be critical. AI Safety Controllers embedded within platforms like MOP will enforce compliance with ethical standards and regulatory requirements.

- **ComPlus Example**: Agents autonomously anonymize sensitive customer data during analytics processes to comply with GDPR while escalating ambiguous cases for human review.
- **LegalDeal Example**: ComplianceAgents validate that all legal outputs align with jurisdictional laws before submission to clients or regulators.

Ethical governance frameworks will ensure that advanced AI capabilities remain aligned with societal values and organisational principles.

The Convergence of Cognitive AI with Blockchain and Quantum Computing

Looking further ahead, the convergence of cognitive AI with blockchain and quantum computing marks a groundbreaking shift in the technological landscape:

1. **AI + Blockchain**:
    - Blockchain's decentralized architecture ensures secure data sharing across distributed systems.
    - Cognitive AI optimizes blockchain operations by enabling predictive analytics for smart contract execution or automating decision-making processes.
    - *Example*: LegalDeal uses blockchain-integrated ComplianceAgents to verify contract authenticity while maintaining tamper-proof audit trails for regulatory compliance.
2. **AI + Quantum Computing**:

    - Quantum computing exponentially accelerates AI training processes by solving complex optimisation problems at extraordinary speeds.
    - Conversely, cognitive AI aids quantum computing development by addressing challenges such as error correction or qubit stability enhancement.
3. **Triad Synergy**:
    - Together, these technologies enable secure data exchanges (blockchain), faster decision-making (quantum), and intelligent automation (AI).
    - Industries such as personalised medicine (e.g., generative chemistry), materials science (e.g., digital twin simulations), and financial modelling stand to benefit significantly from this convergence.

Challenges on the Horizon

While the future holds immense promise, enterprises must address several challenges:

1. **Data Privacy and Security**:
    - Ensuring compliance with evolving regulations like GDPR while leveraging large-scale data integration.
2. **Ethical Decision-Making**:
    - Balancing automation with accountability through human-in-the-loop frameworks.
3. **Scalability Across Domains**:
    - Managing the complexity of deploying thousands of collaborative agents across diverse workflows.
4. **Change Management**:
    - Preparing employees for new roles as cognitive technologies redefine traditional workflows.
5. **Keeping Pace with Innovation**:
    - Continuously adapting architectures and upskilling workforces to leverage emerging technologies effectively.

Conclusion: The Cognitive Enterprise Vision

The future of cognitive AI represents a transformative leap for enterprises like ComPlus and LegalDeal. By advancing through the Agent Maturity Model—from autonomous collaboration at Level 4 to fully self-evolving ecosystems at Level 5—these organisations can unlock unprecedented efficiencies, scalability, and innovation.

For ComPlus, this journey means becoming a leader in telecommunications by delivering seamless connectivity powered by intelligent networks capable of adapting autonomously. For LegalDeal, it means redefining legal services through scalable automation while maintaining the highest standards of practice.

Ultimately, the success of these transformations lies not just in technological advancements but in their ability to empower people—employees making better decisions with augmented intelligence, clients receiving personalised services at scale, and organisations achieving their strategic goals ethically and sustainably. The future belongs to those who embrace cognitive AI not as a tool but as an ecosystem—a living framework that evolves alongside their ambitions.

Catalogue of Architecture Patterns Used in Cognitive Enterprise

---

Foundation Architecture Patterns (Chapter 1)

1. **Cognitive Enterprise Architecture Framework (CeAF)** - A comprehensive and modular blueprint that integrates Generative AI, reasoning, and machine learning models with enterprise data, processes, and systems.
2. **Human-Centric Architecture** - A design approach that places human needs and values at the centre of all architectural decisions, ensuring technology serves people rather than the reverse.

Cognitive Process Patterns (Chapter 2)

3. **Adaptive, Dynamic Processes** - AI-enabled workflows that sense their environment and adjust in real-time to changing conditions, unlike traditional static processes.
4. **Self-Healing Systems** - Networks and platforms that detect problems and implement corrective measures automatically, often resolving issues before users notice them.
5. **AI-Driven Automation** - Architecture that automates routine tasks while reserving complex judgments for humans, transforming productivity across functions.
6. **Generative Design Pattern** - Systems that generate multiple design variations based on parameters, enabling the exploration of solutions that might never occur to human designers.

Core CeAF Component Patterns (Chapter 3)

7. **User Multimodal Interaction Layer** - Architecture enabling natural interactions through multiple channels (text, voice, video) while maintaining context across touchpoints.

8. **Multi-Agent Orchestrator Platform (MOP)** - System coordinating multiple specialised AI agents and workflows to deliver intelligent, context-aware responses.
9. **Pre-Processor Pattern** - Converting diverse inputs (text, audio, images, structured data) into formats that downstream systems can process effectively.
10. **Orchestrator Pattern** - Central intelligence mapping user requests to appropriate actions and coordinating workflows across multiple agents.
11. **Specialised Agents Pattern** - Task-specific AI components (knowledge agents, reasoning agents, action agents) executing specific functions autonomously.
12. **Model Gateway and Hub** - Architecture providing access to appropriate AI models for different situations while managing computational resources effectively.
13. **Data Products and Platform** - Architecture transforming fragmented data into cohesive, trusted resources that drive intelligence throughout the enterprise.
14. **Data Fabric Pattern** - Approach connecting disparate data sources across the organisation, creating a unified network of information that transcends traditional silos.
15. **Knowledge Graph Pattern** - Semantic network mapping relationships between data entities, creating a context that enhances understanding and enables complex queries.
16. **Digital Enabler Layer** - Bridge between traditional systems of record and modern engagement capabilities, enabling personalised experiences while leveraging existing investments.
17. **Application Layer** - Architecture transforming rigid legacy systems into flexible, intelligent capabilities that respond dynamically to changing conditions.
18. **Cloud-Native Microservices Architecture** - Breaking monolithic systems into modular, independently deployable components for greater flexibility and resilience.
19. **API-First Design** - Creating standardised interfaces for business functions, enabling easier integration and reusability across the enterprise.
20. **AI Compute Layer** - Computational foundation for training, fine-tuning, and deploying AI models at scale across the organisation.

21. **Hybrid Deployment Strategies** - Enabling AI capabilities to run in cloud, on-premises, or edge environments based on requirements for latency, data gravity, and cost optimisation.
22. **Active and Intelligent Network Systems** - Architecture transforming traditional network infrastructure into self-healing, adaptive systems capable of self-optimisation.
23. **AI Governance Layer** - Framework ensuring AI systems operate ethically, transparently, and in compliance with regulations through comprehensive controls.

Integration and Data Architecture Patterns (Chapters 3-4)

24. **Event-Driven Architecture** - Systems communicating through events, enabling real-time data synchronization while minimising direct coupling between systems.
25. **Change Data Capture (CDC)** - Mechanisms capturing real-time updates in systems and publishing them as events for synchronization across platforms.
26. **Metadata Management Pattern** - Automatically tracking origins, transformations, and relationships of data assets, making them discoverable and trustworthy.
27. **Ontology Management** - Establishing consistent terminology and frameworks across the organisation, ensuring a common language for data understanding.

Intelligence and Reasoning Patterns (Chapters 3-5)

32. **AI-Driven Decision-Making** - Embedding predictive analytics and reasoning capabilities directly into business workflows rather than treating AI as a separate capability.
33. **Engagement Engines** - Systems powering personalised interactions based on comprehensive user profiles, historical behaviours, and real-time context.
34. **Content Analysis and Generation** - Architecture for understanding and producing content across multiple channels in consistent, personalised ways.
35. **Model Management Pattern** - Handling versioning, deployment, monitoring, and lifecycle management for AI models throughout their operational life.

36. **AI Safety Controls** - Monitoring models for bias, drift, and other potential issues, ensuring systems continue to operate as intended over time.
37. **Human Oversight Mechanisms** - Embedding appropriate human review into AI workflows, particularly for high-risk decisions or edge cases.

References

1. Gartner. (2024). "Top Strategic Technology Trends for 2025." Gartner Research. https://www.gartner.com/en/articles/gartner-top-10-strategic-technology-trends-for-2025
2. McKinsey & Company. (2023). "The Economic Potential of Generative AI: The Next Productivity Frontier." McKinsey Global Institute. https://www.mckinsey.com/capabilities/mckinsey-digital/our-insights/the-economic-potential-of-generative-ai-the-next-productivity-frontier
3. World Economic Forum. (2024). "The Future of Jobs Report 2024." World Economic Forum. https://www.weforum.org/publications/the-future-of-jobs-report-2024/
4. MIT Sloan Management Review. (2023). "Architecting AI-Powered Organisations." MIT Sloan. https://sloanreview.mit.edu/article/architecting-ai-powered-organisations/

Human-Centric AI & Ethics

5. Stanford HAI. (2024). "Human-Centered Artificial Intelligence." Stanford University Human-Centered AI Institute. https://hai.stanford.edu/research/human-centered-ai
6. IEEE. (2023). "Ethically Aligned Design: A Vision for Prioritizing Human Well-being with Autonomous and Intelligent Systems." IEEE Global Initiative. https://standards.ieee.org/industry-connections/ec/autonomous-systems/
7. Harvard Business Review. (2024). "The Human-AI Collaboration Imperative." Harvard Business Review. https://hbr.org/2024/03/the-human-ai-collaboration-imperative
8. The Alan Turing Institute. (2023). "Understanding Artificial Intelligence Ethics and Safety." The Alan Turing Institute.

https://www.turing.ac.uk/research/publications/understanding-artificial-intelligence-ethics-and-safety

AI Implementation & Architecture

9. Amazon Web Services. (2024). "The Machine Learning Adoption Framework." AWS Architecture Center. https://aws.amazon.com/architecture/machine-learning/
10. IBM Research. (2023). "LLM Powered Autonomous Agents." IBM Research Blog. https://research.ibm.com/blog/autonomous-agents-foundation-models
11. Microsoft Azure. (2024). "Responsible AI Principles in Practice." Microsoft AI. https://www.microsoft.com/en-us/ai/responsible-ai
12. Google Cloud. (2023). "AI Readiness Framework." Google Cloud Architecture Center. https://cloud.google.com/architecture/ai-readiness-framework

Knowledge Systems & Data Architecture

13. Databricks. (2024). "Building Enterprise Knowledge Graphs with LLMs." Databricks Engineering Blog. https://www.databricks.com/blog/building-enterprise-knowledge-graphs-with-llms
14. O'Reilly. (2023). "Data Mesh: Delivering Data-Driven Value at Scale." O'Reilly Media. https://www.oreilly.com/library/view/data-mesh/9781492092384/
15. ThoughtWorks. (2023). "Data Mesh Principles and Logical Architecture." ThoughtWorks Technology Radar. https://www.thoughtworks.com/radar/techniques/data-mesh
16. ZDNet. (2024). "Breaking Down Data Silos: The Key to AI Success." ZDNet Technology Insights. https://www.zdnet.com/article/breaking-down-data-silos-the-key-to-ai-success/

17. Deloitte Insights. (2023). "Tech Trends 2023: Legacy Modernisation in the Age of AI." Deloitte Digital. https://www2.deloitte.com/us/en/insights/focus/tech-trends/2023/legacy-modernisation-strategies.html
18. Forrester Research. (2024). "The Modernisation Imperative: Legacy Systems in a Cognitive Enterprise." Forrester Reports. https://www.forrester.com/report/the-modernisation-imperative-legacy-systems-in-a-cognitive-enterprise/
19. IDC. (2023). "Cognitive Enterprise Technology Architecture Framework." IDC Technology Spotlight. https://www.idc.com/research/viewtoc.jsp?containerId=US50455523
20. Accenture. (2024). "From Legacy to Leading Edge: AI-Powered Modernisation." Accenture Technology Vision. https://www.accenture.com/us-en/insights/technology/technology-trends-2024

Glossary of Terms

Active and Intelligent Network Systems: A component of the CeAF that transforms traditional network infrastructure into self-healing, adaptive systems capable of detecting problems, implementing corrective measures and optimizing performance without human intervention.

Adaptive, Dynamic Processes: Business processes that can adjust in real-time based on evolving business contexts, powered by AI models capable of understanding and responding to complex scenarios.

AI Compute Layer: A CeAF component providing the computational foundation necessary to train, fine-tune and deploy AI models at scale, including specialised hardware access and model management capabilities.

AI Governance Layer: A CeAF component ensuring AI systems operate ethically, transparently and in compliance with regulations through controls, oversight mechanisms and explainability tools.

AI Safety Controls: Systems that monitor AI models for bias, drift and other potential issues, ensuring they continue to operate as intended over time.

API-First Design: An architectural approach to creating standardised interfaces for business functions, enabling easier integration and reusability across the enterprise.

Application Layer: A CeAF component transforming rigid legacy systems into flexible, intelligent capabilities through cloud-native architecture, embedded AI and continuous delivery approaches.

CeAF (Cognitive Enterprise Architecture Framework): A comprehensive, modular blueprint that integrates Generative AI, reasoning models and Human-Centric AI with enterprise data, processes and systems to enable cognitive transformation.

Change Data Capture (CDC): Mechanisms capturing real-time updates in systems and publishing them as events for synchronization across platforms.

Cloud-Native Microservices Architecture: An approach breaking monolithic systems into modular, independently deployable components for greater flexibility, scalability and resilience.

Cognitive Enterprise: An organisation that has deeply integrated AI into its operations, enabling intelligence, adaptability and personalisation throughout all processes and customer interactions.

Content Management: A digital enabler with the capability to organise and deliver relevant information across multiple channels in consistent, personalised ways.

Customer 360 Services: Services aggregating information from multiple systems to create holistic customer views, enabling dynamic, real-time personalisation.

Customer 360 Platform: A digital enabler that consolidates customer data into unified profiles for personalised engagement across touchpoints.

Data Fabric: A technology connecting disparate data sources across an organisation, creating a unified network of information that transcends traditional silos.

Data Products: Packages of information created as reusable, governed resources that can be easily consumed by various applications and users.

Data Silos: The isolation of information in separate systems or departments, preventing comprehensive analysis and insight generation.

Digital Enabler Layer: A CeAF component bridging traditional systems of record with modern engagement capabilities, enabling personalised experiences while leveraging existing investments.

Digital Enablers: Systems bridging traditional infrastructure with modern, AI-driven experiences, prioritising engagement, intelligence and personalisation.

Dynamic Graph Augmentation: A technique ensuring knowledge graphs remain up-to-date with real-time information and changing conditions in dynamic environments.

Dynamic Resource Allocation: The automatic adjustment of network resources based on changing requirements, traffic patterns and environmental conditions.

Emotion-Aware Interactions: The use of sentiment analysis to recognize emotional cues in user communication and adapt responses accordingly.

Engagement Engines: Systems powering personalised interactions based on comprehensive user profiles, historical behaviours and real-time context.

Enterprise Service Bus (ESB): A central integration platform managing communications between services in Service-Oriented Architecture, often becoming a performance bottleneck.

Event-Driven Architecture: An approach where systems communicate through events, enabling real-time data synchronization while minimising direct coupling between systems.

Evaluation Framework: A system that systematically assesses AI model performance, accuracy and business impact against predefined metrics and standards.

Explainability Tools: Capabilities enabling organisations to understand and communicate how AI systems reach specific conclusions or recommendations.

Generative AI: AI systems capable of creating new content, insights and solutions rather than simply analyzing existing information.

GraphRAG: An enhanced Retrieval-Augmented Generation technique incorporating knowledge graphs to enable reasoning over interconnected data structures and entity relationships.

Human Annotator: A component facilitating expert input for data labelling, output validation and continuous model improvement in AI systems.

Human-Centric AI (HCAI): A design approach for AI systems that empowers, supports and collaborates with people, ensuring technology serves human needs and values rather than replacing human judgment.

Human Oversight: Mechanisms embedding appropriate human review into AI workflows, particularly for high-risk decisions or edge cases.

Hybrid Deployment Strategies: Approaches enabling AI capabilities to run in cloud, on-premises, or edge environments based on requirements for latency, data gravity and cost optimisation.

Knowledge Graph: A semantic network mapping relationships between data entities, creating a context that enhances understanding and enables complex queries.

Knowledge Management Systems: Digital enablers that transform organisational expertise into actionable insights through automatic knowledge extraction and semantic search.

Legacy Systems: Outdated platforms not built for modern AI or dynamic workflows, often expensive to maintain, rigid and limiting agility.

Legacy Transformation: The use of AI-powered tools to analyse, refactor and modernise legacy codebases more efficiently.

Metadata Management: The automatic tracking of origins, transformations and relationships of data assets, making them discoverable and trustworthy.

Model Gateway and Hub: A component providing access to appropriate AI models for different situations, ensuring optimal performance, accuracy and efficiency.

Model Management: Capabilities handling versioning, deployment, monitoring and lifecycle management for AI models throughout their operational life.

Multi-Agent Orchestrator Platform (MOP): A CeAF component functioning as the "central nervous system," coordinating AI agents and workflows to deliver intelligent, context-aware responses.

Multimodal Support: Capabilities enabling natural interactions through text, voice, video and images across various platforms and devices.

Observability Framework: A system providing comprehensive visibility into AI operations, performance metrics and potential issues through real-time monitoring and detailed logging.

Omnichannel Experiences: Experiences maintaining context and continuity across different touchpoints, from digital platforms to physical locations.

Ontologies: Formal, explicit specifications of shared conceptualizations that define classes of entities, their attributes, relationships and rules governing their behaviour.

Ontology Management: The establishment of consistent terminology and frameworks across an organisation, ensuring a common language when discussing data.

Pre-Processor: A component converting diverse inputs—text, audio, images, structured data—into formats that downstream systems can process effectively.

Regulatory Compliance: Frameworks ensuring AI systems adhere to relevant laws and standards, from data privacy regulations to industry-specific requirements.

Retrieval-Augmented Generation (RAG): A technique combining external knowledge retrieval with generative AI capabilities to ground responses in factual information.

Retrieval-Augmented Reasoning (RAR): An approach performing retrieval operations throughout multi-step reasoning processes rather than just at the beginning.

ReAct (Reasoning + Acting): A pattern combining reasoning with action in an iterative loop, allowing the agent to alternate between analyzing the current state, taking specific actions and refining its approach based on results.

Security Manager: A component safeguarding AI systems through robust access controls, encryption and threat protection while ensuring compliance with data privacy regulations.

Self-Healing Networks: Networks detect problems and implement corrective measures automatically, often resolving issues before users notice them.

Semantic Data Management: A comprehensive layer of meaning created through technologies like knowledge graphs that capture connections between entities.

Service-Oriented Architecture (SOA): An architectural approach where applications expose functionalities as services accessible across different platforms.

Specialised Agents: Components executing specific tasks autonomously or collaboratively, including knowledge agents, reasoning agents and action agents.

Specialised Hardware Access: Provision of efficient computing resources like GPUs and TPUs optimized for AI workloads.

Systems of Engagement: User-centric systems designed for real-time interactivity and omnichannel accessibility.

Systems of Record: Transaction-focused systems emphasizing data storage and retrieval with rigid workflows and siloed data.

Task Decomposition: An approach enabling agents to break down complex problems into manageable subtasks, each handled by specialised components or reasoning patterns.

Technical Debt: Accumulated outdated technology and ad hoc fixes, slowing innovation and increasing costs of adopting new solutions.

User Multimodal Interaction Layer: A CeAF component creating seamless, personalised interactions across multiple channels and modalities, ensuring every touchpoint feels intuitive and human-centred.

About the Author

Shekhar Kulkarni is a visionary enterprise architect and digital transformation leader with over two decades of experience guiding organisations through technological evolution. As the Chief Architect at Deutsche Telekom Digital Labs, he spearheads Digital and AI-driven transformation initiatives and leads cross-functional teams in developing innovative solutions that bridge legacy systems with cutting-edge technologies.

Throughout his career, Shekhar has been at the forefront of successive waves of technological change—from the early days of internet adoption and distributed computing to cloud computing, service-oriented architecture, big data, and now artificial intelligence. This unique perspective across multiple technology transformations has given him exceptional insight into how architectural foundations can either enable or constrain an organisation's ability to evolve.

Shekhar has established himself as a thought leader in enterprise architecture, having developed the Cognitive Enterprise Architecture Framework (CeAF) featured in this book. His work with Deutsche Telekom's Product Innovation and Experience (PIX) team has been instrumental in implementing AI capabilities that deliver tangible business value rather than merely interesting technical experiments.

A passionate advocate for human-centred technology, Shekhar believes that successful AI transformation must balance technical innovation with organisational readiness and ethical considerations. His practical approach to architecture has helped numerous global enterprises navigate complex transformations while maintaining operational stability.

Shekhar holds advanced degrees in computer science, complemented by certifications in enterprise architecture, cloud technologies, and distributed systems design. He is a frequent speaker at international technology conferences and regularly contributes to publications on enterprise architecture, innovation, and digital transformation.

Connect with Shekhar and explore the latest updates to the Cognitive Enterprise Architecture Framework at https://cognitive.enterprises.